Keith Martin on
COLLECTING
PORSCHE

Bob Dunsmore

Cliff Singer and Jerry Seinfeld on the Colorado Grand, in Seinfeld's 1959 RSK.

What SCM'er (since 1997) Jerry Seinfeld has to say about Keith Martin on Collecting Porsche:

"Why anyone, other than me, would be interested in this amount of Porsche drivel I can't imagine! I, of course, read each word as if it were **heart attack nitroglycerine tablet instructions.**"

Keith Martin on

COLLECTING
PORSCHE

Featuring **Jim Schrager** and the editors of

MOTORBOOKS
INTERNATIONAL

This edition first published in 2003 by Motorbooks
International, an imprint of MBI Publishing Company,
Galtier Plaza, Suite 200, 380 Jackson Street, St. Paul, MN
55101-3885 USA

Motorbooks International titles are also available at discounts
in bulk quantity for industrial or sales-promotional use. For
details write to Special Sales Manager at Motorbooks
International Wholesalers & Distributors, Galtier Plaza, Suite
200, 380 Jackson Street, St. Paul, MN 55101-3885 USA.

ISBN 0-7603-1816-6

On the front cover: Sunset 930, by Jeff Dorgay,
www.wallwerks.com.

On the title page: A 1963 Porsche 356 Carrera 2 GS/GT.
RM Auctions

Edited by Peter Bodensteiner
Designed by Mandy Iverson

Printed in China

Surrounded by Old Friends

My relationship with Porsche has already spanned over 30 years. In that time I have witnessed and participated in the evolution of both road cars and race cars, and it's been a fascinating process. Our dealership, Brumos Porsche, has sponsored me for most of my racing career, and our museum houses many wonderful Porsches, from the 550 Spyder through the new Cayenne. It's also full of race cars, from my first championship 914/6 to our current Daytona Prototypes. It's an amazing collection, and each car says something special about Porsche's commitment to excellence.

It's also amazing to see how many of these cars have become highly-desired collectibles, as profiled on the pages of this book, *Keith Martin on Collecting Porsche*.

As a racing driver, I'm always looking to the future, whether to the newest competition-related technology breakthrough or the next model of race car. But when I walk into our museum and I'm surrounded by the incredible history of Porsche, all the memories come back. Standing in that museum, it's like being surrounded by old friends. It's not only the cars, it's also all the people who drove and worked on each example.

For instance, the two cars that started my association with Porsche, the championship winning 914/6 GT and 911, are always on proud display. In 1973, Peter Gregg and I won both Daytona and Sebring in a 911 RS. That win put my name on the map. Two years later we repeated our victory at Daytona, this time driving a new 911 RSR. These 911s are not only great cars to drive, but they also served as the test bed for the 935s.

The 935 was a great car, and I collected many wins with them, including the 24 hours of Daytona and the 12 hours of Sebring. But it is the rare and exotic 936 that I've loved driving the most. It's nicely balanced, with just the right amount of power, and it carried me to my first Le Mans win in 1977, driving with Jurgen Barth and Jackie Ickx. Piloting a factory-entered car at Le Mans also rekindled my friendship with Porsche racing engineer Norbert Singer that had started with our 1973 Daytona effort. Norbert is a wonderful engineer and the father of many of Porsche's most successful racecars.

I personally captured two 24-hours of Le Mans and one Daytona 24-hours behind the wheel of the mighty 962. If you check the history books, you'll find it to be the most successful race car Porsche ever built.

In 2003, I was able to enter the record books again, winning first overall at Daytona in a new Porsche-engined Daytona Prototype. This car is powered by the same motor that has won so many races in the current 911 GT 3.

Of course, you can't talk about Porsche race cars without mentioning their road-going counterparts. The 911 is easily the most recognizable sports car in the world, and has served as the base for a whole generation of race cars. My first street-legal Porsche was a 1969 911S. That car was a real performer, even by today's standards. And they now bring high dollars at auctions around the world.

As I read through *Keith Martin on Collecting Porsches*, I've enjoyed seeing how so many cars I once drove have become so sought after, and how they are now bringing such extraordinary prices. That these Porsches are so highly valued by the marketplace is a tribute to their successes when new and indicative of the high regard collectors have for the marque. But this is far from surprising—you don't have to drive the high banks of Daytona to appreciate a Porsche.

People often ask me which Porsche is my favorite, and I always reply "next year's." It is the continual development of the breed that makes Porsches such desirable automobiles to own and collect. There's something magical about sitting behind the wheel of a 30-year-old car and feeling its connection to the present—and to the future.

—*Hurley Haywood*
Jacksonville, Florida

Hurley Haywood, with his championship-winning 1970 911, at the 2003 Sahlen's Six Hours of Watkins Glen.

Part III: From 906 to 964 and Everything in Between

Part IV: Random Thoughts

The Sum of Many Parts

Just as a car is made up of thousands of pieces, this book represents literally thousands of hours of work and experience by a host of contributors.

The bulk of the profiles of individual cars in *Keith Martin on Collecting Porsche* were written by our resident Porsche guru, Jim Schrager. Restorer and enthusiast Scott Johnston contributed as well, and Alex Leventhal added comments from a legal perspective.

The cast of market reporters is much larger. Their job is a thankless one from many perspectives. They spend long hours examining cars, sometimes in blazing sun, often in chilling rain, and generally far from home and family. Each evaluation of a collector car in this book represents time spent by one of *Sports Car Market* magazine's experts methodically going over the car from front to back. Their charge is to describe the car to you, in writing, as if you were interested in buying the car and they were talking with you on the phone.

"Nice car, shiny paint," doesn't really do it, does it? That's why you'll read sentences like, "Older restoration that is starting to come apart. Pitted chrome. Some rips and tears to seats. Yet overall, seems like an honest car, not tarted up for auction, but not horribly abused in a past life either." It takes a special kind of reporter to be able to look at one hundred cars a weekend and see the strengths and weaknesses in each, and these *SCM* reporters are indeed special.

It's not practical to list each writer with each car they personally reviewed and photographed, so my thanks goes to everyone below for everything they have contributed.

The Market Report specialists represented in this book are Scott Abts, Gary Anderson, John Apen (*SCM* analyst and Ferrari specialist), Carl Bomstead (*SCM* analyst and automobilia specialist), Chip Baldoni (*SCM* analyst and muscle car specialist), Pat Braden, Dave Brownell (*SCM* senior auction analyst), B. Mitchell Carlson (*SCM* analyst and muscle car specialist), Trevor Clinard, Haig Haleblian, Gary Hoisington, Richard Hudson-Evans (*SCM* senior auction analyst), Dave Kinney (*SCM* senior auction analyst), Scott Featherman (*SCM* analyst and Mercedes specialist), Dan Grunwald (*SCM* analyst and American car specialist), Bob LeFlufy, Donald Osborne (*SCM* analyst and Italian car specialist), Terry Parkhurst (*SCM* analyst), Brian Rabold, Marian Savage, Mike Sheehan (*SCM* analyst and Ferrari specialist), Jim Schrager (*SCM* analyst and Porsche specialist), Steve Serio (*SCM* analyst and Lotus/Aston Martin specialist), Phil Skinner, and David Swig.

Of course, without auction companies, there would be no auctions to report on. We are especially appreciative of the auction companies listed below, both due to their encouraging us to share our critical analyses with our readers, as well as their support of *SCM* through their advertising.

The market reports in this book were taken from cars examined at auctions conducted by the following companies: Barrett-Jackson, Bonhams England, Bonhams Europe, Bonhams and Butterfields, Christie's, Coys, eBay Motors, Kensington Motor Group, Kruse International, James G. Murphy, Keith McCormick, Dana Mecum, RM Auctions, Silver Auctions, Spectrum, and The Auction.

Whenever practical, we have credited the auction companies for the photos we have used in the articles. In the market reports themselves, we are here thanking both the auction reporters and the auction companies for the photos used.

The concept of this book was really the brainchild of Tim Parker, Senior Vice President of MBI Publishing Company, and a longtime subscriber to *Sports Car Market*. Like a pesky bee that wouldn't take no for an answer, he kept buzzing around my head every six months or so, wanting to know when we were going to start our series on collecting. So, after five years of his persevering, here it is. Our liaison at MBI has been Peter Bodensteiner, who has helped shape our content. Mandy Iverson has massaged all of these elements into the finished product you see here.

On the *SCM* staff, David Slama has done the yeoman duties of going back through every last issue, from the very first in 1989, and pulling out all the Porsche articles, converting the older ones into digital format. His assignment was the most thankless of this whole process, and he did it with a smile. Of course, that his daily driver is a 1989 Porsche 911 Carrera 4 might explain part of his cheeriness.

Former editorial managers Brian Rabold and Stephen Siegal looked over every article and updated them as necessary.

Bill Neill and Bengt Halvorsen helped with the copy editing and fact-checking, and Kirsten Ononday did a terrific job, as art director, setting the visual tone for the book. She also managed to take about five hundred different graphic styles from our past issues and convert them into a 112-page book that has visual continuity.

SCM legal analyst John Draneas kindly made his handsome 356A coupe available for the photo that accompanies my intro, and professional photographer Bob Dunsmore sent along the photo of Jerry Seinfeld, driving his RSK in the Colorado Grand.

And finally, I want to thank my wife, Cindy Banzer, who is Executive Editor of Sports Car Market magazine, for her longstanding support and encouragement. She has helped build every single issue of the magazine since it started more than 15 years ago, and helped me stay the course through days both good and bad.

If there are any errors or omissions in this book, they are mine alone. If the articles contained within help you to become more effective collectors, and if they make you smile now and then as well, then we've succeeded in what we set out to do.

—Keith Martin

An Insider's Guide to Collecting Porsche

Keith Martin on Collecting Porsche is designed to do one thing: give you the tools to make the right decision when it comes to buying, driving, restoring and selling your Porsche. And it will do all this while providing some real entertainment along the way.

From the latest model Boxsters to the earliest Speedsters, you'll find information essential to purchasing and enjoying Porsches in this book. And whether you're considering a thirty-thousand-dollar 911, a five-thousand-dollar 924 or a million-dollar 917, you'll get the best advice on what to look for and how much to spend.

In our fifteen years of producing *Sports Car Market* magazine (www.sportscarmarket.com), we have always presented no-holds-barred information and personal, yet informed, opinions about the cars that we cover. When we decided to pull together the very best stuff we'd written about Porsches over the years, we chose articles and reviews that you could use to become a better collector.

Every piece has been carefully chosen for its accuracy and pithiness, and has been updated as necessary to reflect current market conditions The market reviews of cars that have appeared at auction were selected because each car described, as well as each sale, has something to teach us

The Question and Answer sections draws on the hundreds of letters and e-mails we've gotten over the years, with topics ranging from the basic, such as, "Should I repaint my vintage 911," to obscure but still important issues like, "Will installing a big-bore kit in my 356 reduce its reliability?"

Jim Schrager has been *SCM's* Porsche specialist for nearly a decade, and the overwhelming majority of the articles here represent his balanced, yet passionate approach to the marque. Jim always seems to have around 20 Porsches in his collection, and he tries to drive as many of them as he can, as often as he can. Porsches and writing about them are his hobby, not his day job, and all of us are the richer for the time he devotes to *Sports Car Market*.

For those of you who have not had the chance to read *Sports Car Market* magazine, get ready for a wild ride with this book. It's quite unlike any other "buyer's guide" or "marque overview" you've ever read. From the start, our goal was to have *Keith Martin on Collecting Porsche* be a "guerilla-approach" to collecting. We want you to know what really goes on in the car market, which Porsches are highly desirable and which are mechanically easily to live with. At the same time, we want to give a loud and clear warning about which cars should be avoided at all costs. (There are Porsches that we'd recommend against owning, even if they were given to you for free!)

Wouldn't you like to know *before* you buy a 928 that major service on one can cost you thousands of dollars? Or that the 2.7-liter engines in the 1975-77 911s had engine studs that were subject to catastrophic failure, leading to complete engine destruction?

At the same time, wouldn't it be reassuring to know that the 1967 911S in your garage is skyrocketing in value, and that even the lowly 914s, especially the 2-liter cars from 1973-76, are a nearly perfect entry-level Porsche, and are going up a little every year?

But that's the way *SCM* approaches the entire collector car market. In short, *SCM's* first commitment is to its readers and to providing them with info that will make them better collectors. *(If you're not already a regular reader of* SCM, *join the other insiders who make up our intense subscriber base. There's a subscription card with a very special offer inside the back cover of this book.)*

There's no need to read *Keith Martin on Collecting Porsche* from front to back in linear fashion. It's designed so that you can jump around from page to page, and section to section, as if you've just come across the world's largest buffet of Porsche-related information. Just pick a section, dive in and enjoy.

—*Keith Martin*

Keith Martin and 1959 356A coupe.

John M. Vincent

PART I
Porsche 356

Since I started out as a British car fan, the Porsche 356 made little sense to me. A proper sports car came with wind in your face as standard equipment, yet the Porsches were mostly coupes. And that squished-Volkswagen body design took a while to get used to. The crazy engine in the back appeared to be covered with tin—why hide the motor? 356s were just fancy Vee-Dubs, right? And they were so far out of my price range that it was easy to just write them off as a rich man's toy. I was interested in a serious driver's car, not a dilettante's totem.

My first drive in a 356 changed all that. How could this small car have so much room inside? How could the flat-four in back be so smooth and so utterly free of vibration? The transmission shifted like the proverbial hot knife through butter and the steering was extraordinarily light and responsive, not heavy like an MG, TR, or Jaguar XK.

Having an engine compartment filled with lightweight tin was a by-product of the air-cooled design, and it meant most of the weight of the all-alloy engine was placed low in the chassis to enhance handling. How clever of those Germans. The power, while never rip-roaring, felt surprisingly good, and the

car was delightfully agile. After a few more drives, I came to realize that the 356 was, in its own way, the ultimate sports car. So full of usable performance, so well-mannered, roomy, and reliable, there was nothing else in the world like it at any price.

Yes, a Ferrari was a fire-breathing monster in comparison, but you wouldn't think of driving one daily, even if you could afford to. The 356 was both great fun and thoroughly usable in everyday life.

Today the 356 attracts attention partly because its now-classic lines set it apart from anything else on the road. But styling alone doesn't explain why the 356 engenders such fanatic loyalty among its owners, resulting in one of the largest single-model marque clubs anywhere, the Porsche 356 Registry (www.porsche356registry.org).

To figure out the great attraction of the 356, you have to drive one, and not just around the block. It will take at least a few hours to really appreciate the fact that this is an old car that doesn't drive like one. And therein lies the secret of its success.

Get your hands on a good 356 and, like so many 356 owners, you may never want to give it up.—*Jim Schrager*

1952 Porsche Type 540 America Roadster

Chassis number: 12 353
Engine number: 40 055

Brooks

This is an unusual example of a significant, yet somewhat mysterious, early Porsche model, the enigmatic Type 540. It has taken decades for marque experts to unravel the numerous questions of the America Roadster, even including such basics as how it came about, who thought of it and why its production was so brief.

Suffice to point out here that the America Roadster—of which perhaps 11 survive—was the model that began to establish Porsche as a street-usable marque also capable of being raced effectively. It provided the initiative, later acted upon by Porsche's prime coachbuilder, Reutter, in creating the best-loved Porsche of the 1950s, the 356 Speedster.

So why so much mystery about this model? Partly because the car was never cataloged. Since it was intended only for American export, the model was not promoted within Europe. In addition, since Heuer, the coachbuilder, lost money on each body built, the production run was cut short after just 16 cars.

In the midst of modestly growing sports car production, Ferry Porsche appreciated that a market existed for a raceworthy Porsche in the United States. In order to obtain light weight and allow for low-volume output without expensive production tooling, the body was aluminum. To save weight, cost and complexity, the doors were hollow, supporting side curtains instead of roll-up windows, and the simple dash panel featured an open glovebox.

Although full-up weight was 1,580 lb, about 122 lb was removable by unbolting the split windscreen and canvas top. Alloy bucket seats were available, as were a small plastic racing windscreen, leather hood straps and headlamp stoneguards. Power was ample, with 0 to 60 in about 9.3 seconds and a top speed of 110 mph.

While the first America Roadsters were fitted with single-grille engine covers, a second batch had twin-grille decklids as well as subtly flared fenders. A third version may have existed with a fixed windshield and partially enclosed rear-wheel arches. Chassis 12 353, the car pictured here, is from the second production series, with a correct twin-grille decklid and flared fender openings.

This example was imported by Max Hoffman in October 1952. Its first owner, Larry Kulok, entered the 1953 Sebring 12 hours race but was unable to start due to transmission failure. This chassis may have been one of two America Roadsters in the 1954 Sebring race which finished an unimpressive 15th and 36th. Today's seller purchased the car from the fourth owner, who owned it for 40 years beginning in 1959. The fourth owner

indicated that the 42,000 miles recorded are probably genuine.

The quick-fill fuel receptacle protruding through the hood panel is highly unusual, and this may be the only America Roadster so equipped. In the late '50s, the car's original color was changed from ivory with green leather to silver with red leatherette. All gauges and lights are working. The tires are slightly oversize at 5.25 x 16-inches rather than the stock 5-inch width. Attachments for the ultra-rare wheel turbo brake-cooling rings have been remade in the original style. The original side curtains, an early replacement top, a tool pouch that looks complete and a period roll bar are all included. The only known mechanical modification from factory specification has been the fitting early in its career of shorter 3rd and 4th gears taken from Porsche 550 sports racing stock.

With a pre-auction estimate of $300,000-$400,000, this car was bid to $290,000 and declared unsold at the Brooks Quail Lodge Auction on August 19, 2000. The thoroughly unrestored condition, as well as the unusual nature of the America Roadster, make this a tricky car to sell.

Unlike the Speedster or even the 550 Spyder, the America Roadster is not a Porsche icon. We don't find hundreds of photos of racing American Roadsters because they were not winners or even consistent contenders. They didn't have the mid-engine placement or lusty horsepower of the 550 four-cam race cars for serious events, or the accessible price and reliability of the 356 Speedster for amateur venues. Even the design of the America Roadster seems odd, with its radiused wheel openings, flowing fender lines fore and aft, cut-down doors and split windscreen looking for all the world as though it was taken right off an XK 120 Jaguar.

This example was old and tired, with deteriorated paint, poor panel fits and a grungy engine compartment. It needs a full restoration before it would be equal to several of the other America Roadsters being trailered around the show circuit. For example, at Meadow Brook in 1998, a positively stunning light metallic silver-green America Roadster was a blue-ribbon winner in the 356 open car class. That fully restored car was rumored to be available for $350,000 or so after the show.

This car now sits on eBay, with a $325,000 opening bid and a reserve somewhere above the opening money. This is a very narrow market, so it is difficult to call. But in my opinion, the crowd at Brooks was correct to hold its paddles on this one.
—Jim Schrager

(Historic data courtesy of the auction company.)

From the November 2000 issue of *SCM*.◆

Year produced	1952
Number produced	16
Original list price	$4,600
SCM Price Guide	$175,000-300,000
Tune-up/major service	$300
Distributor cap	Unavailable
Chassis #	On horizontal bulkhead under front hood
Engine #	Between generator fan pulley and crankshaft pulley on aft-most edge of engine crankcase
Club	Porsche Club of America, P.O. Box 5900, Springfield, VA 22150
Web site	www.pca.org
Alternatives	Jaguar XK 120; Ferrari 250 GT PF Cabriolet; Mercedes 220 Cabriolet; early "C1" Corvette

1952 Porsche 356 (Pre-A) Cabriolet

Chassis number: 15051
Engine number: P31716

In 1952 there were only four Porsche 356 cabriolets sold in the United States out of 294 produced by the Porsche Werke in Zuffenhausen. Back in '52, about the only way to buy a 356 in this country was through New York importer Max Hoffman.

The early cabriolets were among his best-selling cars, helping to give Porsche a foothold in the emerging post-war American sports car market. Today the cabriolets are considered among the most valuable pre-A models due to their limited numbers and unique body styling, different from that of the later 356-A cabriolets introduced in October 1955.

The pre-A cabriolet or "Dame" (literally "Lady" in German) was introduced to the American market through Hoffman in 1952 as Porsche's luxury model. The cabriolet was replete with fully upholstered and carpeted interior, more comfortable seats, a fully lined convertible top and amenities such as an interior dash light and optional Telefunken radio, one of the earliest car radios to offer push-button tuning.

Among the distinguished characteristics of pre-A models is the wider, more graceful rear fender arch that covers more of the tire.

Cars in the serial number range of 15001 to 15116, this example being 15051, were considered interim models, with running changes made throughout the 1952 production run. Early cars had the upright shifter and non-synchro gearbox (changed to the later synchro gearset on this car), rectangular Hella taillight lenses, beehive turn indicators (later models had four beehive taillights) and single backup in the center of the license plate illuminator. Each cabriolet body was virtually hand-built for Porsche by Reutter, making this one of the scarcest 'pre-A' models.

The early cabriolet pictured here was reputedly in the hands of a single collector for many years. At some stage the original engine for this Porsche (1500S with a roller-bearing crank) was replaced by a slightly later 1500 (plain-bearing) engine. A professional restoration was completed about two years ago. More recently, the car underwent a major service including an engine tune and carburetor overhaul. In addition, the transmission was also fully rebuilt with later internals used in the gearbox owing to the unavailability of early components. This cabriolet is also equipped with an original radio. Early examples of the 356 with their simple, unaffected styling, modest performance and VW-driven underpinnings are the cars most true to the original Porsche ideal.

The early 356 cabriolet shown here sold for $35,650 (including buyer's commission) at Christie's auction in Tarrytown, New York, in April 1998, somewhat above the pre-sale estimate of $25,000-$30,000. Although this was a pretty face, the restoration was of uneven quality. Bright shiny paint contrasted sharply with door bottoms that were misaligned with rocker panels. Mistakes that serious force you to worry about the quality of the body work that you can't inspect.

Pre-A 356s, even among the most hearty enthusiasts, are rarely driven. If shod with their original 3.25 x 16-inch wheels and proper period tires, these cars have a genuine "vintage" feel, which means very scary at anything above 35 mph. To make matters worse, they are fragile and, due to a lack of replacement parts, expensive to repair. As a result, there are two ways to enjoy this model: as a dead-stock museum piece or as a fully modernized driver with unique style.

This car qualifies as neither. It no longer has the original, rare (and highly troublesome) roller-bearing 1500 Super motor, but rather a 1953 plain-bearing engine. Although the newer engine is a bit more durable than the original, it is still fragile compared to the big oil-pump motors of the B/C series (1960-65).

The only real advantage to the 1953 motor is that it looks quite similar to the original, with its tiny single-barrel carbs, through-the-shroud accelerator linkage, cross-mounted balance tube, diagonal mount coil and flat-top distributor. Any B/C motor would look different in each of these areas.

Because so few pre-A 356s come up at auction, it is hard to peg a value. And this car, being neither a reliable driver nor a completely original car, would seem a tough sell. I'd say the seller was wise to accept the winning bid and, for value sake, I hope the new owner has the original 1952 engine in his garage.—Jim Schrager

(Historic data courtesy of the auction company.)
From the September 1998 issue of *SCM.*◆

1955 Porsche 356 Silver Bullet Longtail

Chassis number: 47229 17465

RM Auctions

Porsche has built some wonderful cars in its half century as a manufacturer, creating a legacy revered by enthusiasts and an image that is instantly recognizable. Erwin Komenda's first 1948 Gmund coupe is clearly echoed in Porsches right up to today's Carreras and is still effective, efficient and attractive. Porsche's classic profile as a blend of style and substance highlight the marque's purity of design.

Australian Jeff Dutton had well-established credentials as a Porschephile, not only owning barns full of them over the years but also crafting numerous unique creations, including a wide-bodied 356 Speedster and variants of the Turbo, RS and RSR models. Yet his desire to develop a unique Porsche-based automobile that would still be recognizable in the tradition of Komenda's immortal style convinced him to build this car as a Porsche project to end all Porsche projects.

Starting with a mid-engined 914-6, Dutton added a race-prepped 3-liter 279-hp RS-spec engine, breathing through a pair of three-barrel Webers, mated to a close-ratio Type 915 five-speed transmission. A set of full-trick 934 brakes provides retardation to offset the modified engine's urge.

It was not easy to make a Komenda Porsche out of a boxy 914; however, Dutton's solution started with a worn-out 1955 356 Continental coupe. Porsche purists might argue with the approach, but a quick tape-measure survey demonstrated that the dimensions were compatible other than the wheelbase, which was 13.8 inches longer in the 914-6 chassis than the 356 body. While creating a mid-engined Porsche based on the classic Gmund form might seem extreme, it was an exercise with Stuttgart precedent in the 550A Le Mans coupe and the 904.

The Continental's nose fit the 914-6 pan well, but from the doors back the project got interesting. Hot steel sheets were stretched over the space occupied by the 3-liter six to form a gentle curve from the chopped roof, with its 10-inch-high split windshield, to the tapered and flowing tail. The expanse of curved metal between the doors and rear wheel wells was broken up with inset louvered panels, a concept successfully translated from the RSK.

The Silver Bullet is alive with details. Polished scoops replicate rear quarter windows; a polished aluminum engine cover conceals the 915 transaxle; the engine lies below another polished and louvered panel that takes the place of the rear window, accented by a rooftop cold-air intake periscope. This detail is seemingly drawn from the 1996 911 GT1 racer, but in fact was created for the Silver Bullet in 1992. The engine air intake periscope is mirrored by a roof-mounted rear-view mirror and, even more imaginatively, a low mounted rear-view mirror looking through the passenger's door.

This car stands as a work of art while working as a Porsche as well, an attribute not shared with many other customs. The Silver Bullet has completed several high-speed events in Australia and is presented in exceptional condition. In addition to high-speed road events, its custom design and superb execution make it a welcome entrant at rod and custom shows, where it has garnered several awards in its native Australia.

This car was bid to $55,000 and not sold at the RM Monterey sale held August 18, 2001.

There are a band of 356 enthusiasts, known as the Outlaws, who make interesting mild customs. Some of these cars have chopped roofs and fender flares. Others are based on stock bodies with 911 power plants, or more radically, custom four-cylinder 911-based engines.

The Silver Bullet stands apart from these cars. While Porsche-based, it is no more a Porsche than the hot rod Scrape is a 1939 Lincoln. It has stunning looks and prodigious performance, but that can be said of a host of cars, including a brand-new 996.

So what is the purpose of the Silver Bullet, and who is its prospective buyer? It stands as a tribute by Jeff Dutton to Porsche, and with its various visual allusions evokes memories of Porsche's many successes on the race track.

But as a one-off hybrid, it isn't eligible for any vintage event of note; to allow this car into the California Mille or the Colorado Grand, for instance, would be tantamount to insulting every authentic car entered. At a concours, it would have to go into the homebuilt kit-car category, a class we are not likely to see in the near or far future at Pebble Beach, Meadow Brook or Amelia Island.

Further, the new owner would spend half his life explaining what the car is to curious onlookers. Chances are the Porsche guys won't care because it's a bastard child, and the non-Porsche folks won't care because they won't understand the tribute aspect of the car.

This car has since popped up for sale with an asking price of $66,000, which is far below replacement cost. For an enthusiast looking for something unusual with great horsepower and extraordinary looks, it is a good buy. However, it will always be an automotive oddity, with an uncertain value in terms of future collectibility.—Keith Martin

(Historic data courtesy of the auction company.)
From the December 2001 issue of *SCM*.◆

Year produced	1992
Number produced	1
Original list price	N/A
Tune-up/major service	$575
Distributor cap	$20
Chassis #	Wherever the builder stuck it
Engine #	See above
Club	Porsche Club of America, P.O. Box 5900, Springfield, VA 22150 (entry for this car not guaranteed)
Web site	www.pca.org
Alternatives	914-6 body with a 1955 356 engine and a roof scoop

1956 Porsche 356A Speedster

Chassis number: 82186

Coys of Kensington

The first car to carry Ferdinand Porsche's name was the 356. With aluminum fastback coachwork, pressed-steel chassis and the engine behind the rear axle, manufacture began late in 1948 and the 356 made its debut at the 1949 Geneva Show.

Its power came from a 40-bhp, 1086-cc engine mated to a four-speed gearbox, with independent torsion bar/trailing-arm suspension and drum brakes all round. Fuel economy due to good aerodynamics and low weight was excellent. In 1951, 1290-cc and 1488-cc engines were introduced. The following year came an all-synchromesh gearbox and one-piece windscreen.

By 1954, however, Porsche sales in the United States were suffering from the onslaught of MG, Austin-Healey and Triumph, whose cars provided as much exhilaration for a lot less money. It was thus that coachbuilder Reutter penned a minimal shell based on the convertible 356 with low wrap-around windscreen, reduced frontal area and height, removable sidescreens, a lightweight top and more basic interior. Selling at a competitive $2,995 and available with 55- or 70-bhp 1488-cc engine, the 100-110 mph Speedster proved popular on road and track. Weighing 150 lb less than a standard 356, it was also quicker.

The 1957 Speedster pictured here has recently come back to Europe from the United States, where it has resided from new with a well-known Hollywood figure. Finished in white, with a black top and a brown and beige interior, this highly original Speedster has a little less than 80,000 miles indicated on the odometer. The car is fitted with such desirable original items as Rudge knock-off wheels, stoneguards over the headlights and a Bendix radio. It is understood that the car has never been subject to extensive restoration work, and as such its original condition can only be described as superb.

This very original 356A Speedster sold for $66,000 at the Coys of Kensington auction, November 22, 1999, in London, England. This result tells a tale of the value of originality and the rarity and growing demand for Speedsters in Europe.

'50s speedsters were built especially for the American market, and they were a hard sale anywhere else. Who else in the 1950s but Americans could afford such expensive toys? And Speedsters, unlike coupe and cabriolet models, were more toys than cars. The top was more sun umbrella than weather protection, the side curtains hopeless in any kind of rain and the seats beautiful to look at but bereft of padding. Speedsters were great for carefree days in sunny Southern California, but in Europe, owners demanded the sober 356 coupe and cabriolet virtues of comfortable, all-weather sporting transport.

This sale suggests that Europeans may have discovered the Speedster magic, rather than shunning these Spartan toys. Of course, for the most part, today all 356s are sunny-day cars (save for those owned by the diminishing group of the truly devoted who drive their 356s in all types of weather). Once you decide to drive only in ideal conditions, what can make a bolder statement than the impossibly low profile of the Speedster? In spite of being made in rather large quantities (4,243 built), this is still the high-dollar body style of the 356 range, an example of style trumping rarity.

This particular car was prized both for its unusual options and originality. The Rudge knock-off wheels add about $10,000 to the value and the period flat Nardi steering wheel adds up to $2,000. We'll overlook the fact that the radio improperly punctures the dash; an under-dash bracket would be both more correct and more sanitary. The celebrity ownership never hurts, though this one is rather vague.

Original cars, well-optioned and with a decent provenance, can bring good prices, especially when presented to an appreciative crowd with money in its pockets. This car was bought at a price 10% above the high value given for Speedsters in the SCM Price Guide, despite not being a #1 concours car. It reaffirms that when it comes to Speedsters, emotion matters. This car looked right, had the right history and made a price that doesn't seem unreasonable at all.—Jim Schrager

(Historic data courtesy of auction company.)
From the March 2000 issue of *SCM*.◆

Years produced	1954-1959
Number produced	4,243
Original list price	$2,995
SCM Price Guide	$40,000-60,000
Tune-up/major service	$175
Distributor cap	$12
Chassis #	In front compartment, just aft of tire and in front of fuel tank
Engine #	On rear-most portion of engine block, below generator and above crankshaft pulley
Club	356 Registry, 27244 Ryan Rd., Warren, MI 48092
Web site	www.356registry.org
Alternatives to consider	Jaguar XK120, Alfa Romeo Giulietta Spider, Mercedes-Benz 190 SL roadster, 1958 Corvette roadster
Tier of Collectibility	B

1958 Porsche 356A Cabriolet

Chassis number: 151169
Engine number: P730296

Having commenced manufacture with a short run of aluminum-bodied cars built at Gmund, Porsche began volume production of the steel-bodied 356 coupe at its old base in Stuttgart. The work of Ferry Porsche, the 356 was based on the Volkswagen designed by his father. Like the immortal Beetle, the 356 employed a platform-type chassis with rear-mounted, air-cooled engine and torsion bar all-independent suspension. In 1951 a works car finished first in the 1100-cc class at the Le Mans 24-Hour Race, thus beginning the marque's long and illustrious association with *Le Sarthe*.

Constant development saw the 356's engine grow first to 1.3 and then to 1.5 liters; the original split windscreen replaced by a one-piece; and a Porsche synchromesh gearbox adopted. 1955 marked the arrival of the 356A, the newcomer being readily distinguished by its rounded windscreen and 15-inch (down from 16-inch) wheels. There was a choice of 1.3- or 1.6-liter engines, or the four-cam Carrera. Production lasted until 1959 and the introduction of the 356B, by which time a little fewer than 21,000 had been built.

Originally registered in England, this righthand-drive 356A cabriolet subsequently relocated to Northern Ireland, where its owner was Lady Berry, and was purchased by ex-McLaren Formula One driver John Watson in 1989. We are informed that, apart from a replacement engine, the car has no departures from original specification and comes with factory hardtop. Finished in blue with beige cloth interior, the car is offered for complete restoration and without documents.

This project sold for $8,350 (converted at $1.65 per pound) at the Brooks sale in London on December 3, 1998. The car had unusual pre-sale publicity, with a photo and article appearing in the popular British magazine Thoroughbred & Classic Cars.

To my eyes, after having just completed a ground-up restoration on a 1965 356 SC cabriolet, this car looks a long way from ever being a nice car. For starters, it certainly hurts that the engine is wrong. In addition, the hood gap is very poor; it's logical to conclude that it is from another car. Porsche people like to see original panels on their restored cars.

Although a factory hardtop is included, what's needed instead is the nearly irreplaceable soft-top frame. If it is gone, plan on spending several thousand to replace it.

Brooks

Cabriolet hardtops saw little use when new and are today worth as little as a few hundred dollars.

It's hard to justify spending $40,000 or more to bring this car to concours condition, because with the wrong motor, it will always sell at a discount to full #1 money. Further, it can be very difficult working with a car taken apart by someone else. There is no telling how much pain you will endure hunting down all the miscellaneous bits and pieces which are no doubt missing.

To buy this car to part out (or "break it," as the British would say) you will have to find other worse A cabs being put back together, not a trivial risk. The engine, from an early 1964 C with 75 DIN horsepower, is worth about $1,200 as a core.

In spite of all these problems, this car would have sold for about the same price here in the US as it did in England. Any open 356 has a price floor below which it will not fall, no matter how rough the condition.

The best use for this car is as a hobbyist project, fully realizing that the finished car will never be more than a #3 or perhaps #2 driver. I hope an intrepid enthusiast takes the time and effort required to bring this A cab back among the living. However, to give it a professional restoration or part it out would be difficult to financially justify. — Jim Schrager

(Historic data courtesy of the auction company.)

From the February 1999 issue of *SCM.*◆

Years produced (356A)	1956-1959
Number produced (356A Cab)	3,361
SCM Price Guide	$26,000-32,000
Tune-up/major service	$150
Distributor cap	$22
Price of car new	$3,950 (approx.)
Chassis #	Horizontal bulkhead in front of gas tank
Engine #	On rear-most vertical engine case, between generator pulley and crankshaft pulley
Club	356 Registry, 27214 Ryan Rd., Warren, MI 48092
Web site	www.356registry.org
Tier of Collectibility	B

1959 Porsche 356A Super Cab

Chassis number: 151032

RM Auctions

In 1959, Porsche concluded the run of the 356A cars, with their distinctive droopy front fenders, lower headlights and low bumpers.

Even though the cabriolet appears to share the panels of the Speedster, in fact their bodies have almost nothing in common. In further contrast to the Spartan Speedster, the cabriolet was built with a taller windscreen and raised top frame to accommodate drivers of normal stature, roll-up windows and more comfortable seats. The cabriolet has the dash and fittings of the coupe, rather than the hooded three-dial instrument panel and austere interior trim and accessories of the Speedster. The luxurious, fully padded top of the cabriolet is also in stark contrast to the Speedster's simple unlined cloth top.

Approximately 3,367 356A cabs were built during its four-year life span (1956-59), and the refined and elegant cabriolet proved to be nearly as popular as the Speedster. In the US, where the weather was agreeable and racing was a part of the intended use, the Speedster was king. In Europe, the cabriolet far outsold its stablemate. As a more useable and multi-purposed car, the cabriolet has always been highly sought after by collectors worldwide.

The example pictured here has benefited from a thorough restoration, which has included a fully rebuilt Super 1600 engine and new tan paintwork with the correct black leather interior. We understand that this lovely example is in fully sorted mechanical condition, is cosmetically excellent and an overall very solid example.

The car described here sold for $34,100, including buyer's premium, at RM's Arizona Biltmore auction on January 18, 2002.

Color is, of course, an emotive and personal thing, but to my eye it was a pleasure to see this early Porsche painted in something other than white, red, silver or black. However, there did seem to be a touch too much green in the Stone Gray, and it appeared, through a stone chip, that this car might have once been Signal Red.

The car appeared very correct throughout, had excellent door and panel fit (the doors closed with that nice bank-vault ka-lick that Porsches are famous for) and was cosmetically hard to criticize.

Being a cabriolet added to its collector value over a coupe but the more sporting Speedsters are still the darlings of the 356A models. The 1600 Super engine hanging out the back is another bonus. While the 1600 Normal produced 60 DIN brake horsepower at 4,500 rpm, the Super unit was good for 75 horsepower at 5,000 rpm. Fifteen or so horses may not seem like a lot, but it makes a difference in the lightweight

Porsche's scat, upping the top speed from 100 mph to 110 mph and chopping the 0-to-60 time down to the 11-second range. Suspension remained unchanged, with well-developed swing axles at the rear and transverse torsion bars all around. Although some claimed this made for tricky handling, to the adventurous Porsche enthusiast this was yet another skill to be mastered and enjoyed.

As with most all cars of the '50s, foreign and domestic, rust is the enemy. Rocker panels, door posts, floor pans and the myriad nooks and crannies that give Porsche coachwork such rigidity and integrity are all vulnerable to the dreaded tinworm. This car suffered from no such problems, though, and this was reflected in the selling price.

The new owner of this Porsche bought a nice example at a fair retail market level. The fact that it was offered at an auction that had most people waiting and watching for six-figure bidding on the headline exotics may have helped it stay at a rational price level, as happened with several other very clean and show-ready sports cars at the Biltmore that day.—Dave Brownell

Additional notes supplied by Jim Schrager:
This car appeared familiar to me, and upon checking my archives I found it had sold at Barrett-Jackson 2001 for $38,000, and then at Kruse Auburn in spring of 2001, to a dealer, for $28,090. Thus begins another auction mystery.

While not a Porsche Club concours winner, this is a handsome car, with no apparent needs. Why has it failed to find a permanent home? Will we see it again on another auction block, or has it finally landed, as it deserves, in the hands of an appreciative enthusiast?

(Historic data courtesy of auction company.)

From the March 2002 issue of *SCM.*◆

Years produced (356A)	1956-1959
Number produced (356A Cab)	3,367
Original list price	$4,360
SCM Price Guide	$32,000-37,000 with Super engine
Tune-up/major service	$300
Distributor cap	$30
Chassis #	Under front hood on horizontal bulkhead
Engine #	Stamped in rear-most engine case, between generator and crankshaft pulley
Club	356 Registry, Barbara Skirmants, 27244 Ryan Rd., Warren, MI 48092
Web site	www.356registry.org
Alternatives	Jaguar XK 140 drophead coupe, Mercedes-Benz 190SL convertible, MGA
Tier of Collectibility	B

1960 Porsche 356B Roadster

Chassis number: 87985

The Roadster pictured here is a Drauz-built 50,000-mile California car. It was meticulously and comprehensively restored by a Porsche specialist. Presented in Fjord Green with a brown interior, a tan cloth top and chrome wheels, it has seen little use since restoration.

Part of a 50-car collection, this 356 has been consistently and professionally maintained in a climate-controlled environment. Still essentially perfect, it is ready to satisfy its new owner on show fields, weekend drives or in today's popular and numerous historic tour events.

This 356B Roadster sold at RM's Amelia Island auction in Florida on March 10, 2001, for $63,800, including buyer's premium. It was described as being in very nice condition overall, with good panel gaps. The only negative was a few small rust bubbles in the bottom of the driver's door. If the odometer reading (53,068) is accurate and original, the numbers match and the quality of the restoration is consistently high throughout the car, the price is just outside the high end of the current market range.

The B Roadster sits in a desirable position among the many and varied 356 models since it is a direct descendant of the original Speedster, yet has most of the upgrades made to the final editions of the 356 line. It was the last Porsche designed to be driven to the track, have its windshield unbolted, raced, reassembled and driven home.

While Porsche made cabriolets from the very beginning of production, it was the Speedster line, first introduced for the 1955 model year, that opened new horizons for the young auto manufacturer. A stripped-down, lightweight model with laughable weather protection, it was fully competitive in its class in SCCA racing and captured the imagination of the public through appearances in movies like "Hud."

In mid-1958 the Speedster was retired. It was renamed the Convertible D (the D referring to its body builder, Drauz, in Heilbron, Germany), and upgraded with a new, higher windshield, roll-up windows, regular coupe-type seats and a roomier top. The body and chassis of the Convertible D were the same as the Speedster, but the refined cockpit made the car far closer to the Porsche ideal of everyday, all-weather use so central to the marque's image in Europe. The 356A cabriolet continued as Porsche's touring, rather than performance, model.

For the 1960 model year, Porsche introduced the 356B models with a host of sweeping changes aimed at reliability, durability and drivability. A completely revised Convertible D was renamed the Roadster. The top and windshield were nearly identical to the Convertible D but sat atop a body that had all the redesigned elements of the 356B models.

Years produced	1960-1961
Number produced	2,653
Original list price	...........$3,794 (1961)
SCM Price Guide	..........$35,000-45,000
Tune-up/major service	...............$250
Distributor cap	.....................$12
Chassis #	.......On horizontal bulkhead under front lid, just forward of gas tank
Engine #	......On rearmost engine crankcase piece, in between generator and crankshaft pulley
Club	.................Porsche 356 Registry, 27244 Ryan Rd., Warren, MI 48092
Web site	...............www.356registry.org
Alternatives	...........MGB, Triumph TR4, Alfa Gulietta Spider Veloce, Mercedes 190SL
Tier of Collectibility	...................B

Mechanical updates of the 1960 B models over earlier Speedsters included bigger oil pumps, stronger connecting rods, improved shift linkages, finned brake drums, tapered roller bearings for the front axles, improved ZF steering gearboxes and the availability of the high-horsepower Super 90 engine with a counterbalanced crankshaft.

The nomenclature of 356s can be confusing. The 356A Speedster, which evolved into the Convertible D, finally became the 356B Roadster. One performance model, three name variations (Speedster/Convertible D/Roadster). The final 356 body style was introduced with two engine-cooling grilles, leading to the term twin-grille Roadster, used only for the 1962 models (all 1960 and '61 356Bs have a single grille on the engine lid).

For 356 cognoscenti, the Roadster is a natural choice, representing the last of the Speedster line with all of the 356B improvements. While cabriolets shared the mechanical upgrades, once the two are viewed side-by-side, the superior beauty of the Roadster is apparent. The Roadster has, in addition to its chrome-framed windshield, different doors, a different rear cowl and a different top. The distinctions are subtle but unmistakable, resulting in the lighter and sportier look of the Roadster.

Porsche 356s were built to be used on a daily basis, so true low-mileage cars like this are hard to find. As for the corrosion observed, the rust-proofing was so primitive in this era that even otherwise dry, perfect cars can develop rust bubbles at the bottoms of the doors, but this is not difficult to repair. Therefore, given the low miles, even with the bit of isolated rust, the price paid was not out of range for an exceptional machine. Top-notch 356s are continuing to bring prices not seen since the late '80s, as collectors seek out the best of the best.—Jim Schrager

(Historic data courtesy of auction company.)
From the June 2001 issue of *SCM*.◆

1961 Porsche 356B Carrera 2

Chassis number: 154626

RM Auctions

That's no typo—this Carrera 2 is a 1961, the very first Porsche to carry the new Type 587 2-liter, four-cam motor. The car started life as a stock pushrod-powered 356B (T5) cabriolet. After driving it for about seven months as his everyday car, Ferry Porsche returned it to Werks 1, where it was given a transplant: the very first 587 engine, serial number 97001. Afterwards, Ferry Porsche continued to drive the car regularly for several years.

The first four-cam street cars were special-order pre-As, of which relatively few were built. Starting with the new 356A, introduced in September 1955 at the Frankfurt Auto Show, there was an official street-going, four-cam Porsche, the Carrera 1500GS. It was an expensive upgrade, however, costing almost $6,000, or about $1,100 more than the next most expensive street model.

While the factory ignored racing applications of the 356 Carreras, privateers did not, and soon Carrera coupes (mostly in Europe) and Carrera Speedsters (mostly in America) were found on the track. Later, the factory acknowledged the inevitable and put out both race and street versions of the 356 Carreras.

By the time the Type 587 2-liter engine was developed, there was an accepted market for four-cam street cars among those wanting the best in performance. The Carrera 2 became the best-selling of the four-cam street cars, while the racing brothers of this engine went into re-engined Carrera Abarths, late Spyders and, of course, the legendary 904. With a recent full professional concours restoration, this is surely one of the most important 356s known.

Although bid to $220,000, this car was unsold at the RM Classic auction in Monterey on August 15, 1998. As Ferry's personal Porsche, this is certainly a very special machine, but the bid seemed money enough for what is a rather difficult car to use.

To work up a value, let's start with a similar 1964 Carrera 2 cabriolet, in immaculate condition but without celebrity heritage, which sold for $134,500 at Christie's Tarrytown, New York, auction June 15, 1996. This 1964 car had its original four-cam engine in a crate with a nicely detailed 912 engine installed. This is often done with four-cammers due to their reputation of unreliability when used infrequently on the street.

"Unfortunately, many 4-cam motors live up to their reputations as wildly expensive hand grenades."

Years produced	1962-1965
Number produced	88
Original list price	.....................$7,980
SCM Price Guide	.....................$122,500-135,000
Tune-up/major service	.....................$2,000-3,000
Distributor cap	.....................$250 (two required)
Chassis #	.....Stamped in horizontal bulkhead under front hood next to gas tank
Engine #	.....On right side of rear-most engine case, next to fan housing
Club	.....................Porsche 356 Registry, 27214 Ryan Rd., Warren, MI 48092
Web site	.....................www.356registry.org
Alternatives	.....................1964-65 SC Cabriolet 1966 Ferrari 275 GTS, 1958 Mercedes 300SL
Tier of Collectibility	.....................A

Unfortunately, many four-cam motors live up to their reputations as wildly expensive hand grenades. They were always meant as race engines and are rather highly strung to be driven to the mall. Life expectancy on the street can be as low as a few thousand miles between $40,000-$50,000 rebuilds.

Even at 356 events, many who bring their four-cams don't drive them. When the rest of us headed out on the track at the 1998 East Coast 356 Holiday, not a single Carrera made it out of the concours tent. One brave owner started his car in the hotel parking lot, causing an anxious crowd of 356ers to gather just to hear the music.

So this isn't a car for sunny-day drives with its four-cam engine in place. And for this particular car, sticking in an ordinary pushrod engine seems distasteful. In fact, it hints at defilement. This was Ferry's personal car. His hands gripped the beautiful wooden VDM steering wheel, his posterior graced the pleated leather seats.

This Porsche can't be driven regularly and can't be raced without a (historically verboten) engine transplant. So what we have here is a museum car, which makes for a very thin market. In my opinion, this car, at a price in the $150,000 range, would make a great addition to the factory museum in Stuttgart.—Jim Schrager

(Historic data courtesy of the auction company.)

From the April 1999 issue of *SCM*.◆

1963 Porsche 356 Carrera 2 GS/GT

Chassis number: 122561
Engine number: 98016

RM Auctions

Porsche had great success racing 356 Carreras in many different venues. In 1961 at Sebring, Porsche had two class wins with the Carrera 2: the GT class with Ben Pon and Joe Buzzetta, and the Prototype class with Don Webster and Bruce Jennings. After Buzzetta's win, he remarked of the Carrera: "If I had a choice of any one of the Porsches I'd raced to keep for a road car, it would be that one."

The Carrera engine was by far the most technologically advanced powerplant produced by Porsche for the 356. As the Carrera engine not only added more power but was heavier as well, Porsche asked Reutter to build a series of lightweight bodies, which resulted in the GT designation.

The extra power and tail-heavy weight distribution made this a demanding car to drive. The plain-bearing 2-liter engine would happily rev past 7,500 rpm, but Porsche warned customers against exceeding 6,500 for a long period due to excessive fuel consumption and engine wear.

The stunning and rare example pictured here is finished in silver with lightweight blue competition seats, plexiglass windows and a factory-fitted roll bar. Weight-saving modifications of the GT body include aluminum hood, doors, deck lid and deletion of the radio and heater. With 44,000 miles from new, there are less than 500 miles since a complete rebuild. It is totally original except for the paint and some carpeting.

This example's original type 587/2 160-bhp GT engine was replaced at the factory with a 587/3 904-spec engine in April 1964, as noted on the factory Kardex. This 180-bhp 904-spec powerplant remains in the car today. It has recently had a tune-up by well-known four-cam expert Bill Doyle. All numbers match the Kardex for this Carrera, including the 904 engine upgrade.

Richard Freshman purchased the completely original car in 1986. His goal was to preserve this exotic piece of Porsche history, and he worked with well-known 356 expert and historian Ron Roland to do so. This example is eligible for the popular Tour Auto Retrospective.

In 1960, Uli Wieselmann wrote: "Already an enthusiast's carriage of the first magnitude, the Carrera will one day be found only in a few isolated examples in the hands of real connoisseurs. They'll care for it, polish it and drive it amongst everyday cars secure in the knowledge that they possess a product of technical delicacy that's enveloped in romance. No matter how perfect, refrigerators and typewriters can never so aspire."

This 356 sold for $173,250, including buyer's premium, at RM's Santa Monica sale on May 23, 2002. This price, $150,000 more than a decent 356 coupe is worth, was well above "typical" 356 Carrera 2 coupe prices, as well. Nonetheless, it represents a fair market value on what is one of the rarest late 356 cars, the Carrera 2 GS/GT. The explanation of value comes down to what "Carrera 2 GS/GT" means in mechanical terms.

Early Carrera engines were taken straight from the highly successful 550 and RS/RSK mid-engine Spyder cars and placed in standard 356 and 356A coupe (and Speedster) bodies starting in 1955. This was a highly sporting car for the street, with a roller-bearing crankshaft, four cams driven by a nightmarishly complex set of bevel gears and true racing power produced high in the rpm range. This same type of motor even powered Porsche's F1 engines in the late '50s and early '60s.

But the roller-bearing bottom end was not well suited for the street. You had to keep the rpms up or risk lugging the engine, which could cause the roller pins to wear very rapidly. Frequent rebuilds were the norm.

Porsche answered this in 1958 with the first plain-bearing bottom end for a four-cam engine, first in 1500- and 1600-cc sizes. In 1962 the first 2-liter Carrera engines were developed, hence the suffix "2." These Carrera 2 engines were by far the best of the lot and were selected for the fearsome 904 race car, producing 130 DIN hp in GS trim, 160 hp for the GT version and 180 hp in the 904 GTS.

Carrera road cars are called GS for "Grand Sport" and were meant to be the ultimate street car. The GT designation means the car has special lightweight body panels for racing purposes, as well as an engine in a higher state of tune.

A copy of the factory build sheet (the Kardex) is a requirement when dealing with a 356 of this value. Also required is proof the engine is in good running order, as there are just a handful of mechanics in the world able to effectively rebuild a four-cam, and only then at significant expense.

In some ways this is a 356 with all its innate simplicity removed, which now demands V12-Ferrari levels of maintenance hassle and expense. But to a handful of Porsche purists, these four-cam cars are among the most interesting vehicles ever produced by the factory, drawing their engines and inspiration from the world-beating Spyders. As the price paid here indicates, there will always be a strong market for these exotic pieces of Porsche history.—*Jim Schrager*

(Historic data courtesy of the auction company.)

From the August 2002 issue of *SCM*.◆

Years produced	1962-1965
Number produced	445 (approx.)
Original list price	$9,095
SCM Price Guide	$82,500-100,000
Tune-up/major service	$2,000
Distributor cap	$500
Chassis #	On horizontal bulkhead under front lid
Engine #	On rear-most engine case
Club	Porsche 356 Registry, 27244 Ryan Rd., Warren, MI 48092
Web site	www.356registry.org
Alternatives	Alfa TZ-1, Ferrari 355 Challenge
Tier of Collectibility	A

1964 Porsche 356C Coupe

Chassis number: 216900
*Engine number: P*712058*

The Porsche 356C was announced in the summer of 1963 and was the final version of its type before the all-new six-cylinder 911s were introduced in 1965. The steel chassis frame was basically unaltered from the B and the body was the T6 design with twin air intakes on the enlarged rear lid, an enlarged windscreen and rear window and a bigger front bonnet. The interior was also virtually unchanged and in fact quite Spartan when compared to other sports cars of the day. Just two engine options were available, either the 75-bhp 1600C or 95-bhp SC, the former fitted with twin Zenith carburetors rather than Solex. The biggest difference was in the braking,

Christie's

as the C now had four-wheel discs (the handbrake lever operated a drum at the rear), which made a significant difference to the stopping power. In all, some 16,668 356Cs were built, and they were praised for their quality of finish, panel fit, engineering integrity and roadholding capabilities.

This car is a very early 1964 1600C coupe that has had just three owners from new. The car has light ivory paintwork and straight, unmarked panelwork. The interior has black leather seats with dark gray carpeting, a correct steering wheel with full circular horn ring and a Porsche radio blanking plate. Lap belts are also fitted. The indicated mileage is only 33,570 and indicative of the car's original condition.

This less-than-immaculate 356C sold for the eye-opening price of $30,550 at the Christie's Petersen Museum auction on June 17, 2000, in Los Angeles. Does this big price translate to a new level for C coupes, or is the outcome here simply the result of the seller being in the right place at the right time?

C coupes in the common colors of white or red, sans sunroof or the more powerful SC motor, are plentiful. However, the low mileage here is unusual, as most 356 owners found it difficult not to drive their cars.

I rate the condition of a 356 or early 911 by looking at four areas: body, chassis, interior and mechanicals. The exterior of this car had splendid gaps on all the movable panels. This is a big plus, as it can be quite expensive to bring uneven gaps back into line. However, the paint was nothing special. It had been repainted

Years produced	1964-1965
Number produced	13,507
Original list price	$4,295
SCM Price Guide	$17,500-22,500
Tune-up/major service	$300
Distributor cap	$10
Chassis #	On horizontal bulkhead under front lid, forward of fuel tank
Engine #	On rear-most engine case below generator and above crankshaft pulley
Club	Porsche 356 Registry, 27244 Ryan Rd., Warren, MI 48092
Web site	www.356registry.org
Alternatives	Alfa Romeo Sprint, Mercedes 220 SE coupe, MGB-GT, Ford Mustang coupe
Tier of Collectibility	B

somewhere in its life, and the hood was a slightly different shade of white than the rest of the car. Although Porsche calls this color light ivory, as painted on this car I would call it refrigerator white, which is a very bright, clear white with no hint of gray or beige.

The chassis was the car's strong point, being original, tight and straight with no rust or patches. The interior was completely original, which is highly prized. Nothing we have today duplicates the look and feel of the original wool carpets or the sturdiness of the original seating materials. In talking with someone familiar with the car after the sale, I learned that the mechanicals suffered from not being used. While probably not serious, the car needs its brakes redone and new seals installed in the engine and transmission at a total cost of several thousands of dollars.

While this car made a terrific amount of money for the seller, I do not think this sale signals a major shift in the market for 356 coupes. Exceptional low-mileage cars do tend to bring strong money, but we have seen enough similar cars sell to realize that for this car on this day, the auction house was able to generate an unusually high bid.

At least this isn't a 5,000 or 10,000 original-miles car, where every mile driven would bring a huge loss of value. With 34,000 miles, the owner can put 3,000 or 4,000 thousand miles a year on it for the foreseeable future and not diminish its value significantly.
—*Jim Schrager*

(Historic data courtesy of the auction company.)
From the September 2000 issue of *SCM.*◆

356s Melt From The Inside Out

Dear Mr. Schrager: I noticed that a restoration shop profiled in the August 2000 issue of SCM (page 22) listed the Porsche 356 as its least favorite car to work on. Is this shop just weird, or is there something about these cars I should know about? I am seriously considering the purchase and restoration of a 356 and wonder if I am going to run into that attitude elsewhere.—D.Z., via e-mail

Shops which do not specialize in the 356 often find them difficult. The 356, unlike many of its British and American peers, is a complex machine with precision systems and tight tolerances. It does not suffer fools gladly. Here are some of the reasons why.

1) RUST IS MESSY IN A 356
The monocoque body and chassis construction translates into great strength and modest weight, a wonderful combination made possible by the boxed construction of the unibody. But those closed sections are ideal breeding grounds for rust. 356s deteriorate from the inside out, requiring X-ray vision to detect and skill to correct. In a unibody structure, the rust you see on the outside of the car may be only the tip of the rustberg. A shop may quote a fixed restoration estimate and then discover that huge amounts of additional work are needed. This is not a happy event for the shop or the 356 owner.

2) 356s WERE OFTEN HACKED
By the early '70s, the majority of 356s had fallen into disrepair. Many enthusiasts had moved on to the less enchanting but more capable 911. Values were low: Speedsters sold for a few thousand dollars, coupes even less. Given these low values, most repairs made in the '70s and early '80s were of low quality. Restoration efforts today have to undo all that old work. This is both difficult and costly, and harder still to estimate before a car is taken apart.

3) THE MECHANICALS CAN BE TRICKY
The 356 seems straightforward, with its VW-derived air-cooled engine and four-speed transaxle. But those simple parts must be assembled flawlessly or there will be trouble down the road. One of the biggest mistakes a non-356 shop makes is to assume the engine goes together just like a VW. Even something as simple as grinding the crankshaft has its own lore (don't make the radii from the journals to the throws the wrong diameter, or the crank will break). Which pistons and cylinders to buy, among all the aftermarket and OEM choices? Why do the brand-new expensive Weber carbs cause such a big flat spot in the power-band? A non-356 fluent shop can do everything right by most standards, and you can still end up with a car that doesn't run properly, and never will.

4) PARTS ARE EXPENSIVE
When new, a 356 cost as much as a fully loaded Cadillac. Nothing was ever cheap about these cars, and that holds for a restoration as well. Unlike many American and British cars,

The shop you choose to restore your 356 may be more important than the car.

there are no large-scale sources of reasonable quality parts at fair prices. You would think that VW parts would work fine, but other than road wheels for drum-braked 356As and Bs and one particular distributor (the Brazilian Bosch .050), there is little of consequence from the VW that fits.

5) COUPES AREN'T WORTH MUCH
The cost of a decent street restoration begins at about $25,000, but the value of most coupes, when finished, doesn't break $20,000. So the shop owner is put in the lousy position of having his customer upside down in the car from the day it is completed. No shop owner is anxious to do that, if for no other reason than the fact that if the owner doesn't pay, the shop now owns the car and will probably never be able to get its money out.

6) 356s ARE HARD TO GET RIGHT
When new, these cars were built to high standards. While it may not be difficult to duplicate the care with which Chevy built Corvettes in 1964, it is very hard to recreate the body panel fit, interior trim work and paint perfection of a 356. A national concours champion may have $30,000 or more invested in body preparation and paint alone. Not all shops are prepared to complete work at this level of detail, much less for the owner who wants something "close" to this quality at one-third the cost.

The solution is to select the shop to work on your 356 with as much care as you selected the car in the first place. In fact, choosing a shop first, and then having them help you select a car, is not a bad idea. If you feel your local shops don't have enough hands-on experience to do justice to a 356, membership in the 356 Registry (27244 Ryan Road, Warren, MI 48092; $25/year) will introduce you to a host of shops intimately familiar with the cars.

No, the "Wrenching Truth" shop that didn't like to work on 356s wasn't weird, just refreshingly honest. An honest "No, we don't work on those" is much more useful than the casual, "Oh sure, I can restore anything" attitude that can lead to expensive yet disappointing restorations.—*Jim Schrager*

From the October 2000 issue of *SCM.*◆

356s from $16,000 to $150,000

Dear Mr. Schrager: *I'm confused about the spread of prices for open Porsche 356s. At the January Kruse/Scottsdale auction, a red/black 1960 356B convertible in good condition was bid to $26,775 and didn't sell. Another 1960 356B open car, this time silver/red and in better condition, was bid to $52,000 but also didn't change hands. At the Barrett-Jackson auction, a red/black 1955 Speedster in #2 condition with a new motor sold for $42,788.*

I thought Speedsters were the most expensive of all these cars. Why was a 356B bid higher? And, more important, what can I buy for around $20,000, which is all I can afford? – **P.L., Peoria, IL**

The 356 does have a logic to it. First, keep in mind that there are many kinds of 356s, both open and closed.

The low end of the 356 market is inhabited by coupes. Depending upon year and options, decent coupes can be bought in the $16,000 to $20,000 range. These are a great value, but appreciation will be modest due to the large number produced and the fact that coupes are unable to provide the wind in the hair so often required of a sunny-day vintage car drive.

Prices for open 356s range from the teens for beaters to the mid $40,000s for nice drivers, and on up to the $80,000s for very special cars such as Seinfeld's pre-A Speedster or the Speedster that won the People's Choice Award at last summer's Porsche Parade in San Antonio, Texas.

At the very top of the 356 market are cars with the exotic and wildly expensive double overhead-cam motor. These four-cam 356s carry designations such as Spyder, Carrera, RS, GS or GT, and are typically priced in the $60,000-$150,000 range.

Cabriolets and Speedsters

Casual observers often fail to notice the two distinct lines of open cars: cabriolets and Speedsters. Although they share the same chassis and engines, the bodies and interior appointments are quite different. Also, they were built in different numbers, for different uses, and today have rather different values.

Cabriolets are based on the coupe body, have a thickly padded top, two small back seats, a coupe dashboard and a coupe windshield set in a body-colored frame. When new, they were the most costly body style in the line; now they are the cheapest way to buy an open-air 356. They are heavy, luxurious, and to my eye, not as attractive as Speedsters. And unlike Speedsters, they were never meant to be taken on the track. In good #2 condition, they typically change hands in the range of $35,000-$50,000.

Speedsters, on the other hand, seem anxious to arrive at the starting grid. With their removable chrome-framed windshields and minimal interior appointments, they were always just a few steps away from looking the part of a race car. At the track, their lighter weight gave them a genuine advantage. Good Speedsters will bring $35,000-$40,000 for pre-A cars and $38,000-$50,000 for 356As.

Since the mid-'80s, Speedsters have been the most valuable 356. Built in both pre-A ('54-55) and 356A models ('56-58),

Color can make a big difference in price.

Speedsters are the only series-produced Porsches with very low windshields and side curtains rather than roll-up windows. In late 1958, Speedster bodies were upgraded with roll-up windows and a higher windshield. These cars are known as the Convertible D in honor of the coachbuilder, Drauz. At the time, they were seen as a great improvement over the Speedster. Today, Convertible Ds, of which only about 1,330 were built, are worth quite a bit less than the Speedster. They fall into the $36,000-$40,000 range.

In 1960 Porsche made a major change to the 356. The Speedster tradition was carried on in a new removable-windshield open car, this time called the Roadster. As with all descendants of the Speedster, the doors and rear body were of a subtly different shape than cabriolets, the unique Speedster dash was used along with a simple, light, unpadded top and there were no back seats.

The three cars that confused you this winter in Phoenix help us understand today's market. They were of three different styles: cabriolet, Roadster and Speedster. The 1960 356B bid to $26,775 at Kruse was a Cabriolet. It was a nice enough car, but cabriolets were built in large numbers (about 14,400 in total), and these models don't have the sporting attitude or racing pedigree of the Speedster and its descendants.

The other open 1960 356B, bid to $52,000, was a Roadster, finished in the unusual and highly desirable color of silver trimmed with a red leather interior. The price bid may seem high but is market correct for a superb example and evidence of the continuing rise of Roadsters. Total Roadster production from 1960 to 1962 is about 2,900 cars (versus about 4,200 Speedsters). These cars have much better weather sealing and creature comforts than Speedsters, and are therefore more practical to use regularly. *(Please remember that any high bid on an unsold car may reflect wishful thinking on the part of the seller rather than an actual cash offer.—Keith Martin.)*

The '55 Speedster that sold for $42,788 at Barrett-Jackson fits in between these cars and is the hardest to explain. You are correct in thinking that Speedsters have generally been worth more than Roadsters. Part of this car's lower value can be explained by the fact that it was a pre-A, rather than the more durable and drivable 356A. Still, this price was probably on the low side by a few thousand dollars for such a nice example and, if the car was complete and correct and drove well, was a relative bargain.

If you are serious about a $20,000 budget, I'd recommend a nice coupe rather than a beater cabriolet. You can easily spend $20,000 restoring a ratty 356, and I've seen twice that much spent without too much trouble. If you can slide up to $30,000 or so, a good cabriolet will bring you the added bonus of top-down driving. At $45,000 you should find a handsome Roadster if driving is your most important objective. The same money will buy a decent Speedster if you don't mind the inconsequential weatherproofing.—*Jim Schrager*

From the April 1998 issue of *SCM*.◆

Mystery Motor Discount

OK, so you've found that great 356 coupe and you realize that these cars are a rather good buy. The owner tells you the motor runs great and was rebuilt just before he bought it. But of course, he has no paperwork to back that up. In your test drive, you verify that the car seems to run well enough, and besides, if you get stuck with an engine problem, it's no big deal to rebuild it yourself or have your brother-in-law who once worked on VWs do the honors for you. No problem, right?

Wrong. Dimensionally, the 356 case is very similar to the 36-hp VW case, yet the Porsche produces from 60 to 95 hp. Although it has four bearings, it is in effect a three main bearing engine, even though in a perfect world you'd need five to fully support a high-performance crankshaft. The result is that the crankshaft flexes, and especially for the higher horsepower S-90 and SC motors, cranks can and do break. You want to avoid this, as a broken crank often takes the case with it when it goes. Due to the high level of vintage 356 racing these days, the supply of both cases and cranks is limited and getting smaller (read that as ever more expensive).

The neat aluminum pistons make for a lively engine but tend to wear out with shocking regularity. Some mechanics never replace just the rings in a 356, so certain is the wear on those snappy aluminum pistons that spend their lives waging a war fighting against tough steel rings. It doesn't take much imagination to realize that the ring lands get oversized rather quickly.

What you have is an overstressed engine that needs to be assembled very carefully to have any chance of even medium-term survival. In addition, parts are expensive, at about $1,800

A certified rebuild may be money in the bank.

for either a new crank or a new set of pistons and cylinders (Ps & Cs as we call them). Then we get to heads that can cost $500 each to redo properly. When all is said and done, you can easily have $6,000 in parts and $2,500 in labor doing a no-excuses rebuild that will take the car back to its original reliability.

So, the bottom line is that cars with certified rebuilds (i.e., with receipts carefully documenting the work) are always worth more than 356s that just run nice. Thus the term *mystery motor discount*. If it's a nice car but has a mystery motor, you should subtract a few thousand dollars from your offer as a hedge against the day when it is time to rebuild.—*Jim Schrager*

From the April 1997 issue of *SCM*.◆

Mystery Photo

The evolution of Porsche's new SUV had very humble beginnings.—**Michael Glauberman, Huntingdon Valley, PA**

Hans *en route* to the concours with his priceless '53 Conestoga "Jolly." Note the beater tow car.—**Richard J. Castiello, Chevy Chase, MD**

Abner Butterchurner's Amish relatives never did figure out how he made those trips to the Big City so quickly.—**Chris Atkins, Washington, MO**

Having no idea how hard Sierra Nevada winters could be, Hans and Bertha signed on with the Donner Party for the trip to California.—**Jeff Hepner, Washington, PA**

"Short Bob's Porsche Chuck-wagon."—**Eric and Cynthia Meyer, Santa Barbara, CA**

Ken Leach gives a helping hand to classmate Meriwether Lewis, who suffered horsepower failure.—**John Mitchell, Lake Oswego, OR**

Before the introduction of the camber compensator, Dr. Porsche's remedy for 356 rear-end oversteer was the factory option Conestoga wagon. Improved handling ingeniously

Amish relatives go motoring according to Chris Atkins.

combined with pantry facilities: the ultimate driving machine.—**Norman S. Vogel, San Francisco, CA**

Instead of a toaster, what one receives for opening up a checking account at a Wells Fargo branch.—**Dan Hampton, La Crosse, WI**

I think Porsche is working too hard on their new slogan, "Back to the Future."—**Marni Lynn, Kewaskum, WI**

Well, Sophia's papa didn't make a mistake when he bought her the Porsche and camper for her 16th birthday. She parallel parked it her very first try.—**Bob Lynn, Kewaskum, WI**

Chip and Layla von Whoopsburg decide to trace their roots back to the Old West.—**David Parish, via e-mail**

Go west, my boy. Go west to Berlin!—**David Parish, via e-mail**

Covered wagon being pulled by rare *Zuffenhorsen*.—**Bruce Tarsia, via e-mail**

And this month's winner of a truly remarkable 1/18 scale model from USAppraisals is Chris Atkins, for revealing a previously unknown segment of Amish history.—*Keith Martin*

From the January 2001 issue of *SCM*.◆

Buy a C, Not a B?

Dear Mr. Schrager: *I am looking for a 356B or C coupe for about $10,000. I think that I should buy a decent, non-rusty, fully functioning example. However, I have heard that if you are going to buy a 356, be sure to buy a C, not a B. Why?*—**F.B.B., via e-mail**

Finding a decent running and driving 356 will end up being more important than whether it's a B or a C. And unless you find a steal of a deal, I just don't think that $10,000 is going to get the job done.

Consider this story. A good friend and long-time multiple 911 owner set out last year to find an above average, but not perfect, 356B or C coupe to beat

Either a 356 B or C in good condition is a sound investment.

around in. This guy knows his cars and put a $14,000 ceiling on his purchase. Based in Colorado, he used half a lifetime worth of frequent-flier miles and dragged himself all over the United States looking at cars. He would call me from the road, right after he had looked at one of these $12,000 gems that had been represented on the phone or by e-mail as "a very nice, correct car that needs nothing." He would tell me what a worthless pile of junk it was, and after a while he began to wonder if he would ever find a decent car.

After several months of this torture, I suggested that he raise his sights a bit. Maybe spending $18,000-$20,000 initially would get him a far superior car. He refused to listen to me and spent another six months in search of the elusive 356 Holy Grail: no rust, good panel fit, drives great, $14k. Finally, he moved his target price up a few thousand, and quickly found a very sweet 1963 B Super coupe for $17,500, which he drove home from California to Colorado. He has been thoroughly enjoying the car since.

Most Porsche owners have been fairly successful in their day jobs, and that success has come about partly because of an understanding of the value of time. Yet take these same people and put them on the track of a 356 or early 911, and they will spend literally hundreds of hours trying to save $2,000 or $3,000. Or worse, they sucker themselves into the dream of a cheap restoration project.

A fellow in our local PCA region bought a project 356 SC coupe with serious rust, a gutted interior, heavy accident damage and a questionable motor for $5,900. He thought it was the deal of the century until he started to restore the car. Now he realizes that after all his hard work, he will be very lucky to get out with what he has invested in the car, in spite of the fact that he is doing his own welding, body and paint work. After three years of hard work, he has never driven the car. Even worse, when he is finally done, unless all the work is done to the absolute highest standards, buyers will shy away from a car that has had so much work done to it by a non-professional.

Bottom line: For $10,000, you will generally only see 356B and C coupes with one or more major flaws, such as rust, the

need for imminent engine work, a lousy interior, a tatty paint job or, if you are especially unlucky, several of the above. I'd raise your price range or get ready for a very long search.

Now, let's assume that you've seen the light and are prepared to pay $15,000-$18,000 for a 356 coupe. Which model to buy?

Many enthusiasts see the 356C/SC models (1964-65 model years) as the finest of all pushrod 356s. The C and SC are nearly identical to the 356B cars from the 1962 model year on (known as the T-6), but they have disc brakes and somewhat revised engines. The 356C/SC cars are identifiable by their wheels, with larger vent holes, a smaller bolt pattern and flatter hub caps—no more VW wheels with baby moons or raised center hubcaps with enameled emblems.

There are just two engine choices for the C/SC cars: the 75-horsepower C motor that is very similar to the earlier Super, and a slightly hotter Super 90, now called the SC, and rated at 95 horsepower. The point of the C/SC engines was not horsepower, but torque. The C engine had more torque than the old Normal and yet the same top end as the old Super, while the SC was much better at low rpm than the old Super 90 and still had a bit more at the top end as well.

However, a C/SC car will generally sell for $3,000-$4,000 more than a B in equivalent condition. In my opinion, that makes the B a better value. The drum brakes on the Bs are very powerful, so don't look for a noticeable change in dry stopping power with the discs.

The B had three engines, all 1600 cc: the 60-hp Normal, the 75-hp Super and the 90-hp Super 90. The higher horsepower motors trade low-end torque for high-rpm power. In any event, a well-sorted B engine has a delightful power band.

Facing facts, you're really not going to buy a 40-year-old car for daily driving. More likely, you'll take it out on nice days to Porsche club picnics and vintage rallies. So the overall feel of the car, the condition of its suspension, the smoothness of the gearbox and its state of tune are much more likely to influence your enjoyment than whether it is a B or a C.

So, I say target a minimum of $15,000-$18,000 and look for a nice B coupe, perhaps an older restoration that has begun to mellow. If you keep the car for a few years, it will probably be worth a little more than you paid for it, which is certainly more than you can say for a new 996.

Both the B and C coupes will never be wildly collectible. While a treat to drive, and offering a pallet-full of vintage car sounds, smells and feel, there were a lot of them produced. Like MGBs and TR6s, they are great cars for the hobbyist and deliver plenty of fun for a modest amount of money. It's condition you should be looking for when you buy, though, rather than model.—*Jim Schrager*

From the May 2001 issue of *SCM*.◆

Door Fits & Color Combos

Dear Mr. Schrager: *I noticed a neat 356 coupe at a recent Porsche swap meet. It was a 1963 356B, silver/red interior, with chrome wheels (4.5 inches in front, 5.5 inches in back) It had a 1600 Super engine, and was driven about 150 miles to the show by its owner, so I presume it runs well. The door fit on the driver's side was quite far off all the way around. The paint was older. The car was noticeably lower in the front than the rear. The interior was vinyl, and quite decent, but by no means new. The carpet was a loop pattern. The price was $17,900.*

*My questions are: How big a deal is the door fit problem? Is the carpet correct? Are the wheels correct? Does the color combination have any effect on value? Is this a good motor to buy? What was wrong with the front end? How fair is the asking price?—**R.F., Kalamazoo, MI***

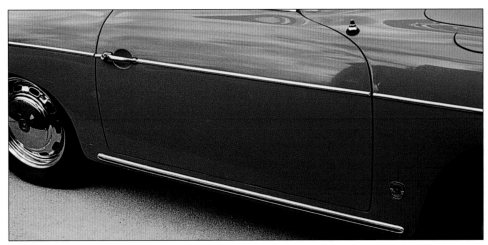

The fit of the door can be a guide to overall body condition.

You are in luck, as I was at the same Porsche swap meet and looked this car over fairly carefully. Let's go through your points, starting with the most important one.

Door fit. The way the doors (and hood and engine cover) fit on a 356 is of paramount importance in valuing the car. Poorly fitting movable panels speak of the double whammy of previous damage, poorly repaired. Much of the value in a 356, unless it has the exotic four-cam Carrera motor, is in the body. The cost to repair the door fit is about $2,000, not including paint.

The paint on the car was tired, with cracks, small dings and chips on many panels. You can spend anywhere from $300 to $10,000 to repaint a 356. This one needs to be taken down to bare metal to see what lurks under the deteriorating paint. Budget about $4,000 on paint, and you'd end up with a very nice, but not concours, job.

The fact that the car is down at the nose is not unusual. This is caused by the front torsion bars sagging with age. 356A, B and C models have adjustable front suspensions, so this may be a simple matter to correct. The different-sized wheels are wrong, but reproduction five-lug VW chrome wheels are available in the original 4.5-inch width for about $70 each.

Carpets for these cars are expensive, with the original

> "But more **important** than the original design spec is the current condition of the motor. **How long** since the last rebuild? **Who** did the work? **How well** has it been maintained? Do we have records?"

German square-weave wool replacements costing about $900 installed. This is an important detail, and anything less than the proper pieces will devalue the car.

Regarding the engine, you need to have an independent evaluation performed by taking it to a mechanic or having a knowledgeable enthusiast drive the car. If the engine is a 1600 Super, as the script "S" on the back of the car indicates, that's a plus. Porsche offered three motors for the street in the 356B models: the Normal, at 60 horsepower, the Super (75 hp) and the Super 90, with 90 hp. (All these are 1600 cc, and all horsepower ratings are DIN.) Many Bs were Normals, making this Super more rare as well as more powerful. But more important than the original design spec is the current condition of the motor. How long since the last rebuild? Who did the work? How well has it been maintained? Do we have records?

Color choice is always highly subjective. About one-half the Porsches of this vintage are painted either red or ivory. I believe that an unusual color such as silver, here in combination with a red interior (which is both proper and rare), adds to the value of this car, perhaps by $1,500.

However, the asking price seems way out of line, given the condition. If this were a nice #2 B coupe, in these pretty colors, I'd say it would be worth about $17,000-$18,000. Given the cost to bring this car to #2 condition, anything much more than $8,000 would be too much. If the seller won't come off the asking price significantly, I'd say keep looking.—*Jim Schrager*

From the September 1998 issue of *SCM*.◆

Spend More, Get More

Dear Mr. Schrager: I took your advice and bought my first Porsche, a 1971 911T coupe, signal orange/black, with a five-speed, S-deco package, Fuchs alloys, Carrera chain tensioners, much original paint, an original interior in nice shape, 87,000 miles. I am very pleased with the car. It is everything you said it would be: fun to drive; easy to handle; great, smooth power; distinctive; and, for the first year at least, no hassles. I paid $12,000 and felt it was a good buy.

A good 356 Cabiolet (above) is easier to find, and easier to sell, than a coupe.

I plan to keep this car and now want a 356, ideally as nice as my 911. From your columns, I have a good idea of the mechanical issues involved in owning a 356. I would like to find a nice B/C coupe, as I understand they are cheaper than open cars. I've been told by some buddies to hold out for the biggest motor. I'm not in this to make money, but

I don't want to get buried, either. Will a big-engined B/C coupe be a good choice for me? *—J.P., via e-mail*

The 356 B/C coupes, particularly the final T-6 body style built from 1962 to 1965, are great cars. However, I recommend you buy an open 356. While a Roadster or cabriolet will cost about twice as much as a coupe, the open car will be cheaper in the long run.

First, restoration costs for a coupe and an open car are about equal. Because it is hard to justify spending $35,000 on the restoration of a coupe that will only be worth about $20,000 when done, people usually cut corners or do the work themselves. And most hobbyist restorations have major hidden flaws, which will seriously lower the value or will cost several thousands to make right.

Next, the strong interest in collector cars has pulled many non-traditional 356 buyers into the picture, and most love the idea of wind-in-the-face motoring. The open-car experience is much more vivid in comparison to what we get from the closed cars we drive every day.

Because of their popularity and value, there are more nice open 356s available than there are coupes. Big appreciation for drop-tops in the '80s and the continued appreciation of the late '90s has meant that many more open 356s than coupes were given first-class restorations.

Cheaper cars usually sell easier, so you'd assume coupes would be hot property. But open 356s break that rule. Even at twice the price of a coupe, all else being equal, it is easier to sell a well-done open 356.

So while an open car will cost more, you'll have more first-class 356s from which to choose. And, when it's time to move on, you'll find more willing buyers and a better chance to get top dollar.

As engines go, the pressure to get the "big" engine can be misleading. All pushrod 356B/C engines are the same size, 1600 cc. Increases in power, given the same engine displacement, generally slide the power band higher in the rev range, sacrificing low-end torque in the process. This is certainly the case with the 356. The 60-hp Normal redlines at 4,500 rpm, the 75-hp Super and C engines at 5,000 rpm and the Super-90 and SC at 5,500 rpm.

So if you enjoy screaming your 35- to 40-year-old toy up to the redline at each shift, then the higher horsepower motors may be for you. But I find many 356 owners enjoy the low-end grunt of the 60-hp Normal for everyday driving.

Among our four 356s are S-90, SC, Super and Normal engines. My current favorite is a box-stock 1962 B Normal. It's a delight around town and still has plenty of power for the freeway. I always appreciate the silky torque down low and find few occasions to rev beyond the 4,500 redline.

Whichever engine you choose, if you still want a coupe, plan on taking your time. We have a near-concours 1963 B coupe that I love, but it took years to find. And, as an investment, it won't perform as well as an open car. The previous owner of our B coupe unhappily discovered he couldn't recover most of his extensive restoration costs. His loss was our gain.

Buy what you want, but don't say we didn't warn you.
—Jim Schrager
From the August 1999 issue of *SCM.*◆

How to Value a Car That Isn't For Sale

Dear Mr. Schrager: *I attended the 356 Registry Holiday in Michigan in August, and I enjoyed your valuation workshop. I particularly liked the outdoor lecture, as you took us through the value of a 356C with sunroof. You arrived at an estimate of $35,000 for that car and when looking at all the price guides, it seems high to me. Can you (again) take me through how you came up with that value?—L.B., Cleveland, OH*

Sky Blue 356C, not for sale today.

The 1964 356C with sunroof that we viewed at the 356 Holiday was an exceptionally strong example, an "end-of-the-world" example. More than just another pretty car, it was a cost-no-object restoration on a 356 in rare colors (Sky Blue/red) with an original interior, even more unusual because of its sunroof.

What made this car so special? To start with, the body lines were razor sharp from every possible angle. This means if you stood in front or in back of the car and looked down its length, you saw absolutely no waves, bulges, creases or distortions; the doors appeared to flow directly from and into the front fenders and rear quarters; the wheel wells were proper in both shape and size and identical on both sides.

The gaps on the movable panels were among the best I have ever viewed. For comparison, we are in the process of restoring a 356C with original paint. The gaps on the Sky Blue car at the Holiday were better than the factory panels. How? They were perfectly true from edge to edge, and actually a bit closer than I've seen on original cars.

The Sky Blue car's original vinyl interior showed some wear, but I prefer this to new vinyl or leather. Vinyls available today feel softer and spongier than the original. Part of the joy of an old 356 is the feel of that sturdy old vinyl. To upgrade to leather is acceptable, but incorrect for the car and to some, makes it less valuable than the original.

A sunroof is a rare option in a 356. We guess the percentage of cars thus equipped to be less than 5% of coupe production. Sunroofs in these old cars are rather cranky and must often have their delicate aluminum slides realigned or rebuilt. Cables, which often stretch and break, were not available for years, and reproductions often require modifications to fit. One of the most troublesome parts of the sunroof is the headliner for the sliding panel. Any bend in this flimsy frame causes the roof to jam. To find a sunroof that operates as silently and smoothly as this one is a rare occurrence, and worth a premium.

The condition of the paint on this car was superb. But the color, a non-metallic light/medium deep blue, made this car

> "Part of the joy of an old 356 is the feel of that sturdy old vinyl. To upgrade to leather is acceptable, but incorrect for the car and then some, less valuable than the original.

stand out, even in a field of well-presented 356s. This is a sophisticated color and, no doubt, not to everyone's taste. But I would argue that to the right buyer, this unusual and correct color combination adds to the value of the car. Not only is it a correct factory color, it is also the original color of this car.

So how to value this machine? The best way is simply to find an identical car and watch it sell. But I have never seen a Sky Blue/red 356C with sunroof in this superb condition sell. So, instead, we find the price of a comparable car and add on for the special features of the one we are trying to value.

For example, I recently saw a very strong #2 1960 T-5 356B Normal coupe, in silver/red, sell for $20,000. This gives us a starting point to value the Sky Blue car.

I'd make five additions to the silver car that sold for $20,000: first, for the extra superb condition of the Sky Blue car, next for the sunroof, the T-6 body, the C disc brakes, and finally for the C engine (equal to a Super). I added $3,000 for each of the five additions to the $20,000 and arrived at a total of $35,000.

Alternatively, I also saw a 1961 T-5 B Super with sunroof, in Signal Red/black, in #1 condition, sell for $26,000. To this car, I'd make three additions; first, for the color combo of Sky Blue/red, next for the T-6 body and finally for the disc brakes. The same $3,000 for each item brings us to $35,000.

Of course, these figures are just estimates, and we can argue about how much each difference is worth. But to me, $35,000 is a reasonable number. By the way, this Sky Blue C was driven by its owners from Georgia to the Holiday and went on to win the People's Choice Award. I also understand it is not for sale. But if you want it, I suggest starting at $35k.—*Jim Schrager*

From the October 1998 issue of *SCM*.◆

A Nasty Parts Car Brings $6,600?

Dear Mr. Schrager: *I recently saw a righthand-drive 1960 356 B S-90 coupe sell on eBay for $6,660. It was red with a black interior, and thoroughly rusty. It reportedly hadn't run in years and had been parked outdoors in a field. It needed everything. I budgeted it as a parts car, and when the bidding hit $3,000 I dropped out. I was very surprised to see it sell so high, particularly as it was a right-drive model. What gives here? Are all these tired old coupes worth that kind of money? Won't the buyer be way upside down after he fixes this buggy?*—**T.J.M., Omaha, NE**

Fright pigs here, valued jewels in Britain and Japan.

I also watched this car sell on eBay and was surprised by the outcome. I spoke with the seller and he indicated the car was going to Japan. Therein lies the secret that allowed this rusty relic to fetch such big money. Japan is a right-drive country, and original righthand-drive 356s are quite rare. Hence in Japan, Great Britain and Australia, they bring a surprising premium. Nonetheless, in my opinion this was an over-the-top price. I understand that the sale was successfully completed (something you can never take for granted with an online auction) and the seller should be quite satisfied with the outcome.

One great advantage of the Internet is the ability to put your product in front of an international audience; you could advertise a rusty right-drive 356 coupe for $6,000 in your local *Auto Trader* for the rest of the century and never hear your phone ring.

Dear Mr. Schrager: *I am interested in buying a 356 coupe and have been reading your previous columns. I am just beginning to learn about the cars. I spent a day last week test driving two 356B coupes: a 1600 Normal and a 1600 Super. I was shocked to walk away feeling like I drove two slightly different VW Beetles. Do they all feel this way? You write as if these are fun cars to drive, but the ones I tested were sloths. I was careful not to abuse these cars on the test drives and tried to shift them at about 3,500 rpm. What gives?*—**T.J.B., via phone**

First, you need to adjust your driving style. While I applaud your gentleness with other people's machinery, 356s produce power high in the rpm range. This, coupled with a rather long throw to the gas pedal, means you have to push a long way down and consciously drive in the higher rpm range to make them come alive. You simply can't drive a 356 like a Corvette.

Drive the car easily while it is cold. Then, once it is warmed up, put the car through its paces. Stay away from the redline in first gear but, once into second, take it up to the redline, shift and do it again in third. You should get a good feel for the power this way.

The tach is an especially important instrument in a 356. The green bands, which start at either 2,500 or 3,000 rpm and run to the redline, show you where the power is produced. If you push hard on the gas pedal prior to being in the green zone, don't expect much response from the engine.

In addition to the driving-style issues, there are many reasons why a particular 356 may seem slow. The accelerator linkage may be out of adjustment far enough so that the carbs are only partially opening. This will have a serious effect on horsepower. The car you are testing may also be way out of tune, have a worn distributor or incorrect carburetors or be comprised of an eclectic and probably mismatched set of internal engine parts. There are many unsorted cars out there.

A good 356 will feel light and lively and, most of all, fun to drive. The controls will be easy and direct, and once you realize the power resides above 3,000 rpm, you'll find the car great fun.

Even a standard-issue 356 Normal should pull strongly all the way up to (and beyond) its 4,500 redline. This makes the car feel sporty and is one of the really endearing parts of the 356 package. Even better, if it is a properly rebuilt motor, it should run for years at high rpm with no ill effects.—*Jim Schrager*

From the January 2001 issue of *SCM*.◆

> "You simply **can't drive** a 356 like a Corvette. If you pushed hard on the gas pedal prior to being in the green zone, **don't expect much** response from the engine."

Two 356 Coupes, Cheap. I Pass.

A broker called the other day trying to sell a '62 356B and a '64 356C coupe. The B was the desirable T-6 body with a fresh motor, rusty body and chassis, and tired interior. The C had cheapie fresh paint, "no rust visible above or below" (his words), a lousy interior and tired mechanicals. The broker wanted $9,500 for the pair.

There are three ways to look at these cars: as restoration candidates, as parts cars or as fixer-drivers. A look at the economics will show why I didn't take long to pass on the deal.

Parts car or daily driver project?

Forget Restoration

As restoration candidates, most coupes don't make sense in today's market. A very nice, straight, restored C coupe sells for about $20,000, yet the cost of restoring one, even without going wild, will quickly approach that number.

Let's take a quick look at a typical restoration. Start with an engine rebuild, and without getting too crazy you've spent $5,000. Body work to make the seams straight and clean up previous damage would probably be $2,000. This is very important to 356 buyers who love their hood and door gaps to be Lexus-style near perfect.

A decent, but not concours, urethane paint job will cost $2,500. Include new rubber for windows, doors, hood and door sills at $600; a complete interior re-do with original materials $4,000. Be certain to use the expensive German square weave carpet, as anything else is an instant give-away to a cheapie job, but do not use leather on the seats, as almost all coupes had vinyl anyway.

Rebuild the brakes for $1,000 (almost always required when the disc brakes sit unused for a few years); replace or replate the chrome and aluminum trim, $2,000; add a new battery, tires, shocks, muffler and all the miscellaneous bits and parts, $1,400.

At this point we've spent $18,500 and have not spent a dime on the transmission, steering gearbox or any of the understructure such as longitudinal members, front or rear floor pan sections, battery box or rear torsion bar area. And it's rare not to need work on one or more of those parts.

We started with the C because it is worth about $3,000 more than the B when done. But restoring either one doesn't make any sense.

Not Parts Cars Either

If we appraise this package for parts, this is what we come up with. The tired engine, $1,000; the fresh engine, $2,000; the two transmissions, $750 each; disc brakes on the C, $750; drums on the B, $500; the seats will each bring $150, for a total of $600; each of the four instruments as a core is worth $40, as are the steering wheels, for a total of $400 more. We are now left with fairly rusty, stripped bodies and we have spent a lot of effort to obtain a grand total of $6,750 for all the major pieces of our cars.

None of the remaining body parts are worth much. With luck, we'll break even for our time and effort taking the cars completely apart, talking to dozens of people on the phone selling all the pieces, and packaging and shipping everything all over the country.

So Just Drive Them?

That leaves the only real option for these cars as daily drivers for someone handy who wants to do his own restoration. Somewhat surprisingly, this is a fairly lively market. However, the initial purchase price on one of these must be very low to seduce the purchaser into believing the entire project can be done on the cheap.

I'd pay about $3,000 for the rusty B coupe with the good motor (cars with rusty chassis parts are hard to sell), and maybe $5,000 for the C that doesn't run too well (cars that don't run are hard to sell). Oops, that still doesn't add up to $9,500.

Both of these cars deserve good homes and I hope they are lovingly restored someday. But as a money-making proposition, I pass.—*Jim Schrager*

From the July 1997 issue of *SCM*.◆

> "There are three ways to look at these cars: as restoration cadidates, as parts cars, or as fixer-drivers. A look at the economics will show why."

Upgrades Can Be Downers

As enthusiasts, our urge to upgrade our cars is nearly irresistible. Perhaps it stems from hours spent poring over J.C. Whitney catalogs when we were supposed to be studying 12th grade biology. Or maybe it's just the American make-it-faster affliction manifesting itself in our German cars.

Bolting parts onto a 356 that purport to make it a better car is pretty easy. But in my opinion, stock is best, and few of the upgrades come without significant problems attached.

Big-Bore Kits

A common engine enhancement for 356s is the installation of a big-bore kit.

These piston sets, originally made by NPR (Nippon Piston Ring), are now available from other suppliers who have copied the Japanese kit. Popular when 356 values were low, these sets allowed you to save a few hundred bucks off the price of the original Mahle parts while adding about 150 cc of displacement, bringing the stock 1,582 cc to between 1,720 cc and 1,780 cc.

The oversized pistons can be a source of continuous trouble and even lead

Installing a big bore kit, not as simple as it looks.

to engine failure. Some mechanics believe these sets cause vibrations that accelerate crankshaft destruction. The more immediate problem, though, stems from a lack of care in setting the compression ratio when installing non-original piston sets.

The compression ratio is set in a 356 engine by adding thin shims between the bottom of the cylinders and the crankcase to adjust the distance between the top of the piston and the head. To properly accomplish this, the engine is test assembled out to the heads and the combustion chamber filled with fluid and carefully measured. Many 356 heads have been flycut to get the cylinder-to-head mating surfaces flat, adding to the difficulty of obtaining a factory compression setting.

If the compression ratio is set wrong, the result is either a very quick car that blows itself to bits in short order or a slug. Compression too low won't generate the power originally called for, and a too-high compression ratio will generate excess heat and loads beyond design tolerances.

If a big-bore kit is installed by an expert, then this upgrade might perform as well as the original parts. But especially with too much compression, I've seen engines that ran hot, resulting in a broken crankshaft or a blown rod. It wasn't a pretty sight.

Switching to Webers

Weber carbs are another popular addition. These are fine carbs (I know Alfa guys swear by them) and I have seen superb mechanics with lots of patience get the Webers set up so performance will just about equal the stock Zenith (used on Normal, Super and C engines) or Solex (Super-90 and SC engines) carbs. Armchair enthusiasts (and Weber-carb marketing gurus) claim you can buy a set of Webers pre-jetted for your 356, bolt them on and suddenly start smoking your rear tires at stoplight drags. But the reality is that 60-, 75-, 90- and 95-hp engines have different heads, valve sizes, piston designs and camshafts, which means that no single carburetor type or size works for all.

Porsche had three different carburetor set-ups and two different carb types (Zenith single-barrels and Solex twin-barrels) to cover the 356 line. When engines changed, so did the carbs. For example, a 1963 B Super has Zenith carbs and produces 75 hp; the 1964 C has Zenith carbs and produces 75 hp. The Zenith carbs, identical on the outside, are different on the inside for these two engines. Even the insides of the intake manifolds differ.

The Porsche factory did its homework when it built these cars. If you buy Webers, plan on working hard to make them right.

Switching to 12-Volt

Here's another instance of an unnecessary change from stock. Many 356s are offered for sale with the phrase "upgraded to 12-volt system" in the advertisements. 356 owners with stock six-volt systems often complain about dim headlights or a slow-turning starter. But consider that when new, 356s with their stock six-volt systems earned a reputation for being true all-weather cars that were started and driven regularly in the snow as well as the heat of summer. So what's gone wrong over the years?

The six-volt systems work well when the fuse box and wire ends throughout the car are corrosion free, all the ground straps are making proper contact, the battery terminals are clean and the cables are tight. If you have a strong battery (I recommend an Optima leak-proof model, which fits with no alterations), a working generator and a correctly adjusted voltage regulator, six volts should be plenty. If all the preceding check out but your starter still cranks slowly, it's probably a bad bushing in the starter or an ignition switch that needs replacement.

I currently own four 356s, each of which is regularly started and driven in the winter. Their well-maintained six-volt systems work just fine.

Next month: tire and suspension upgrades.—*Jim Schrager*
From the December 2001 issue of *SCM*.◆

The Nuts and Bolts of Tires and Shocks: Modifiying Your 356

Wheels, tires and shocks are mostly bolt-on items and allow you to set your 356 up in a variety of configurations, from comfortable weekend cruiser to tooth-rattling, autocross-spec buckboard. Each choice has its pluses and minuses; there is no free lunch when it comes to 356 handling upgrades.

356 suspension options include ride-height adjustments and changes in torsion bars. While it is fine to lower your 356 a bit, over-lowering induces excessive harshness for street use. Stay to within an inch or two of factory specs for street use. You can also install stiffer torsion bars, but avoid this unless you will be driving only on the track. Ride quality deteriorates quickly with stiffer springs.

Installing Koni shock absorbers is a popular option. In the old days, this expensive shock (about $100 each) solved the fade problem that allowed a standard absorber to become soft when on the track or driven hard over difficult terrain. Armchair enthusiasts, upon driving their first Koni-equipped car, are often shocked to realize the price for this extra damping is a stiff ride. Although Konis are adjustable, they need to be partially removed to accomplish this. And even on the softest setting they can be quite harsh.

In the old days of stock 4 x 15-inch wheels and 165/80/15 tires, Konis weren't so bad, as the high sidewall and small tread area of the tires allowed for some of the compliance the Konis took away. But today, with 5-inch-wide wheels and high-performance Z-rated 195/60/15 tires, be careful or you can quickly turn your 356 into a bone-jarring sled.

I prefer the stock Boge shocks. At about $50 each, they deliver a supple ride around town and on the highway. Would I use them for racing? No, but who am I trying to impress here? My wife, so she will enjoy riding with me as much as I enjoy having her along. Other shock options are KYBs, at $25 each (firmer than Boges), or Bilsteins, at $75 apiece and similar in firmness to Konis.

Wheels and tires work in close concert with the shocks and springs to deliver a compromise between reasonable street performance and go-cart-style firmness. Let's start with wheels, where the choice is simple. Every 356A, B and C came with 4 x 15-inch wheels. Today, for drum-brake 356A/B cars, we have a choice of the original size or the larger VW repro 5 x 15-inch

(about $75 each). C/SC cars with disc brakes have a different bolt pattern and use the stock 4-inch wheel or the 1968 and later 912/911 5-inch wheel.

But there are problems going to the 5-inch wheels. Repro VW wheels, available in chrome only, fit well but look wrong due to different vent panel and vent hole designs. There are no reproductions of 5-inch C/SC disc brake wheels, so you have to hunt the swap meets and salvage yards to find them. Both will rub a bit in front at full lock, but that's not a serious problem.

Rather than the nearly correct 165/78/15 Michelin XZX or Dunlop SP20 tires available today, I find a slightly smaller diameter modern tire to be a good compromise between road holding and ride comfort. My favorite is a 185/65/15 Pirelli P400. At about $50 each, these are comfortable tires with a rather low speed rating, which is still much faster than I drive. Other widely available sizes are 195/65/15 and 195/60/15, each requiring 5-inch wide wheels.

Installing a set of Porsche 356C/SC disc brakes on a drum-braked 356 will hurt originality but is an acceptable upgrade. 356 front drum brakes have two hydraulic cylinders and therefore two leading shoes per wheel, and the swept area is very large for the weight of the car. The drums are a clever blend of alloy outers with deep cooling fins, and a pressed-in steel lining. Most do not realize that the drum brakes, when properly adjusted, stop the car on dry pavement just about as well as

The eternal dilemma: ride quality or performance?

the discs. The discs do better when fade is an issue or when driving in wet conditions. Parts and labor on a disc brake conversion run $2,000-$3,000.

When built, 356s offered a state-of-the-art combination of performance and roadability. Today, if you are willing to accept the design as originally conceived and executed, this humble swing-axle suspension can still deliver an astonishingly compliant ride together with delightful handling on the street. Certainly more modern suspension designs can reach higher levels of ultimate adhesion on the track. But turning a 356 into a track competitor capable of banging wheels with the latest designs will eliminate the dual-purpose nature of the vehicle.

My advice is to stick with stock and enjoy the handling of your car the way that Ferdinand Porsche designed it to perform.
—*Jim Schrager*

From the February 2002 issue of *SCM*.◆

356s Cross the Block

"On-site auction reporting is the trademark of SCM. When an SCM expert attends an auction, his job is to personally evaluate the cars crossing the block, taking note of everything from the chassis number to the originality of the seat stitching. They analyze each car as if they were going to buy it for themselves.

As you'll see in the 356 reports below, SCM experts

don't hesitate to call a prince a prince and a toad a toad.

Their reports are always honest, sometimes witty, and always make you feel as if you were there looking at the car with them."

— *Keith Martin*

356 Pre A's & A's

#50-1955 PORSCHE 356 PRE-A 1500 SPEEDSTER. S/N 80329. Black/black. LHD. Nicolas Cage collection. New top. Appeared to be a very good example. Panel fit, straightness, paint quality and detail level high throughout. Cond: 2. **SOLD AT $71,500.** *Upper end of SCM Price Guide. Since Seinfeld is taking a break from the limelight, maybe it's the Cage cars that will gain an extra $10,000 from celebrity status. The popularity of the star is indicated by the premium of the price.* **RM Auctions, Amelia Island, FL, 3/00.**

#1037-1955 PORSCHE 356 SPEED-STER. S/N 80705. Red/black leather. LHD. Odo: 64,166 miles. Older repaint shows lots of flaws, stainless and chrome trim complete, but weak. Well-worn interior, rubber mats show wear. A Speedster, just as you saw them 25 years ago when they were only old Porsches. Very honest presentation. Cond: 3-. **NOT SOLD AT $40,000.** *Lots of potential bidders mistook this combination of early 1970s restoration and repairs to be original, as the patina of age has given credence to its look. It's not all original, and that's okay. Just don't pay more thinking that it is.* **eBay/Kruse, Atlantic City, NJ, 2/02.**

#1013-1959 PORSCHE 356A Convertible D. Body by Drauz. S/N 85731. Eng.# 72251. Red/tan leather. LHD. Odo: 75,855 miles. Nardi wood steering wheel, 1600 Normal motor, full chrome wheels and caps. Full of Porsche accessories, very nicely restored car, fully detailed chassis, engine compartment spotless. Cond: 2+. **NOT SOLD AT $45,000.** *One of 1,330 Convertible Ds built. Methinks the chandelier held the high bid on this one. Very nice restoration, well presented; however, this clearly wasn't a Porsche crowd. The right car, the wrong venue.* **eBay/Kruse, Atlantic City, NJ, 2/02.**

#335-1959 PORSCHE 356A Cabriolet. S/N 152189. Silver/red. LHD. Odo: 31,907 miles. Idaho plate. Floor pan looks good. Underneath clean and undercoated. Shift-lever paint chipped. Horn button cracked. Trim on left door loose. Overall, a nicely done restoration. Cond: 2. **SOLD AT $38,610.** *Driven to the auction from Idaho by an SCM subscriber. Less than half the price of the twin-grille roadster at this auction, but will provide much more than half as much fun. A reasonable way into the world of open 356s.* **Barrett-Jackson, Los Angeles, CA, 6/02.**

#116-1959 PORSCHE 356A 2-door coupe. Body by Reutter. S/N 107872. Light yellow/chocolate brown leather. LHD. Odo: 34,547 miles. Pirelli P600 tires, California black plates. Very good fit and finish. Excellent chrome. Tidy and complete. Some wear to driver's seat bolster. No radio. Chrome wheels. Cond: 2+. **SOLD AT $30,500.** *This was a nice example, however, the money paid was*

clearly over the top. Irrational exuberance hits the Porsche market, with no Alan Greenspan to put the brakes on. Time for short selling? *RM Auctions, Monterey, CA, 8/00.*

#772-1959 PORSCHE 356A Convertible D. Body by Drausz. S/N 86205. Cream tan/ black. LHD. 1600 Normal motor, new paint, top, seats, carpet. Good panel fit, no Bondo found, chrome wheels, chrome bumper overriders, a very appealing car. Cond: 2. **SOLD AT $41,340.** *Fair price for good Convertible D. This car is as cute as a bug, has loads of curb appeal and is one of just 1330 built. Fair money for an honest car. Barrett-Jackson, Scottsdale, AZ, 1/00.*

#207-1955 PORSCHE 356 Sunroof Coupe. S/N 54119. 4-cyl. 1582cc. 70 hp. Burgundy/beige vinyl. LHD. Odo: 116 miles. 4-speed. Bucket seats. Factory steel wheels. Good paint overall with a surprising amount of orange peel and some dust showing (dirty spray gun?). Panel fit and interior fair, chrome could be better. Cond: 3. **SOLD AT $26,400.** *One of only a few pre-A 356's to have a factory sunroof. Updated carbs but original manifold and carbs included with purchase. Strong price for decent car considering the many minor flaws and inattention to details. RM Auctions, New York, 9/00.*

#389-1955 PORSCHE 356 2-door Speedster. S/N 80187. Speedster Blue/beige with blue stripes. Beige top. Odo: 76,878 miles. Cost $2,995 new from Hoffman of New York. Full bare-metal restoration completed 1992. Stored in New Mexico since 1993 and still mainly presentable cosmetically. Correct 1500 Super replaced with 1600 Normal engine. Cond: 1-. **SOLD AT $42,660.** *Very reasonable for a Speedster. Their prices continue to be all over the map, from $25,000 for beaters to near $100,000 for trailer-queens. This car should be easy to upgrade to concours-competitive standards. Barrett-Jackson, Scottsdale, AZ, 9/00.*

#84-1957 Porsche Speedster. S/N 84115. Eng. #676754. Light blue/red leather. LHD. A really, really close inspection revealed that the car was lightly skinned in Bondo all around—not due to rust but for smoothness of finish. Factory Rudge chrome wheels. Flawless restoration. Cond: 1. **SOLD AT $88,125.** *The Jerry Seinfeld Speedster at its second auction this year. At Barrett-Jackson it pulled down $92,880. Was immediately resold for a $10k-$15k premium, but seller decided color didn't fit his collection. Sent to Christie's, sold to an SCM subscriber who plans on keeping the car. Christie's, Tarrytown, NY, 4/01.*

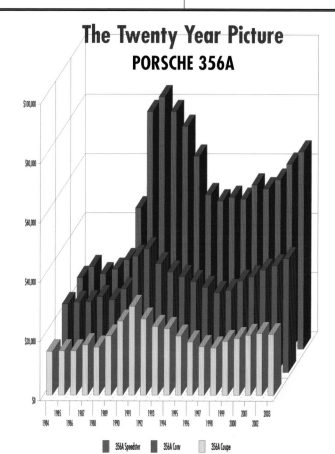

The Twenty Year Picture
PORSCHE 356A

356A Speedster   356A Conv   356A Coupe

This value guide is provided courtesy of Cars of Particular Interest. CPI is the guide most often used by Credit Unions and Banks when dealing with loan values of collectible domestic and imported cars; www.BlackBookUSA.com.
From the May 1998 issue of *SCM.* ◆

#381-1957 PORSCHE CARRERA GT Race Coupe. Body by Reutter. S/N 56476. Silver metallic/tan. Odo: 3,631 kms. From TV personality Jerry Seinfeld's collection. Said to have cost him $120,000. G&W Motorwerke of VA restored early 1990s. Fully prepped for historic racing. Cosmetically perfect, apart from amateur-looking attempts to seal leaks to rear side windows. Cond: 1. **SOLD AT $64,800.** *Wrong engine, wrong brakes mar a visually stunning presentation. Car would have brought double if correctly configured—however, wouldn't be nearly as much fun on the track. Purchased by an active SCMer. Barrett-Jackson, Scottsdale, AZ, 1/01.*

356 B & C

#205-1960 PORSCHE 356B Coupe. S/N 108921. White/red vinyl and velour. LHD. Odo: 18,823 miles. Sunroof. Documented to be the first Super 90 made by Porsche. Originally a factory demonstrator assigned to Herr Kling. Car looks as if Kling enjoyed using it. Cond: 3-. **SOLD AT $10,800.** *Car sold way to cheap, was a great buy for someone, perhaps we will see this car again. Worth at least $5,000 more than the amount paid. Barrett-Jackson, Los Angeles, CA, 6/02.*

#275-1962 PORSCHE SUPER 90 Roadster. S/N 89740. Black/black. LHD. Twin-grille roadster. Fully restored to a very high standard, with excellent paint, chrome and panel gaps. Can't reasonably fault in any way. No reserve. Cond: 1. **SOLD AT $92,880.** *Spirited bidding for this car. It had terrific eyeball in triple black, was rare (one of 248 built) and was brilliantly presented. Donated to the Petersen to be sold as a fund raiser. Huge price, but twin-grille roadsters keep climbing and this one had the added value of chrome Rudge knock-off wheels, worth about $10K extra. Barrett-Jackson, Los Angeles, CA, 6/02.*

#290-1964 PORSCHE 356C Coupe. S/N 129222. Red/black. LHD. Odo: 24,433 miles. Fuchs alloy wheels. Rust under door jamb rubber. Headliner faded. Heavy black undercoating hiding damage. Steering wheel cracked. Lots of rust on left jack lift, covered with Bondo. The more you look, the more you don't want to look. Cond: 4-. **SOLD AT $16,740.** *A surprising price for this car with needs. Car came with rare 4.5" early 911S Fuchs alloys worth about $1,500 by themselves. Maybe L.A. is 356-crazy. Barrett-Jackson, Los Angeles, CA, 6/02.*

#4-1961 PORSCHE 356B 1600 SUPER Cabriolet. Body by Reutter. S/N 155425. Red/cream vinyl. LHD. Odo: 2,397 miles. Nardi wood steering wheel, Blaupunkt AM/FM/SW radio. Good paint, with some orange peel. Most chrome good, windshield surround weak, some rubber gaskets torn and drying. Ill-

fitting seat upholstery. (There are no modifications mentioned here.) Cond: 3+. **SOLD AT $42,300.** *Fair enough money for a driver if a fun summer car is all the buyer wants. Beware at resale time, however, as the Porschephiles will cut you up and leave no prisoners until the noted flaws are remedied. Christie's, New York, NY, 5/02.*

#119-1963 PORSCHE 356 GS/GT CARRERA 2 Coupe. S/N 122561. Eng.# 98016. Silver/gray and blue. LHD. Odo: 43,692 miles. Close-ratio five-speed. 587 engine replaced by 907-spec four-cam in 1964. Competition seats, plexiglass windows, roll bar. Aluminum hood, doors and decklid. Older restoration. Kardex correct. One of the most hallowed Porsches around. Richard Freshman car. Cond: 2-. **SOLD AT $173,250.** *Porsche fanatics go nuts over these cars, and this one is arguably among the best, with its stellar provenance. Fitted with alloy/steel composite wheels, an exceptionally rare option. RM Auctions, Santa Monica, CA, 5/02.*

#220-1961 PORSCHE 356B Cabriolet. Body by Reutter. S/N 155 126. Black/black. LHD. Original New Mexico car with ground-up restoration complete with receipts for bare-metal respray, new top and interior. Claimed original pans. Fitted with improper 912 engine. Reproduction chrome wheels. Cond: 2. **SOLD AT $36,300.** *All the money for a pretty Cabriolet in good colors with a wrong motor. Black was a rare color in 1961 and it was unclear if the color was correct for this car. Regardless, this Cabriolet, if well put together, will be a joy to drive with the 90 hp engine. RM Auctions, Phoenix, AZ, 1/00.*

#716-1960 PORSCHE 356 SUPER 90 2-door Roadster. Body by Drauz. S/N 87432. Red/black. Black cloth top. LHD. Odo: 80,793 miles. Wood steering wheel, chrome wheels, chip on driver's door glass, good panel fit, some orange peel, paint chips with touch-ups. Small tear on front of top. Full chrome wheels with "moon" caps. Cond: 3. **SOLD AT $38,690.** *Just the right amount of money for this car; both buyer and seller should go away happy. The S-90s are picking up a little in value, and it's certainly more fun to own a 356 than to spend your time watching your Internet stock tank.* **Kruse, Auburn, IN, 9/00.**

#839-1964 PORSCHE 356 SC Coupe. S/N NR217695. Yellow/black leather. LHD. Odo: 86,508 miles. "Original unrusted pans," Pirelli P3 tires in good shape. Major rust bubbles on front of hood, doors, trunk. Blaupunkt AM radio. Good glass, un-hateful interior, mediocre panel fit. Cond: 4. **SOLD AT $15,900.** *Another cute little bomber you can't afford to restore, so keep driving it and enjoy it. Minor to major problems everywhere you look. Bid was fair enough to seller, and the new owner's repair shop will be overjoyed.* **Kruse, Auburn, IN, 9/00.**

#62-1960 PORSCHE 356B Roadster. Body by Reutter. S/N 86850. Eng. #600

123. Red/tan leather. Beige fabric top. Odo: 46,545 miles. Sharp car with fresh restoration and upgrades including wooden steering wheel and leather upholstery. Logical heir to 356 Speedster but more civilized. Cond: 1-. **SOLD AT $76,375.** *Continued proof that Porsche fanatics will step up for brilliant examples. An over-the-top price for an over-the-top car.* **Christie's, Pebble Beach, CA, 8/01.**

#40-1960 PORSCHE 356B Roadster. Body by Drauz. S/N 88576. Silver fabric top. Odo: 10,901 miles. Precise door and panel fit, very good original interior, excellent repaint, goodies included leather, chrome horn ring steering wheel, chrome rims, Blaupunkt radio, Hazet tool kit. Sold at no reserve. Cond: 1-. **SOLD AT $52,875.** *Given the popularity of B roadsters and the quality of this restoration, another $5,000 wouldn't have surprised.* **Christie's, Pebble Beach, CA, 8.01.**

#281-1965 PORSCHE 356C Cabriolet. S/N 162145. Eng. #731722. Red/tan leather. Tan cloth top. Odo: 39,277 miles. Factory 12-volt, German square-weave carpeting, tools, jack and owner's manual included. Missing steering wheel center. Pitting in vent window surrounds. Shows better than it actually is when opened up. Very good paint. Cond: 3+. **SOLD AT $44,550.** *356Cs and SCs continue to march up the value guides. They are extremely user friendly, and relatively cheap to operate—an unusual combination in the world of vintage cars. A high, but not crazy, price.* **RM Auctions, Monterey, CA, 8/00.**

#607-1961 PORSCHE 356B Coupe. S/N 110509. Red/black leather. LHD. Odo: 52,711 miles. Severe rust on door pillars, scads of surface rust and poor paint, front of hood rusted away. Cautionary sign on doors: "Please do not open." Vendor claimed engine ran well. Cond: 5-. **SOLD AT $2,756.** *A tribute to the optimism of the human spirit. Possibly restorable by a highly skilled body man who charges off his own time at $1 per hour. Otherwise a hopeless mess.* **Bonhams & Brooks, Beaulieu, UK, 9/01.**

#86-1964 PORSCHE 356C Cabriolet. S/N 159154. Black/burgundy leather. Black cloth top. Odo: 49,314 miles. A very sweet restoration. Very well sorted and preserved throughout. Factory Kardex, original motor, four-wheel disc brakes. Cond: 1. **SOLD AT $50,600.** *More than the price guides say you should pay for a #1 car. The color is right, the top goes down and there are many events to use it in.* **RM Auctions, Monterey, CA, 8/01.**

#63-1965 PORSCHE 356SC Coupe. S/N 219791. White/black leather. Odo: 85,581 miles. Sharp inside and out with excellent hood and door fit. White not the most flattering color for any car and may have affected bid. Four-wheel discs standard on these final year 356s. Excellent show and go vintage Porsche. Cond: 1-. **SOLD AT $24,200.** *Very honest 356. An excellent way to enjoy a vintage Porsche. Honest car can get a crowd excited. Fair price to both buyer and seller. RM Auctions, Phoenix, AZ, 1/01.*

#280-1960 PORSCHE 356B Cabriolet. S/N 153606. Red/black vinyl. LHD. Odo: 50,298 miles. Reutter body, Optima AM/FM cassette, Nardi wood wheel. Left front fender shows signs of sectioning. Some high spots on fender. 1600 Super 90 motor. Restored recently, but will not be a show contender. Cond: 3-. **NOT SOLD AT $25,000.** *Plenty here for the Porsche Club crowd to pick apart, but at least it is a cosmetically complete and decent-looking example. As a driver, this one should have brought at least $3k or $4k more. eBay/Kruse, Ft. Lauderdale, FL, 1/02.*

#1074-1964 PORSCHE 356C Cabriolet. S/N 160310. Black/tan leather. LHD. Odo: 29,588 miles. Nardi wood wheel, Blaupunkt AM/FM cassette. All tools and books, one owner for the past 20 years. Large wave in hood paint. Owner states original leather, but most likely from a restoration 20 plus years ago. Very nice chrome. Miles said to be actual. Cond: 3+. **SOLD AT $31,800.** *Time to be aware of a trend that I often see with cars from the 1960s—the 20- and 30-year-old resto bits being represented as original. They have the patina of years of use, and most sellers just don't know the difference. Solid price. eBay/Kruse, Ft. Lauderdale, FL, 1/02.*

#131-1960 PORSCHE 356B SUPER Coupe. S/N 110476. Slate grey/light gray vinyl. LHD. Odo: 47,227 miles. Sunroof. Hood fit off, panels wavy. Rusty area between dash panel and window seal. Fair-quality repaint. Jambs poorly finished, paint starting to crack in some areas. Chrome starting to pit. Interior in presentable condition. Underhood needs detailing. Cond: 4+. **SOLD AT $18,700.** *Seems a bit much for a car that appears to have a questionable-quality cosmetic upgrade. RM Auctions, Amelia Island, FL, 3/02.*

#86-1965 PORSCHE 356 SC Cabriolet. S/N N/A. Dark blue/light gray. LHD. Impressive restoration completed 3,000 miles ago. Complete with tools, jack, owner's handbook, records, receipts and photo documentation. Hood fit way off. Hard to fault in any other area. Matching-numbers car. Cond: 2-. **SOLD AT $45,100.** *The SCs are the most sophisticated of the 356s, which to some makes them the least interesting (think Healey BJ8 versus 100/4). RM Auctions, Amelia Island, FL, 3/02.*

#8-1964 PORSCHE 356C Coupe. S/N 216900. Eng.# P*712058. 4-cyl. White/black vinyl. LHD. Odo: 33,571 miles. Chrome disc wheels. Older restoration holding up we Window rubbers splitting. Decent panel fit, rear of

passenger door a little lumpy. Interior clean but not spectacular. Seems like an honest driver. 3 owners, claimed original mileage. Cond: 3+. **SOLD AT $30,550.** *While this was a nicely patinated car, it is in need of a thorough cosmetic restoration. There are better 356C coupes, although probably with higher mileage, out there for less. Strong price, seller should be very happy. Christie's, Los Angeles, CA, 6/00.*

#103-1961 PORSCHE 356B S90 Coupe. S/N 115202. Eng.# 600501. Silver metallic/black. LHD. Odo: 79,816 miles. Cracked wind shield. Various modern competition features include roll bar, fire system, wide rear tires, larger oil cooler, electronic ignition. Large quantity of spares. Cosmetically good. Offered with FIA papers, restoration invoices. Cond: 2. **SOLD AT $21,752.** *Viewed realistically, any race car bought at auction can be assumed to need a complete going through. If everything turns out to be in tip-top shape, you've grabbed the golden ring. More likely, you'll spend another $10k, but still be in the car right. Bonhams, Nurburgring, Germany, 8/02.*

#131-1964 PORSCHE 356SC Coupe. S/N 129243. Champagne yellow/red. LHD. Odo: 69,430 miles. Garish original color scheme looks like strawberries and custard. Good paintwork and panel fit. Nice original interior with corduroy seat centers. Chrome okay. Cond: 2. **NOT SOLD AT $14,550.** *Champagne Yellow is a highly desired color, though it is not a standard combination with the red interior. Bid too low for the last of the 356s with the most powerful and driveable SC engine. Would take about $18k to buy this in the States. Bonhams, Nurburgring, Germany, 8/02.*

PART II
Porsche 911

When the Porsche 911 appeared in 1965, it was a a Bauhaus-school styling exercise set in motion. Its lines were clearly derived from the 356, yet the car was startlingly fresh and inviting, its sheet metal taut and exciting. I was 15 when the car was launched, and I predicted to all my friends that the purity of its lines would never be eclipsed. Little did I realize how right I was. While Mies van der Rohe was revolutionizing architecture with his "less is more" philosophy, Ferry Porsche's young son Butzi used the 911 to do the same thing to automotive styling and functionality.

The cockpit, outfitted in luxurious materials including short-nap wool carpeting, sturdy vinyls, and thick rubber floor mats, was made for serious driving. All the controls were within close reach of the driver. Five large dials provided the data-monitoring system.

Like the 356, the 911 was air-cooled, which allowed most of its weight to fit low in the chassis. But that's where the similarities stopped. Not a single part in the flat-six engine was carried over from the previous model. New for the 911 was an eight-main-bearing alloy crankcase, enlarged cooling capacity, a race-bred dry-sump oiling system, and a pair of single overhead cams. Also introduced was a five speed transaxle and a fully independent rear suspension.

The outcome of this mechanical refinement is response. The unassisted (for the first 25 years of production), yet never heavy, steering, the robust and enjoyable power band, and the consistently superb brakes all contribute to the unique manner in which a 911 responds. Ride quality is delivered in addition to, rather than at the expense of, road-holding capabilities. As attractive as the cars are, ultimately, the 911 is a driver's machine, a finely-honed tool that a beginner can feel comfortable in, and that an expert can extract astonishing performance from.

The basic 911 concept—a 2+2 coupe with superb power, a roomy cockpit, and excellent durability—was so right that Porsche has kept it in production for over 40 years. During that time, it has become one of the most highly developed machines in automotive history. Enthusiasts have never tired of it.

Today, a new 911 stands at the pinnacle of usable automotive performance. But more importantly, a used late-model 911, or earlier vintage model, can be the ultimate enthusiast's bargain. Used 911s are now affordable cars for nearly every enthusiast, with some selling below $10,000. But what will really surprise you about a used 911 of any vintage— even a 30-year-old one—is how well it drives when properly set up and how reliable it is.

You really can drive one of these wonderful vintage machines every day, to just about anywhere. And that is the point, isn't it?—*Jim Schrager*

1967 Porsche 911S SWB 2.0L Coupe

Chassis number: 118-0-0138

It was evident to Porsche management in the late '50s that the 356 series was rapidly becoming dated and reaching the end of its development potential, so in 1959 Ferdinand Porsche began designing a new car. A number of criteria were laid down: The car would have no more than a 2,200-mm wheelbase and would carry two adults and two children.

The new model was introduced at the Frankfurt Show in September 1963. It was a significant advance on the outgoing car, providing greater performance, space and refinement. The new engine, a 1991-cc opposed six-cylinder unit, was designed by Ferdinand Piech, Dr. Porsche's nephew. Situated in the rear to maximize space efficiency, it produced 130 bhp.

The 911 "S" was Porsche's top-of-the-range sporting model throughout the late 1960s and early 1970s, a period when the purest and most desirable versions of the 911 were produced. The 911S boasted a higher fifth gear, anti-roll bars front and rear, Koni shock absorbers and ventilated disc brakes, later also receiving alloy front brake calipers. The engine was also improved with higher compression and improved breathing, which produced 160 bhp. Only 4,689 of these high-specification short-wheelbase 911Ss were produced in coupe form in 1967-68.

Another 1,160 of the less-desirable, from a performance standpoint, 911S targas were built. Of the coupes, probably fewer than 100 were available in righthand drive. (In 1969 the wheelbase of the 911 was lengthened, reducing its agility and starting the overall softening that was to dilute the sporting essence of Piech's original design.)

This 1967 model is especially desirable as its date of manufacture qualifies it for historic rallying, a practice at which the 911 excels with its power and agile handling. Described as in overall excellent condition, it has had only two owners from new, the second undertaking a sympathetic restoration.

This short-wheelbase 911S sold for $15,985 at the Coys of Kensington Chiswick House sale in London on May 15, 2000. Although offered as a 1967 car, the third digit of the serial number shows that Porsche considers it a 1968 model. However, since it was manufactured in late 1967, it will still qualify for events with a 1967 build-date cut-off. This is also a rare righthand-drive car, which will usually bring a premium in the UK.

The "early" 911 period is typified by the original body style,

before the imposition of federally mandated collision bumpers in 1974. There are two series of 911S models in this period: the short-wheelbase, Weber-carbed, 160-hp models of 1967-68, and the long-wheelbase, mechanically fuel-injected models of 1969-73. The fuel-injected models had growing displacement and horsepower ratings of 2.0L/170 hp in 1969; 2.2L/180 hp (1970-71); and 2.4L/190 hp (1972-73). The longer wheelbase helped reduce the pitching at highway speeds and improve the balance of weight distribution. However, the short-wheelbase 911 has an elemental raw appeal and edgy feel to the handling that many prefer to that of the more refined, later cars.

The original non-S, 130-hp, 2.0-liter 911 engine has a sweet midrange powerband. The S version trades that midrange for greater top-end speed. As a result, an early S is not ideal for puttering around town and easily fouls spark plugs; keeping a deep socket and a set of spare plugs in the boot is a good idea. But for high-speed applications, the upper rpm power is a delight as these engines willingly rev to redline and make every driver feel he is on the Mulsanne Straight at Le Mans. For any historic event with a late '60s cut-off date, a well-prepared 911 is sure to be competitive, as few if any 2-liter cars from the period offered the performance and roadability of a 911S.

The price paid here is a bargain if the mechanicals check out; the car has its correct, original engine (not mentioned in the catalog) and is in decent cosmetic condition, as well. While it appears that the car is not up to the PCA concours standard set here in the United States, in some ways this makes it a more usable vehicle. Besides, you can leave your fancy trailer and feather duster at home and just drive the car to events.

In the 911 world, condition of the chassis and body are more important than the engine, as the engines are generally strong and the cost to rebuild one ($6,000 to $8,000) is far less than the expense of rust repairs and factory-quality refinishing. Early SWB 911Ss were rare to begin with, and most were run hard and put away wet. Of the non-race car Porsches, this is the segment of the market showing the most appreciation. Assuming this car ran out well, this was a good buy in a usable early S, and it should appreciate at the front of the 911 market.—Jim Schrager

(Historic data courtesy of the auction company.)

From the October 2000 issue of *SCM*.◆

Coys of Kensington

Year produced	1967-1968
Number produced	4,689
Original list price	$7,074 (1967 base)
SCM Price Guide	$12,500-15,000
Tune-up/major service	$300
Distributor cap	$13
Chassis #	On horizontal bulkhead under front lid, just aft of gas tank
Engine #	On vertical fan housing support passenger side of engine
Club	Porsche Club of America, P.O. Box 5900, Springfield, VA 22150
Web site	www.pca.org
Alternatives	BMW 2800 CS, Mercedes 280SL, Jaguar XKE, 2+2, 1967 Corvette coupe
Tier of collectibility	A

1972 Porsche 911E Coupe

Chassis number: 9112200948

The Porsche 911 is one of the most timeless designs in motoring history. This unconventional and charismatic car has evolved at a rapid pace throughout its production life. The 911S was Porsche's top-of-the-range sporting model throughout the late 1960s and early 1970s, a period when the purest and most desirable versions of the great 911 were produced. Initially available in 2-liter guise from July 1966, it boasted a higher fifth gear, anti-roll bars front and rear, Koni shock absorbers and ventilated disc brakes, later also receiving alloy front brake calipers.

In 1969 all 911 models had their wheelbases increased and the S variant developed a healthy 170 bhp, giving it excellent performance: 0 to 60 mph in just seven seconds and a maximum of 135 mph. Naturally the 911S found its way into competition and was successful in its class in all the major events, including Le Mans, the Targa Florio and the Tour de France.

Coys of Kensington

This example, a 1972 911E, originally a 2.4-liter model, was purchased by the previous owner in 1988 and handed immediately to marque expert Chris Turner, at which point the more desirable 2.2 S-specification engine fitted to the car was extensively rebuilt before a comprehensive restoration was performed by Gantspeed Engineering. More recent work includes overhaul of the fuel system, with a new fuel pump and injectors, a rebuilt injection pump and intake stacks with rebushed butterflies. The car is resplendent in black with a matching black interior.

This 911 sold for $20,865 at the Coys of Kensington sale in London, November 1999. This result points out the disparity between the US and European markets. For American purists, the substitution of the smaller engine, even done to "S" specs, would be a real price-killer. In Europe, where the 2.2L is regarded as having more "snap" than the 2.4L by many owners, the change didn't affect the price at all.

The 1972 and '73 2.4-liter cars are the final years of the small-bumper bodies. Aside from the Carrera RS, which displaces 2.7 liters, they have the largest engines of all the original bumper cars (1965-1973). 1972 is also the first year of the stronger 915 gearbox, which replaced the original 901 box that could no longer handle the torque of the bigger engines. To many early 911 enthusiasts, cars from these last two years are the ones to own.

This car has the 1970-71 2.2-liter S engine, which may seem

Year produced	1972-1973
Number produced	5,298
Original list price	. . . .$9,178 (1962 base price US)
SCM Price Guide	. . . .$10,500-12,000
Tune-up/major service	. . . .$250
Distributor cap	. . . .$17
Chassis #	. . . . .On embossed plate in front compartment, mounted on horizontal bulkhead next to hood latch
Engine #	. . . . .On vertical engine casting, passenger side of fan housing
Club	. . . . .Porsche Club of America, P.O. Box 5900, Springfield, VA 22150
Web site	. . . . .www.pca.org
Alternatives	. . . . . .Ferrari 308 GTB, Corvette C4 coupe, Jaguar XKE coupe, BMW 633 CSi, Mercedes-Benz 450SLC
Tier of collectibility	. . . . .B

like a letdown. However, the 2.2 and 2.4 engines are highly similar: Both have mechanical fuel injection and identical cylinder diameters; the 2.4 achieves its extra displacement by being stroked for longer piston travel. Many tuners believe the "short-stroke" 2.2-liter cars are a bit sharper off the line than the 2.4 models. Of course, for sustained high-speed work, the extra displacement of the 2.4 comes in handy. But for sprints to the dry cleaners or through the local club's autocross course, the punch of a crisp 2.2 can be quite satisfying.

The 911E model is a bit of a sleeper, as many do not realize that the E has the bigger brakes and appearance group of the S. So this E, with the S engine, has the full mechanical complement of an S.

However, this 911E has a number of non-original items in addition to its engine, such as the Carrera RS stripe on the engine cover, the seven-inch Fuchs alloys and perhaps the color. In the US, this car probably would not have made so much, despite its reputed excellent condition. But in the UK, where good, rust-free cars are rare, decent 911s tend to bring more, sometimes substantially more than here in the Colonies.

These early 911 cars are slowly being rediscovered as the great all-around cars that they are. I expect prices will continue to rise. This one, bought at well below restoration cost, should provide many hours of driving pleasure, and might even be able to be sold for a profit within the next 24 months—but only in Europe.—Jim Schrager (Historic data courtesy of the auction company.)

From the July 2000 issue of *SCM.*◆

1973 Porsche 911 Carrera RS 2.7 Touring

Chassis number: 911 360 0093
Engine number: 663 0112

Where two-seat GT cars are concerned, there can be little doubt that the Carrera RS of 1973 stands in good company. Porsche took over in sports car racing where Ferrari left off in the early 1970s. After winning the World Sportscar Championship in 1970, '71 and '72, the FIA swung from Sports-prototypes to more production-based machinery. To be homologated, each manufacturer was required to build at least 500 identical copies.

To build the Carrera RS, Porsche took the 2.4-liter 911S and subjected it to a myriad of improvements. The steel bodyshell was lightened by using thinner-than-standard steel for many components. Lightweight glass was used in some cars. The RS Carrera's characteristic ducktail spoiler was added to keep the rear end planted at top speed, now some 150 mph. The basic 2.4 S engine was enlarged to 2.7 liters through increased bore

and the mechanical fuel injection was recalibrated, but it was otherwise just like the 2.4 S, using identical cases, cams, heads and crankshaft.

Making its debut at the Paris Motor Show in 1972, the Carrera RS delighted the sales staff as customers found the car so appealing the entire 500-unit production run was sold out. Two additional runs were added, plus a handful of race cars, bringing the total production to 1,580.

Some 200 of these RSs were lightweights, but the vast majority, such as the example featured here, were equipped with full touring interiors and body fittings of the 911S models. These full touring cars were known officially as RSLs, with the L standing for luxury.

This Carrera RS was delivered new in November 1972 to a bus driver in Geneva, Switzerland. This proud purchase was his only major possession and he drove it carefully for only 50,000 kilometers (about 31,000 miles) in the next 26 years. In the late '80s, he sold it to an Englishman.

The third and present owner bought the car in 1996 and commissioned famed Porsche racer Nick Faure to complete a full major service prior to shipping the car to the US. According to the owner, the current mileage of 83,000 kms (52,000 miles) is believed to be correct. The engine and transmission are original to this RS and the spare, tool kit, jack and compressor are provided. The car has had a host of recent improvements, including updated chain tensioners, new Bilstein Sport shocks and stainless steel heat exchangers.

This well-kept Carrera RS sold for $69,300, including buyer's premium, at RM's Monterey sale on August 18, 2001. Two years ago, this price would have seemed steep. Today, it represents a modest bargain for the buyer. With its high degree of originality, this Porsche is a top contender to rise at or above the head of the market.

The auction company lists the production number, which is placed on the chassis before it is assigned a serial number, as being 103 2838. In the early days of the 911, the production number was the serial number. Starting in 1968, though, the production number became a separate sequence, as serial numbers added codes indicating the car to be a T, E or S.

The production number is completely hidden from view and requires removal of the lower knee pad on the passenger side of the cockpit for inspection. As Carrera RSs are easy to fake, inspecting this hidden number is one of the best ways to authenticate a car. There is no published list of production numbers; however, the factory will verify individual production numbers for particular cars. This is a real car.

This RS, painted light yellow, which has quite a strong green tint to it, looks to be very original. Important touchstones are the full deco strips on the rocker panels and front and rear bumpers, original Recaro sport seats and correct six-inch and 7 x 15-inch Fuchs alloys, rather than the seven-inch and eight-inch sizes that, although wrong for this early RS, are often seen as replacements. The centers of the wheels on this car are brightly anodized, which is correct even though the wheel centers were often painted to match the graphics. For any color other than Grand Prix White, the Carrera graphics were an option. Note that these side images are placed too low on this car's body, indicating they were added later.

The Carrera RS has emerged as one of the most collectible street Porsches of all time. For an early 911 enthusiast, it represents the ultimate race-bred street car, in some ways the Ferrari SWB of the Porsche world. Especially for high-speed European vintage events, it is a reliable and adrenaline-filled way to race through the countryside and perhaps end up with a podium finish as well.

The price paid was fair in the current market and it would not seem out of line should this car get resold in the near future for more.—Jim Schrager

(Historic data courtesy of the auction company.)
From the November 2001 issue of *SCM*.◆

Year produced	.1973
Number produced	.1,580
Original list price	.$10,500
SCM Price Guide	.$42,500-62,500
Tune-up/major service	.$300
Distributor cap	.$20
Chassis #	On horizontal bulkhead under front hood
Engine #	Stamped into alloy engine block near right side of cooling fan
Club	Porsche Club of America, P.O. Box 5900, Springfield, VA 22150
Web site	www.pca.org
Alternatives	BMW 635 CSi, Corvette Sting Ray coupe, Alfa Romeo SZ, Ferrari 330 GTC
Tier of Collectibility	A

1970–1973 911S: Affordable Classic

The E-type and the 911 share the distinction as two of the most recognizable sports car shapes of all time. Both cars conceptually leapt ahead of the competition when introduced and both had teething troubles in their infancy.

But after eight years of production, the E-type had lost its edge and had become somewhat dated, while the 911 was just reaching the first of several pinnacles in its long history. Porsche's continual refining of the original 911 concept is precisely what makes the 2.2-liter and 2.4-liter such appealing cars today.

With the introduction of the 2.2-liter S in the 1970 model year and the 2.4-liter S in 1972, gone was Porsche's previous standard of attempting to extract the maximum horsepower per liter from its production engines. The 1969 2.0 S with 85 hp/L had the highest output for any normally aspirated standard production Porsche. These super peaky engines had to be revved mercilessly and were too noisy and tiresome for most drivers.

With 1970 and later 911s, Porsche strove to deliver maximum driving performance rather than maximum volumetric efficiency. For example, the 2.2 S achieved 82 hp/L and the 2.4 S, 81 hp/L. This transformation was completely successful and these last models of the true S (especially the 2.4 S) are considered the finest of the pre-SC production models. These are easy cars to live with on a daily basis, their performance is unequalled by many supercar contemporaries, they have comfort (ease of entry/exit) and they have a practicality and a robustness that is legendary.

As with the purchase of any 30-year-old car, there is no substitute for a careful inspection by an expert. Porsche was not fully galvanizing the bodies in the '70s so look for signs of rust or poor repairs. The 901 gearbox of the 2.2s should be smooth, light and quiet. The 915 gearbox of the 2.4 and later cars tends to be notchy and often has balky synchros. A bit of transmission bearing whine is common, and cars can run with it for years.

The engines suffer lead-footed fools gladly and truly love to rev. A puff of smoke on a cold start which clears up in a few seconds is common but not universal and

> "These are easy cars to live with on a daily basis, their **performance is unequalled** by many supercar contemporaries, they have comfort and they have a practicality and a robustness that is **legendary.**"

Years produced	1970-1973
Number produced	4,691 (2.2 S); 5,094 (2.4 S)
Original sale price	$8,200-11,000 depending on year and options
SCM Price Guide	$12,500-14,500(2.2 S); $14,000-17,000 (2.4 S)
Current value	Cond: 3, $10,000-15,000; Cond: 2, $15,000-20,000
Tune-up/major service	$90/hr=$450
Distributor cap	$12
Chassis #	Left-hand windscreen pillar, stamped plate next to hood latch and stamped on body in trunk next to fuel tank
Engine #	Right-hand vertical surface of cooling fan supporting on block
Club	Porsche Club of America, P.O. Box 5900, Springfield, VA 22150
Web site	www.pca.org
Alternatives when new	Alfa GTV, Jaguar E-type, Mercedes-Benz 280SL, Dino 246, Corvette
Alternatives now	Later 911SC, Corvette coupe, Jaguar E-type coupe, Mercedes-Benz 280SL, BMW 3.0CS
Tier of Collectibility	B

seems to happen after long periods of storage.

Oil pressure should be at least 10 psi per 1,000 rpm with the oil warmed. Oil pressure can drop to near zero at idle, depending on the type of dry sump lubrication system. The original Bosch mechanical fuel injection system is the best fuel system for the car even though many have had Webers fitted. The Bosch system works well and is very efficient if it isn't inactive for a long period of time.

Decent-condition #3 drivers can sometimes be found under $10k, but you will probably have to be quick to snag one at this price. And much under $10k, you will probably be getting some sort of project. Over $15k should buy you a very nice driver. Over $20k and you are into the realm of low-mileage original cars or superb restorations. These cars are scarce and may take a lot of searching to find.

Make certain that if you are paying for an S you are getting an S by checking all of the numbers carefully. Owning a good car will be an enlightening experience.—*Scott Johnston*

From the January 2000 issue of *SCM.*◆

1985 Porsche 911 Cabriolet "Slant Nose"

Chassis number: WPOZZZ91ZFS51400

The Porsche 911 is probably the single most recognizable car shape in the world, an instant "Classic." For those who wanted to feel the wind in their hair while enjoying 911 motoring, Porsche manufactured for many years a "targa" version of its immortal coupe. This "targa" incorporated a rollover bar behind the cockpit as crash protection.

In the early 1980s, Porsche, like many other car manufacturers, believed that bureaucracy, particularly in America, would prevent a truly open car from being built. When its designers saw that this was not going to happen, they set to work and swiftly came up with the classic cabriolet. This 911 Carrera, with its simple one-handed hood operation, without having to fasten or release any buttons, proved an instant hit, especially in the US. Another welcome feature, the rear panel carrying the transparent rear window, can not only be opened by pulling a zip fastener but is entirely detachable and can be replaced if the vinyl becomes damaged or scratched.

By this time, the 911 itself had been well developed into a fast, comfortable, fine-handling car with its six-cylinder air-cooled 3.2-liter engine, which gave well over 200 hp at some 5,900 rpm.

RM Auctions

> *"Porsche finally solved the Achilles' heel of the 911 engine, the pair of hydraulic cam chain tensioners, with the 3.2 liter six of the Carrera."*

This 911 Carrera cabriolet sold for $33,000 at the recent RM auction in Monterey, California, August 28, 1999. The 911 Carrera, built from 1984 to 1989, was the final run of the original flared body that began with the 1978 911SC. Both the 911SC and the 911 Carrera were tremendously popular cars with quick and reliable powertrains.

Porsche finally solved the Achilles' heel of the 911 engine, its pair of hydraulic cam chain tensioners, with the 3.2-liter six of the Carrera. While earlier 911s had a sealed tensioner that eventually leaked and collapsed, the Carrera introduced a tensioner pressure-fed from the engine oil supply, essentially ending tensioner failure. Because the 911 is an interference design, should a tensioner fail, the valves can hit the pistons and do tremendous damage.

We can tell some important facts about this Carrera but need more data before we can make an informed judgment on the price paid. The letters ZZZ in the chassis number alert us this is a gray-market car. We can also see that this car was built as a regular 911 cabriolet, even though it now sports a slant nose and highly modified Turbo-style bodywork.

What we can't see is whether the modified bodywork was completed by the factory, as part of the Special Wishes program or by some aftermarket firm somewhere. We also aren't told if the body is executed in steel of fiberglass—another important issue.

At 70,000 miles, this isn't a low-mileage Porsche, but the 3.2 engine has proven to be robust. I would like to see maintenance records to insure the valves have been adjusted more or less on schedule, to prevent premature valve wear. Otherwise, unless the car has been raced, the powertrain has a life expectancy in excess of 150,000 miles.

The price paid for this car, by any measure, seems quite high. Assuming this isn't a factory car and following the rule that all body modifications to a street car only diminish value, the seller should be quite pleased with his day at Monterey.—Jim Schrager

(Historic description courtesy of the auction company.)

From the November 1999 issue of SCM.◆

Years produced	1984-1989
Number produced	22,283
Original list price	$37,500 (US delivery)
SCM Price Guide	$20,000-23,000
Tune-up/major service	$200
Distributor cap	$20
Chassis #	Under front hood, stamped in horizontal bulkhead, just aft of gas tank
Engine #	On passenger's side of cooling fan, stamped on a vertical fan support member
Club	Porsche Club of America, P.O. Box 5900, Springfield, VA 22150
Web site	www.pca.org
Alternatives	Ferrari 308, Mercedes-Benz 560SL, Corvette C4
Tier of Collectibility	C

1989 Porsche Carrera Speedster

Chassis number: WPOEB0913KS173790
Engine number: 64KO6495

RM Auctions

The six-cylinder boxer engine was a concept originated with the first 911 prototype in the early '60s. Thanks in large part to Porsche's engineering prowess, this aluminum-alloy, air-cooled engine remained a Porsche staple, developing and evolving while remaining true to many of its original design principles. By 1989 the engine had grown from its original 2 liters to 3.2 liters. Power increased proportionally, from 130 hp in 1963 to 231 hp (DIN) by 1989.

Not unlike the engine, many facets of the 911's original design remained consistent—unit-body construction, rear-mounted engine, dry-sump lubrication, independent suspension, four-wheel disc brakes and excellent ergonomics, all enclosed by an aerodynamically effective fastback body. Popular targa-top and convertible versions were also offered by the early 1970s.

The 1989 911 Carrera Speedster, with its steeply raked, low-cut windshield and cockpit cover, was inspired by the original four-cylinder 356 Speedsters produced in the '50s. With its stout 3.2-liter engine and its much improved G-50 transmission, the 1989 Carrera Speedster is likely the most collectible of the 1980s Porsche variants since only 2,065 examples were built in a single model year. Of this total production run, only 823 arrived in North America.

The particular 911 Speedster offered here is notable for two key reasons: The car has covered only 1,260 miles since new and remains virtually in showroom condition, and it was custom factory ordered in Aquamarine Blue to match the standard color of the first owner's 1958 356 Speedster.

This Turbo-look, wide-body Speedster also features an interior in gray leather and a complementing dark blue convertible top. Other optional equipment, according to the Porsche Cars certificate of authenticity, includes a Blaupunkt Charleston AM/FM stereo with cassette, cruise control and air conditioning. Other than a new factory battery and Michelin Pilot tires, this Porsche time-capsule car is exactly as it left the factory in 1989.

This striking 911 Speedster made $74,800, including commission, at the RM Amelia Island, Florida, auction, March 11, 2000. This Price Guide-busting result speaks to the superb condition of this car matched with a highly appreciative audience.

Even though only 2,065 1989 Speedsters were built, there are always a handful for sale. It is not unusual to have the factory wide-body option, as 1,894 were so ordered. The ultra-low mileage does make this example a bit unusual, but the vast majority of 911 Speedsters have covered under 10,000 miles as, unfortunately, most were bought for speculation rather than driving. The sophisticated color of this car is eye-catching, as most 911 Speedsters are Guards Red, black or Grand Prix White.

The chassis and all of the mechanicals are identical to any other 1989 911 Carrera, and that means quick and bulletproof. The Speedster package shaves about 90 pounds off the weight of a coupe, but the Turbo-look option puts most of that weight back on. The top on a 911 Speedster, known for its modest wet-weather protection, is only meant for occasional use, so this is a car best saved for sunny-day drives.

One of the principal reasons 911s have been so successful is the overwhelming practicality packaged with their performance. These are cars that can be driven to work without worry, and over time, the comfort and accessibility makes them cars that get frequent use. The Speedster takes away a chunk of that practicality and as a result, whether in its 356, 911 Carrera or C2 version, it has never been a high-volume seller.

The 356 Speedster has risen atop the 356 value chain, and the 911 Speedster has as well. But for 911 Speedster owners, it's been a bit of a wild ride. Many of these cars sold new for upwards of $100,000, yet today nice cars can still be found in the low $50,000 range. While the price made was way over our Price Guide numbers, remember our Price Guide assumes a #2 car, while this example enjoyed the 50-100% premium often afforded a #1.—Jim Schrager

(Historic description courtesy of the auction company.)
From the May 2000 issue of *SCM*.◆

Years produced	1989
Number produced	2,065
Original list price	$69,800 (base)
SCM Price Guide	$43,000-48,000
Tune-up/major service	$600 (including valve adjust)
Distributor cap	$50
Chassis #	Stamped in horizontal bulkhead aft of gas tank and on aluminum tag just aft of front bumper, both in front trunk
Engine #	Stamped vertically on engine case on passenger side of engine cooling fan
Club	Porsche Club of America, P.O. Box 5900, Springfield, VA 22150
Web site	www.pca.org
Alternatives	Mercedes-Benz 560SL, Corvette C4 ZR-1, Ferrari
Tier of Collectibility	B

1978-1983 Porsche 911 SC
Coupe, Targa, and Cabriolet

Get a good SC in the first place, and maintain it properly to perserve its value.

While the automotive world suffered through the 1973-77 era of dramatically tightened emission-control laws, Porsche was busy building, piece by piece, the better mousetrap that would become the 911SC. Starting with the dramatically simplified CIS fuel injection of the '73 911T, the SC included the flared body of the 1974 Carrera, the engine block from the 3.0-liter Turbo in 1975, the galvanized sheet metal developed in the 1976 cars and the improved interior ventilation system introduced in 1977. By its introduction in 1978, the 911SC, with its 3.0-liter six-cylinder boxer powerplant, was arguably the best serial production sports car on the market. Even today, many Porsche enthusiasts feel it offers the perfect combination of creature comforts (just enough, without the car becoming a luxo-barge) and sterling performance.

Further, the 911SC has an extraordinarily robust drivetrain, even by Porsche standards. Engines, if properly maintained and serviced, regularly go 200,000 miles before overhauls. Our 1981 targa had original paint and 155,000 miles when we sold it. We now have a 38,000-mile dead-original '83 SC and a 98,000-mile cosmetically challenged '78 model. If you were blindfolded, all three would feel exactly the same from behind the wheel.

Now that these cars are reaching 20 years of age, we are seeing some head stud breakage, which is not trivial and costs about $3,000 to repair. The original, old-style chain tensioners need to be replaced every 10 or so years. A better option is to convert to the later pressure-fed style (approximately $900). Cruise-control modules fail, turn-signal levers wear out, fresh-air blower motors in the ventilation system pack up and air conditioning systems, unless upgraded, are marginal.

This was a highly successful car built in large numbers, so chances are prices will stay stable for the foreseeable future. However, we are seeing more collectors

> "Even today, many Porsche enthusiasts feel the SC offers the perfect combination of creature comforts (just enough, without the car becoming a luxo-barge) and sterling performance."

willing to pay a premium for documented, unmodified, low-mileage (under 75,000) cars. Avoid $10,000 SCs with fiberglass body add-ons or cars that look like they've been run hard and put away wet. The difference in price between a pig ($7k) and a jewel ($16k) is just too small to justify buying a car with significant needs.

For pure appreciation, the 1983 cabriolet is the best bet, as this was the first 911 cabriolet and had limited production in its first year. Serious drivers prefer the coupes due to their greater chassis rigidity; the sunroof cars are a good compromise for those who want an open-air feel without worrying about weather sealing or cowl shake.

I never hesitate to recommend an SC for a first-time Porsche buyer. They still have some of the edgy enthusiast-oriented feel of the earlier 2.0-2.4L cars while adding a host of improvements and durability enhancements. The SC is a car with big performance, limited depreciation (a well-kept car simply won't go down in value) and tremendous reliability that you can enjoy driving every day.
— *Jim Schrager*

From the September 2000 issue of *SCM*.◆

Years produced	1978-1983
Number produced	68,080
Original list price	. . . . .$22,665 (as tested, 1978)
SCM Price Guide	. . . .$16,000-22,500
Tune-up/major service	. . . .$600
Distributor cap	. . . .$13
Chassis #	. . . . . .Under front hood, on horizontal bulkhead, just forward of gas tank
Engine #	. . .On alloy vertical web to right of fan
Club	. . . . .Porsche Club of America, P.O. Box 5900, Springfield, VA 22150
Web site	. . . . .www.pca.org
Alternatives	. . . . .Corvette C4, Mercedes 380/450/560SL, BMW 6 Series, Jaguar XJ-S
Tier of Collectibility	. . . . .B

1984-1989 Porsche 911 Carrera Coupe

The 1984-89 Carrera, as the final iteration of the original "widebody" normally aspirated 911, is a good choice for someone looking for an affordable sports car coupled with a high degree of refinement, reliability and sparkling performance.

Comparisons to the 1978-83 911SC are natural, as they share nearly identical bodies and interiors. But the Carrera has many significant improvements, starting with a 3.2 rather than a 3.0-liter engine. The Achilles' heel of the 911 engine—hydraulic chain tensioner failure—was solved in 1984. While tensioners on previous models carried their own limited reserve of hydraulic fluid, Carrera tensioners have a steady stream of engine oil fed directly via two small oil lines visible at the rear of the engine. Changing to electronic engine controls in 1984 resulted in lower emissions, higher horsepower and better gas mileage.

Improvements continued in following years. The shifter was redesigned in 1985, reducing lever throw. The air conditioning system, vastly improved in 1984, was improved again in 1986 by redesigning the dash to accommodate larger vents. In 1987, a hydraulic clutch and a new gearbox, the G-50, with improved synchronizers were introduced.

Carrera engines are durable, but watch for worn valve guides, often more the result of poor maintenance than poor design. Connecting rod bolts have been known to let loose, but this generally occurs on cars that have been raced or autocrossed. Obviously, Carreras with flares, spoilers and faded racing stickers on the doors are not your best choice.

Driving a Carrera is a civilized and comfortable experience, although not as vintage as earlier 911s. As their horsepower comes higher in the rpm band than the 911SC, a generous application of the throttle is required

Years produced	1984-1989
Number produced	36,834
Original list price	$31,950 (1984); $51,205 (1989)
SCM Price Guide	$17,000-25,000
Tune-up/major service	$600
Distributor cap	$13
Chassis #	Under front hood, on horizontal bulkhead, just forward of gas tank
Engine #	On alloy vertical web to right of fan
Club	Porsche Club of America, P.O. Box 5900, Springfield, VA 22150
Web site	www.pca.org
Alternatives	Corvette C4/5, BMW M3-M5, Ferrari 308 QV
Tier of Collectibility	C

> "Especially with late-model 911s, the factory **really knew what they were doing** when they set these cars up; unless you're Hurley Haywood heading for Daytona, **stock is best.**"

to get to the fat part of the torque curve. These cars are quiet and ride well, so long as no one has added the sport suspension pieces that cause a serious deterioration in ride comfort.

Personally, I prefer the 1987-89 models, as they were the most refined, but the earlier 1984-86 versions can be had for just a bit more than a 911SC. One of the upsides to owning a 911 is that stock and upgraded performance parts are widely available; one of the downsides is the number of 911 owners who bolt these parts on for a go-fast look to the detriment of the overall performance of the car. Especially with late-model 911s, the factory really knew what it was doing when it set these cars up; unless you're Hurley Haywood heading for Daytona, stock is best.

Porsche 911 Carreras are a tremendous blend of performance and durability for the money. With so many built, the collectible factor for a Carrera coupe is negligible at best, but as a lively daily driver with few vices, these cars are hard to beat.—*Jim Schrager*

From the August 2001 issue of *SCM*.◆

1992 Porsche 959

Chassis number: WPOZZZ95ZJS9002

The Porsche 959 was conceived by the Stuttgart marque in 1985 as a practical road-going application of the ultimate in racing technology.

Its specification remains unparalleled, with a detuned 450-bhp version of the 2.85-liter 956/962 Le Mans-winning twin turbocharged engine; variable split four-wheel drive with computer-controlled programs for dry, wet, icy and off-road use; automatic height and ride control; lightweight Kevlar/aramid composite body; ABS racing brakes giving in excess of 1.25 G deceleration; automatic tire-pressure loss sensors; run-flat tires and more. The list seems endless.

But being a Porsche road car, the 959 was also comfortable with climate control, electric heated seats, stereo system, electric windows and mirrors and, most importantly, service intervals of 12,000 miles with oil changes necessary only every 6,000 miles. The car steam-rollered its opponents in the Paris-Dakar Rally of 1986, finished seventh at Le Mans that year and also won the IMSA GTZ class.

The road-going 959 had a top speed of over 200 mph, acceleration of 0-60 mph in just under 3.8 seconds and 0-125 mph in 8.2 seconds. One road tester described acceleration as having two stages: "brisk" with the first turbo engaged and "manic" with the second.

Porsche built a limited run of just under 200 cars in 1988-90 and eight additional cars in 1992-93. These final versions, built for a handful of selected long-term customers, incorporated various improvements. This car, delivered in December of 1992, is finished in the classic and understated combination of metallic silver with a black leather interior. The car is unmarked and virtually in as-new condition, having less than 25,000 miles in total.

All services have been carried out by the factory and, most importantly, the car has been regularly and carefully used. The file includes a letter dated June 1997 from the factory confirming the car's as-new condition. The car is currently road licensed in the UK.

Offered by its second owner, this is a unique opportunity to acquire a rare Series 2 959 in superb order. The 959's attractions of very limited production, exotic specification derived directly from race-winning cars and practicality make it by far the most collectible of all modern-generation road-going Porsches.

It took $203,391 at the Bonhams & Brooks Monaco Grand Prix sale, May 21, 2001, to drive this 959 home. The price is reflective of the current market for these supremely complex exotics and takes into account the exclusivity of the Series 2 specification against the rather high miles (remember, while 25,000 miles may be like-new for a regular car, for a collector car it's as if you had driven the car to the moon and back).

The 959 was developed as a way to show the commitment of the factory to the 911 for years to come. American-born Porsche CEO

Years produced	1988-1990, 1992-1993
Number produced	208 (approx.)
Original list price	$275,000
SCM Price Guide	$150,000-175,000
Tune-up/major service	$3,000 (approx.)
Distributor cap	Included in above
Chassis #	On horizontal bulkhead under front hood
Engine #	Stamped into alloy engine block near fan shroud on passenger side
Club	Porsche Club of America, P.O. Box 5900, Springfield, VA 22150
Web site	www.pca.org
Alternatives	Ferrari F40, Jaguar XJ 220, McLaren F1
Tier of Collectibility	A

Peter Schutz was responsible for the decision to keep the 911 in production and wanted a showcase to prove the car fully able to perform at all levels against all comers. The 959 was a sublime way to convey this message.

However, it is handicapped as a road car in two important ways. First, due to the original Group 3 regulations, the engine was smallish, at only 2.85 liters. The car was still wickedly fast, but later road-going twin-turbo 3.6-liter engines produce as much power with greater ease. The tremendous complexity of the car required a program of maintenance available only at the factory. This is fun if you live in proximity to Stuttgart and have a convenient way to stay in contact with the folks building these fabulous cars, but it makes things hard for those of us in export markets. You can own one, of course. It's the driving and maintenance that becomes worrisome.

How about the appreciation potential for such a landmark car? While we haven't seen any significant increases in value, neither have these cars declined in value. By comparison, just ask a 1992 Testarossa owner how his car is doing in the marketplace. The 959's racing history and limited production ensures that you're unlikely to find any bargain-basement deals. Unlike, say, 904s that could be had for $6,000 in 1970 because nobody cared about them, the increased sophistication of the collector car market is likely to keep the 959 above $200,000 for the forseeable future. Spectacular cars like the 959 no longer drop quietly from view.

However, partly because it has a 911-based body shape, the 959 is unlikely to emulate the 50-fold increase of the 904 (now worth $300,000) over the next 30 years. Rather, it will stay, like a Ferrari F40, as a definitive statement of one of the supercars of its era, and it will always make a highly prized addition to any sophisticated Porsche collection.

Further, should you ever be at a cocktail party and have the owner of a McLaren F1 sidle up to you, proposing a race for pink slips, you can simply reply, Sure. I'll pick the course. How about the Baja 1000?—Jim Schrager

(Historic data courtesy of the auction company.)

From the October 2001 issue of *SCM*.◆

930 Turbo: A Porsche for Mr. Leadfoot

The 930 Turbo was Porsche's first serial-production muscle car. And like its American counterparts that sacrificed driveability in their ferocious pursuit of raw horsepower, the 930 Turbo marked a radical departure from the traditional 911 virtues of lightness, finesse and modesty.

Porsche 356s and early 911s through 1973 do a lot with a little, and I admire that. Although the 911s have smallish powerplants, ranging from 2.0 to 2.4 liters, they extract horsepower from their flat-sixes in a very efficient manner and are quite lively to drive. Despite diminutive outside dimensions, they have loads of room inside. Without exotic suspension pieces or gargantuan tires, excellent road holding is delivered along with, rather than instead of, decent ride quality. No power assists to any of the controls are required because the cars are so well balanced. Shifting gears is a true joy. In essence, they are a definitive point-to-point GT car, equally as comfortable in urban traffic as on twisting mountain roads.

Goes like the wind, rides like a truck.

In most cases, you can fix anything that goes wrong yourself, short of a complete engine rebuild. Ownership is less a display (sometimes vulgar) of how much borrowing power you have amassed than a statement of how much automotive wisdom you have acquired.

None of the above is true with a Turbo. They go very fast when on boost but trade off every other traditional Porsche virtue to do so. The Turbo in my warehouse is a US-model 1976 930 sunroof coupe, silver with black leather and in very nice condition. There is nothing especially unusual about the car except that it is completely stock. No toilet-bowl-sized turbo upgrade, no boy-racer muffler, no body aero gee-gaws, no double-wide wheels and monster tires. It is well cared for, to be sure, with glossy paint and an original interior in excellent condition.

Introduced in 1975, the 911 Turbo was Porsche's response to the need to homologate the wildly powerful Turbo for FIA GT competition. Of course, the CanAm 917-10 and 917-30 cars with their turbocharged flat-12s had demolished all competitors. How wonderful to have a Porsche Turbo for the street! The original street Turbo engines for the US market displaced 3.0 liters and produced 245 horsepower. In 1978 they grew to 3.3 liters and added an intercooler to make 20 extra horsepower. Zero to 60 times of about 6.2 seconds were a bit slower than the Carrera RS's 5.7. But above 60 miles per hour, the Turbo had giant reserves of power. For example, when *Road & Track* tested the 1976 Turbo, it just barely got into second gear at 51 miles per hour, and just out of second at 85 miles per hour while exercising the car in a 0-to-100-mph sprint. It did not use fourth gear at all.

My Turbo would be a perfect car for everyday driving if I lived in Montana and had to drive 100 miles on the Interstate every day to work. At 95 miles per hour, the car is steady and serene. But below 70, where most of us do the vast majority of our driving, the Turbo is harsh, sluggish and heavy. Below 50 miles per hour, driving the Turbo is a chore.

The four-speed transmission is clunky to shift. The good news is that within US speed limits you won't shift often. If you want to be "on boost" at normal highway speeds, things happen very quickly in first gear, and when you get to boost in second you're already at the speed limit. Third and fourth are both distant overdrives here, efficient devices for collecting expensive traffic tickets.

Because of all the complexity and requisite plumbing stuffed into the engine compartment, along with the air-conditioning equipment, there is little room for the home mechanic to fiddle. Changing the distributor cap on my Turbo can be a two-hour job, and my car doesn't even have the giant intercooler, standard from 1978 on. To change the spark plugs, begin by removing the air-conditioning compressor. It will take a while; I know.

The Turbo is not for those with faint egos. Between the giant fender flares and the whale tail, the car screams "look at me!" Finesse? Brute force is more like it. The strangest part is that when off boost, say below 3,500 rpm, it's a dog. There is more weight and less torque than a similar 911SC (1978 to 1983).

But wait, it gets worse, as the fewer gear ratios of the Turbo four-speed versus the 911SC five-speed make that lesser power seem even further out of reach. The giant (and stiff) tires make most 930s ride like heavily laden pickup trucks on anything but a perfectly smooth race course tarmac.

If you must have a 930 Turbo, avoid gray-market cars. By now, many years after their importation, they can be difficult to smog. Don't consider any cars that don't have good service histories, either. A 930 with a mysterious past simply can't be cheap enough. Have any prospective acquisition inspected by someone fluent in Turbos. In today's market, expect to pay $35,000 to $45,000 for a best-in-the-world example, and $25,000 to $35,000 for a nice car with no bad stories.

Despite all the above, I enjoy having my stock Turbo as an example of a direction that Porsche took in the late '70s that was so diametrically opposed to everything it had done before.—*Jim Schrager*

From the September 2002 issue of *SCM*.◆

What's the 411 On My 911?

Dear Mr. Schrager: I am looking at a 1966 911 five-speed coupe, dark orange with a black vinyl interior and loaded with options, including sunroof, air conditioning, gas heater, fog lights, rear-window wiper, headrests, wood-rimmed steering wheel, chrome wheels and AM/FM Becker radio. It seems to be quite rust free, with a generally straight body and a surprisingly decent interior. The car runs but has trouble starting. The seller knows little or nothing about the car. The price is firm at $5,500. I know you like the later, long-wheelbase 911s the best, but this one seems like a good buy to me. What do you think?—**N.S., Evansville, IN**

Educate yourself before buying an early 911.

For those new to the 911 hobby, I tend to favor the 1969-73 911s, as these 2.0, 2.2 or 2.4 long-wheelbase cars have many improvements over the early cars. However, I have a special place in my heart for the 1966 911. They were the first cars brought into the US and came equipped with an unusual amount of standard equipment and some special trim not available again.

For example, a strip of real teak wood in the middle of the dash and a beautiful wood steering wheel were standard in 1966. By 1967, the wood dash was gone and the wood wheel a rare option. All 1966s had fog lights under the front bumper and an auxiliary gas heater, both unusual as the years went by.

The sunroof is a rare option for any early 911. Air conditioning was usually dealer-installed and often didn't work too well. You can check on the quality of the installation by seeing if it has a second condenser in one of the front wheel wells. If it does, it was one of the better attempts. The underdash A/C vent units were quite fragile, with parts hard to find then and nearly impossible today.

Tangerine was not an official US color, so there is a chance your car started out in Europe. This isn't a big deal, as there was no real difference between a US and European car back in those pre-smog, pre-D.O.T. days. Most interiors were fitted with sturdy black vinyl which can still be in one piece 35 years later if well cared for.

The 1966 911 produces 130 (DIN) hp. Based on the later VIN you sent, the engine should have Weber carbs. This is a sweet early engine, with great mid-range torque and excellent tractability. However, you need to keep an eye on the cam-chain tensioners. The older cam-tower castings are difficult to convert to the updated Carrera hydraulic chain tensioners, so if you buy this car you'll want to install a fresh set of Turbo-style chain tensioners and release guards that protect your engine from complete tensioner collapse. While you are in there, update the ramps and put in a new set of chains. Plan on about $1,000 for parts and labor.

Early 911s came with 4.5"-wide wheels straight from the 356, and 165/15 tires are about the only proper fit. Later 5.5" wheels will bolt right on and modern 185/65/15 or 195/60/15 tires work well. There were no alloys in 1966, so the chrome wheels on your car were standard with all 911s that year.

Carefully inspect the turn signal and rear stop-light lenses, as these one-piece units are no longer in production. If the lenses are cracked, and they all get that way sooner or later, replacement is expensive, with good used units bringing about $300-$400 each.

I worry about cars that have been sitting for a while. Starters and alternators go bad, ignition switches wear out, gas tanks rust, fuel pumps get tired, carburetors gum up and distributor advance plates get sticky. One or more of these systems may be responsible for your hard-starting problems. I'd start with the ignition switch and work my way back to the engine.

The good news is that many body and interior parts are available at reasonable prices from similar-year 912s, which are rarely worth even a modest restoration these days. Further, good news is that the prices of the earliest 911s (1965 and 1966) are slowly starting to move up. Excellent cars are bringing $15,000, fueled as much by demand here in the US as in Europe, where import taxes in some countries are waived when cars get to be 35 years old.

Although the later 911 models are better all-around cars and easier to live with, for those new to Porsche, this one, at just $5,500, could be a fun way to join the marque. And you'd be buying a car whose value can go nowhere but up.—*Jim Schrager*

From the May 2000 issue of *SCM*.◆

Soft Rear Window Targas, Collecting 993s, and Buying on eBay

Dear Mr. Schrager: *Which is better, soft or hard? In reference, of course, to the long-term value of a 911 Targa with a soft rear window versus the glass rear window. (I know, at first you thought it had something to do with Viagra, gold chains and manual shifters.) I've always loved the look of these open-backed Targas but have only seen them as 912s. Do you know how many were produced and would you say, all things being equal, the soft rear window is worth a premium over the standard Targa?*

Also, I own a 1996 993, silver/black, six-speed, with less than 23,000 miles. Do you imagine these cars will be considered premium 911s to own in the years to come due to their styling and being the last air-cooled 911s?
—M.L., via e-mail

911 Targa "hard back" is valued at about $2,000 less than the "soft back."

For 1967, the first year of production, there was no glass rear window available, and all 718 911 and 483 911S Targas were built with the removable plastic rear window. Porsche developed the glass rear window starting in the l968 model year to solve two problems: first, the unexpected body flex of the Targa, and second, to eliminate the maintenance needed by the delicate plastic rear window. Given a choice, buyers in 1968 and 1969 overwhelmingly chose the glass-rear-window model. By the end of the 1970 model year, all Targas came with glass rear windows.

Because the soft rear window was an option and cars with it do not have a separate chassis number, it is not known how many were made beyond the first year of production. For the same reason, the number of early 911 coupes with sunroofs is not known. Evidence derived from observation, however, suggests that both options are rare. I'd value a soft-rear-window 911 Targa at about $2,000 more than one with a glass window.

"993"

Regarding your 993, as the last of the air-cooled 911s, it will always have a special place in the hearts of Porschephiles, but probably not in their pocketbooks. It will take years before the 993 stops depreciating and starts to increase in value.

To compare, consider the 911SC, another landmark Porsche. It shows little sign of heading back up in value, even though it is more than 20 years old. Prices have been stable, and it is a great car, but there is little collector interest. The real value-killer here is production numbers. Over 60,000 SCs of all flavors were produced. In the world of Ferraris, the 308/328 is derided as a "mass-production" car, and just 10,000 of those were made. Further, when the 348 was introduced, it looked, for better or for worse, completely different from the 328 it replaced. By comparison, all 911s share visually similar characteristics, further depressing their collectibility.

If you like your 993, by all means keep it and enjoy it. But it will depreciate just like a used car for maybe 20 or 25 more years before the price will start to strengthen. And really, aren't there a lot of other sports cars you might want to enjoy during the next

two and a half decades? Even the most valuable mass-produced Porsche, the 356 Speedster, needed 25 years after production ceased for its values to climb above $10,000, and that was a car produced in far more limited numbers than even a single year's output of the 993.

eBay Caveat

During the past several months, I've written about my positive experiences buying and selling parts and literature on eBay. Recently, however, I have received a disturbing number of letters from Porsche enthusiasts who have bought cars on eBay, sometimes with disastrous results.

There is a common theme to these horror stories: misrepresentation, either through ignorance or treachery on the part of the seller. Some actual examples: A supposedly rebuilt engine delivered with an obvious crack in the block, a freshly restored 356 with floor pan rot "repaired" using Bondo and undercoat, major body damage artfully disguised with computer photos taken from just the right angle, and a 1963 Super 90 356 with a completely wrong 1600 Normal engine from 1959, a fact the seller failed to disclose.

No picture on a computer monitor can substitute for a hands-on examination of a car or for personal references. When bidding, first take a look at the seller's feedback, and contact a few previous buyers. If the seller has no feedback, be very, very careful.

Second, if you are serious about a car and the reserve seems reasonable, offer to have the car inspected, at your expense, before the bidding ends. Alternatively, you can try to make your high bid contingent upon an inspection, but this is unwieldy for most sellers.

Some sellers won't be interested in having their cars inspected. If this is the case, exit that screen and walk away from the computer. The instant thrill of buying a car with the click of a mouse will quickly fade and be replaced by months of remorse as you struggle with a lousy car purchased at a lousy price. Be careful.—*Jim Schrager*

From the February 2001 issue of *SCM*.◆

What About the 912?

Dear Mr. Schrager: *I've seen 1965-69 912s at under $5,000 that seem like pretty good cars. This represents a 40% discount or so from a 911. I believe the 912 is the same basic body, interior and suspension as the 911, although of course less powerful. Doesn't this four-cylinder car still deliver much of the six-cylinder Porsche experience at a discount price?*—**B.J., Syracuse, NY**

Many of us started our Porsche ownership careers in a 912. I have fond memories of my Irish Green/tan 1966 912 coupe and the nearly identical sand beige/black one owned by my best friend way back in 1970.

When new, 912s were a bargain. The 912 is a real Porsche—designed by Porsche, built in the Porsche factory and powered by an engine designed and built by Porsche. The 912 is virtually identical to the 911 except for the engine, a few instruments on the dash and the 912 script on the engine cover.

In 1966, the 912 was priced at $4,690, compared to $6,490 for the 911 (notice the clever transposing of numerals). This meant the 911 cost a cool 38% more than the 912 for its two extra cylinders. This significant discount in price explains why an estimated 30,000 912s were sold between 1965 and 1969, as opposed to about 20,000 911s.

The 912 is fitted with a slightly de-tuned version of the four-cylinder pushrod engine used in the final 356SC, still a rather highly stressed package producing 90 DIN horsepower out of 1.6 liters. Over time, it has become evident that the 912's durability was compromised by the lack of an oil filter and a crankshaft supported by three main bearings around four throws when five would support the crank much better.

To make matters worse, and perhaps because of their lower price, 912s often fell into the hands of those unable or unwilling to maintain the high-performance engine with the regularity it demanded. After 30 years of suspect maintenance, the result is that 912 engines regularly break, often in spectacular fashion. Many spin their gland nuts off the flywheel end of the crankshaft, some burn holes in their pistons and others launch rods hither and yon through cases, heads and even sheet metal.

Reading Porsche's internal memos from the early '60s, we discover that Porsche was aware of these design flaws in the 356 (and later, 912) engines. In Dirk-Michael Conradt's superb book *Porsche 356, Driving in its Purest Form* (published by Beeman Jorgensen, 1993), an internal memo is presented which shows broken crankshafts as #3 on the list of customers' reasons for selling their Porsches (pages 126-127). It's rather shocking that breakage of such a crucial and expensive part would rank so high on the list of 14 areas needing improvement.

These problems were skillfully solved in the 911 series: eight main bearings (for six crank throws), a full-flow oil filter and a repositioned oil cooler. The result is that an old 911 can still be quite reliable. But the vast majority of 912s haven't received the care they need, and the result is often a significant amount of deferred repairs.

Looks like a 911, goes like a 356.

Today, it costs plenty to make a 912 right. A rebuild will often include new pistons and cylinders (about $2,000 for the OEM set) and extensive head work (up to $1,000 for both sides). Used cranks can be touchy if not machined correctly, and you can spend up to $1,700 for a new one. A new oil cooler and various other important internal parts will bring the parts and labor tab to between $6,000 and $8,000 for a really first-class job.

This means the cost of a good rebuild is often more than the entire car is worth. Since so many 912s were produced, we are not in danger of suddenly facing a shortage. In my mind, 912 values will stay low for a long time.

Of course, there is another way around the 912's engine longevity problem. You could simply slip a 911 engine in the 912's nearly identical engine bay. This idea sounds good in theory, but in practice, by the time you buy a good used 911 engine and piece together all the minor electronic components and other bits required, you've probably spent about as much as if you had sold your 912 and purchased a decent 911 instead. And there is no way that a 912 with a swapped engine will ever be worth as much as an original 911.

I'd consider a 912 only if it has had the good fortune to have had a very thorough overhaul with the best parts, and lavish care thereafter. This would include yearly valve adjustments and oil changes every 1,000 to 1,500 miles. If you can find a 912 like this, and get a substantial discount from a 911 in similar condition, then it can be a good first Porsche.

Otherwise, if your budget can handle it, the superior engineering in the 911 will deliver both more power and greater durability. In the end, that usually makes the 911 a much better value, as well.—*Jim Schrager*

From the March 1998 issue of *SCM*.◆

Restore a Porsche For Love, Not Money

Dear Mr. Schrager: *I have recently gotten involved with Porsches, having been a long-time VW collector. Your columns help me think about how to invest wisely in these wonderful cars. I am generally a very realistic, some might say cynical, person and in your writings you seem to have the same somewhat jaded perspective.*

I work with these cars for love, not money. I am a neurosurgeon and bringing these old cars back on the road gives me the same thrill that helping my patients does. How do I balance my joy of restoring an old 911 against your steely eyed value judgments?

A project waiting to be put to the budget test.

I have a 1957 356A non-sunroof coupe that needs restoration, a 1980 911SC coupe, a 1971 911E with a rusty chassis and a 1968 911L coupe, white/black, that runs, but barely. The turn signals and taillight lenses on the '68 are cracked, the engine leaks and smokes, the interior is both not original and very tired, the body is lumpy and there is rust underneath.

I feel I bought the 911L for a song at $4,000 and am anxious to restore this car to its previous glory. How should I proceed?—**Dr. W.H., South Bend, IN, via phone**

You should begin by selling the car. I recommend eBay. I would list the 911L at no reserve and start the bidding at $1. Your 911L will reach about $1,500 or so and you will have just saved yourself at least $10,000 and countless hours of wasted time.

Now that we've solved your immediate dilemma, let's talk about the heart versus the head. Fooling around with Porsches is not my day job. I do it strictly for the love of these old cars, and in many cases, I do things which make virtually no sense other than when understood as acts of passion.

However, your passion does not have to be spent in a destructive fury. It can be constructive, but you have to educate yourself, be disciplined and employ judgment. There is nothing quite like the satisfaction of completing a restoration. To maximize those good feelings when restoring a Porsche, here are a few rules to follow.

First, only one restoration at a time. No sense doing this '68 911L, that '57 356A and the other '71 911 all at once. Focus your efforts on a single car. You'll find it is hard enough to complete just one, much less three or four.

Second, only restore a special car. If an early 911, it should be an unusual model or color or have some special options. If a 356, it should not be a non-sunroof coupe. It should also be a car that you will be happy owning for a long period, because the completed car should remain in your collection to produce a satisfactory return on your emotional and financial investment.

The third rule is that before you spend a dime, write a thorough budget with carefully researched costs. Compare the projected costs with the value of the finished car. Only with this splash of cold water in your face should you seriously consider starting a restoration.

The reality is that your '68 911L will never be a highly desirable Porsche. It isn't an open car, doesn't have any unusual options, isn't a rare color and, due to the impact of emission controls, is a year both Porsche and most enthusiasts would rather forget. In addition, yours is a rusty relic that will never be equal to a clean, original car.

Here's some simple math:

Chassis rust repairs	$2,000
Body work to remove lumps	$2,000
Non-concours street paint job	$3,000
Rebuild engine/carbs/trans	$6,000
(not primo, but good running standard)	
Refinish alloys, new tires	$1,000
Rebuild brakes (complete)	$1,000
New interior, original materials	$3,000
Good used taillights, turn signals	$1,000
Miscellaneous stuff I forgot	$2,000
Original cost of car	$4,000
Total invested	**$25,000**

When completed, your car would be very hard work to get even $15,000 for.

I'm not trying to be cynical in telling you not to restore this car. Instead, I'm asking you to exercise a bit of judgment and discipline to avoid years of wasted effort culminating in a financial apocalypse.

You'll feel much better about your automotive hobby if your Porsches are chosen in light of realistic costs and probable future value as well as pure love. It doesn't take a brain surgeon to figure that out, does it?—*Jim Schrager*

From the September 2000 issue of *SCM*.◆

Finish the Restoration on this 1969 911T Targa

I'm looking at a 1969 911T Targa five-speed that was waylaid on its way to a concours restoration. The car has a stunning burgundy paint job on a straight, rust-free body. Although the seats and top need re-covering, the dash has no cracks, carpets are good and an original AM/FW/SW Blaupunkt radio resides in the dash. The entire underbody has been meticulously scraped of original undercoat and refinished in gloss black POR-15. Mechanically the transmission is in place, but the engine consists only of the two crankcase halves.

What isn't needed here?

The seller lost interest after working on this car for 10 years. He is firm at $4,500. The urethane paint job alone seems worth the price. A car that has had so much careful work completed really turns me on. How can I say no?—**G.J., Boston, MA**

At first blush, this sounds like a way to end up with a 911 for under $10,000, nicely beating my target of $12,000 to $13,000 for a well-sorted '69-'73 911T. But let's write a budget before we write the check.

The car is in Florida and you are in Boston, so there will be at least $750 in transportation.

Great place for an engine.

You can find complete bolt-in engines priced reasonably, as racing enthusiasts often upgrade their cars. I recently saw a running '69 911T engine complete—except for the flywheel, clutch and pressure plate—for $1,500 in Los Angeles. Add $400 for crating and shipping and it's yours.

We'll need a good, used flywheel, clutch, pressure plate and throw-out bearing; this will run about $460. Plan on new oil-tank lines ($100); updated turbo valve covers and gaskets ($135); Carrera tensioners, new chains and ramps ($510); and new oil-return tubes ($120).

It needed a new bumper and reflectors.

The Weber carbs will need rebuild kits ($195), and the plastic velocity stacks crack after 25 years ($138). Half-shaft boots and clamps ($35) and new trans main seal ($19) are must-do items. Labor to install the flywheel, insert the new tensioners, chains, ramps, rebuild the half-shafts, disassemble and rebuild the Webers and re-install the engine will be about $1,400. So far we are at $10,262 and counting.

Check your door pockets.

Because the car sat immobile for so long, plan on a complete brake overhaul, including pads ($82), bleeder screws ($83), soft brake lines ($60), hard brake lines ($75), master cylinder ($73), caliper repair kits ($70) and labor ($435). You'll also need to pull the gas tank and have it cleaned and sealed (about $220, including labor). Total now: $11,360.

Various bits of body trim will require replacement, such as the horn grilles ($46); front and rear light lenses ($300); rear bumper reflectors ($50); front, side and rear decos ($320); carpet trim rails ($58); hood emblem and base ($26); left and right door stops ($41); hood shocks ($24); good, used OEM rear-view mirror ($90); new seat belts ($47); and a good, used, leather-covered steering wheel ($150).

You won't want to be without an owner's manual ($61).

The alloys need polishing ($400), you'll need new tires ($320) and you'll need to add a spare wheel, tire and jack ($125). Most likely you will have to have the period Blaupunkt radio serviced ($95).

The targa top needs to be replaced, with materials and labor for $355, and the same trim shop will do both front seats in vinyl for $380. An Optima 800 battery runs $129; four stock Boge shocks are $525 installed.

By my count, we are now at $14,902. We have not spent a dime on the transmission, so I hope it's quiet and the synchros are good.

In addition, cars with targa tops can be hard on the interior door panels. Are the two vinyl-covered cardboard pockets on each door in good shape? I hope so, as they cost about $100 each if they're rotten. How is the rubber on the targa seals? These pieces can run $400. If we need door pockets and targa rubber seals, we are at $15,702, including taxes, license or insurance.

Sadly, we have proven once again that it rarely pays to bring a project car back to life unless it's a rare and valuable model or you are willing and able to do much of the work yourself. Not only will you break the budget, but you will have to wait for months to discover if you like the way the car drives. I'd scratch this one and find a 911 you can drive home, unless you are really looking for a DIY project, and the pleasure you will get from putting the car together yourself will outweigh the financial results.—*Jim Schrager*

From the July 1999 issue of *SCM*.◆

Poor Old Porvair

Dear Mr. Schrager: *I just found what seems like a bargain, a 1971 911E Targa, Sand Beige with a black interior, for $6,000. It is powered by a 140-hp Corvair motor which works pretty well; however, the custom exhaust system is rather noisy.*

The chassis is supposedly rust-free, but the driver's fender had rust and has been somewhat haphazardly patched by the owner. There is a rust hole in the driver's door jamb and the bottoms of the doors have rust bubbles.

The original motor is included in the deal. It was rebuilt by the owner and when re-installed, it would not run well. I figure to fix the original motor and then sell the Corvair engine for about $1,000. Is this a good deal?— **P. D. K., Denver, CO**

A perfect candidate for the Porvair treatment.

A decent '71 E Targa without rust and running well would be a good deal at $6,000. Since you sent the seller's phone number, I called him and had a long chat with him about this unusual car.

Here's what happened to the original engine. Apparently, an injector malfunction led to oil contamination, causing a spun bearing and ruining the crankshaft.

The owner located a good used 911T crankshaft for $100. However, the T crank is not counterbalanced, while the 2.2E and S are. So the T crank, while of the proper dimensions, is not designed to handle the higher revs an E or S can deliver.

The owner indicated he did not use new pistons, cylinders or rings. Generally, those parts are replaced in a rebuild. Also surprising was that the original cases were used without being repaired. After a spun bearing, which generally spins in its mount inside the case, the cases need to be align-bored at the very least, or carefully re-welded and machined, or perhaps even replaced.

I asked the owner which shop manual he preferred when doing all this heavy engine work and he said he used the one in the local library. I noted that an aftermarket manual, such as a Clymer, is only about $25. He said it was easier to just go to the library and copy all the torque specs and so on. This gave me some idea of the budget the owner was working under.

(It may sound as though I am making this story up, but really, folks, it's all true.)

So how did this original 911E engine run when put back in the car? To no one's great surprise, not very well. In fact, it wouldn't idle at all. The next logical step would have been to troubleshoot the electrical and fuel systems with the engine in the car.

But instead, this intrepid do-it-yourselfer decided to pull the Porsche engine and stick in the Corvair powerplant. Now he's stuck with a non-running 911 engine and a Porvair.

You can run diagnostics on an engine when it is in a car, but very few with it out, sitting on the ground. Given its catastrophic earlier failure and the apparent lack of expertise in its reassembly, the only prudent course of action would be to immediately re-rebuild the engine. I'd budget about $5,000, which would include a proper used crankshaft, very careful work on the cases and a set of new pistons and cylinders.

The rest of the car needs rust repair and paint, also not a minor task. The interior has sagging seats and needs new carpeting. The targa top has a rip. The wheels are chrome steel discs in excellent condition, but from a 912. Most people will prefer the correct five-spoke Fuchs alloys wheels.

The Corvair engine was installed with an adapter kit used primarily for dune buggies. With more weight (about 80 lb) and fewer horses (140 versus 155), the flat six from Detroit tends to erode the sparkling performance of the 911.

I consider the 2.2E (1970-71) a delightful car to drive. The E retains most of the torque of the T yet has a higher-revving nature without the peakiness of the stock S. In addition, the E has the bigger S brakes. I find the Targas becoming more desirable since 911s are used as sunny-day drivers rather than daily transport. The color, a non-metallic camel tan, is one of my personal favorites but may hurt the value a bit, as it is not widely appreciated.

The highest and best use for this Porvair would be for an enthusiastic young owner with much more time than money to make it an in-depth educational project over the next several years, driving it with the Corvair engine while taking apart the original engine for a rebuild and carefully scrounging cheap but usable parts from swap meets and the classified ads in Panorama, the monthly publication of the Porsche Club of America.

As it sits, I might pay $5,000 for the package, sell the original engine as a core for $1,000 and end up with a Porvair to tool around in for $4,000. You should buy this car only if you are willing to do nothing but drive it and intend on keeping the engine lid locked shut at Porsche club picnics. If you try to make it into a no-excuses 911E with the proper Porsche engine, you'll find yourself solidly buried well before completion.—*Jim Schrager*

From the November 1998 issue of *SCM.*◆

A 911 for the Intellectually Challenged

Item recently found on *eBay*: *"1971 Porsche 911T, A Rare Beauty, Low Reserve. A REAL HEADTURNER. I've had this car for three years and have loved every minute of it. I just bought a Model A and my wife says it's her or one of the cars. It took awhile, but I decided on the car (who would cook?)."*

These first few lines of this online ad really show promise. A comedian selling his 911 so he can step up to a Ford Model A? It makes perfect sense, doesn't it? Sell your modern high-performance road car for an ancient, low-performance antique, best suited for heavily rutted dirt trails.

"In the time I've had the Porsche, I haven't put any money into the car because it is very dependable. I've had a general service done and just had the wheels rebalanced."

Now this really inspires confidence. At best, we are talking one oil change in three years. Shame on any of you who don't change the oil at least once a year. How anxious would you be to buy a 911 from someone who is proud of the fact that he hasn't put any money in it? It's a sure sign of a know-nothing owner and a car with plenty of deferred maintenance awaiting its new owner.

"The exterior is Pearl White and had black accenting throughout. One of the nicest things about the car is that the P-O-R-S-C-H-E lettering on the rear is gold plated, and looks awesome."

Pearl White isn't an original 1971 color. All '71s had bright trim. Gold lettering was a frequent factory option in 1971. It is hard to imagine that the letters on the engine lid represent the nicest thing on a 911.

"The bra pictured does come with the car and I have a car cover also included."

These two items are worth about $50 each at any swap meet, so their inclusion here is of little importance. Bras, if left on for days at a time, are one of the most destructive accessories ever sold. We just looked at a pristine 1986 911 Carrera Sunroof with 43,000 miles that had a bra left on to protect the front paint. It ruined the paint instead, and the original paint on the front fenders and hood had to be repainted.

"The body does have some very minor nicks, but nothing to worry about!"

Well, that depends. Might some of these "nicks" actually be small signs of rust poking out from behind the paint? We need to know the location and description of all these flaws. All flaws are not created equal.

"The interior is black and in good shape, with a leather steering wheel, and the two back seats are fully functionable."

I wonder what kind of function the seller thinks he is able to host in the back seats? Does he mean the seat backs move up and down, as they are supposed to? No one much larger than an eight-year-old can hang out in the back seats of a 911 for more than a few minutes.

"The dash is in great shape, one small crack, but otherwise awesome."

To most 911 aficionados, any crack in the dash decidedly removes said appurtenance out of the "awesome" category.

"Blaupunkt (original) stereo."

Nope. No stereos in 1971. Just a single speaker in the dash.

Good luck trying to inspect a car at an on-line auction.

"The driver's seat needs a screw in one of the brackets (nothing major)."

Well, nothing major until you try to fix it. These screws are placed through the hinges and can strip out the metal imbedded in the backrest. To fix it, you need to take the backrest apart and weld in a cage nut. Since a '71 has just two screws on each side supporting the backrest, it is vital they both work.

"Not too much to say on the engine. I'm not a Porsche expert, but I've been told that the 6-cylinder engine in the car is the biggest and fastest possible engine that Porsche made at the time..."

We finally agree on something: You aren't an expert. The 2.2-liter 911T engine is a delightful motor, but it had the lowest six-cylinder Porsche engine horsepower rating of its day.

"It has a lot of power and goes very fast (trust me)."

Oh, we do. Your statements so far give us plenty of reasons to trust what you say.

"The odometer reads a little over 50k, but I'm not sure if it is 50k or 150k. The mechanic thought by the way the engine sounds it is 50k, but wasn't definite."

It's highly doubtful that we have a 50k-mile car here. If it is a 150k-mile car, that's getting to be lots of miles on a 2.2L without replacing the pistons and cylinders and getting inside the cases for bearings. We need to hear about rebuild history.

"I've been watching the bids on Porsches of this calibur (sic) and I saw one sell last week for $19,000. I have a low reserve because I need to keep my wife around."

I think you need to look a bit closer at the bidding for Porsches like yours. $19,000 buys a tremendous amount of early 911T.

Four bids were submitted ranging from $6,000 to $7,100, money enough for a T coupe in average condition with unknown history. The time limit expired with the reserve unmet, so this car was declared unsold. Somebody dodged a bullet on this one. Be careful out there.—*Jim Schrager*

(All information in italics was taken directly from the seller's description on the eBayMotors auction site.—ED.)

From the June 1999 issue of *SCM.*◆

1973 911T Winter Beater

Every year about this time, I start poking around for a winter beater. Here in the Midwest we put our nice cars away when the salt flies. However, I find it impossible to go for months without my Porsche fix, so a proper winter vehicle is both a challenge and a necessity.

In August an ad in the Chicago Tribune caught my eye: "1973 911T coupe, full engine/transmission rebuild, updated tensioners, no chassis rust but body, paint and interior tired, $5,700." I called and the seller sounded both honest and reasonable. I asked him for his bottom dollar: $5,500 would buy the car. He also mentioned that he was getting a good volume of calls. I thanked him, made a few notes on our conversation and decided to pass. By my calculations, $5,500 was just too rich.

In September, the car appeared again, this time at $5,000 I called and he told me that while several tire kickers stopped by, nobody wrote a check. I again asked bottom dollar and this time he said $4,500. (The receipt for the rebuild alone was about $6,000.) He said three more people were coming to look at the car.

I thought about all this while we were talking and decided I could only go $4,000. He countered with exactly the right response: "Thanks for your offer, but it's less than I'll take today. However, if you are serious, give me your phone number and if no one else steps up, the car is yours for $4,000." This response tests my desire for the car (will I stop him and say, "Okay, I must have the car at your price"), while at the same time keeping me warm as a possible buyer.

I held my ground and left my phone number. He called in a few weeks. The 911 was mine if I wanted it.

I have made it a practice in the last few years not to look at or drive most of the cars until after I've closed the deal. I know it sounds crazy, but there is a certain thrill to buying these wonderful old cars without actually seeing them first. I usually get them inspected by a good shop and sometimes obtain photos. Even though this car was just 100 miles away, I didn't see it before sending my cashier's check. I had it brought home on a flatbed truck.

When the car arrived, it was pretty much as advertised. It ran fine, just like a fresh '73 T should, shifted well and so on. The wheels were not original Fuchs, but fakes; however, they had nice new Dunlops. The interior was worse than tired, as it had been redone in wrong materials and then worn out again. It has a good pull-out cassette radio that works well. All in all, I was happy.

If no one else steps up, it's yours for $4,000.

So what's this car worth?

I value an old beater like this for its parts, as they are often worth more dead than alive. I figured the nicely rebuilt engine at about $2,600; the rebuilt type 915 transmission (used from 1972 to 1986) about $1,200; the wheels and tires, $400; and the rust-free chassis with clean title maybe $1,200 (for someone who wants to build a race car or 911 hot rod). As parts, the whole package adds up to about $5,400, as long as I am willing to spend an afternoon pulling the engine and transmission myself.

Is this car worth saving? Yes, but only if you are willing to do part of the work yourself. The fenders, doors and quarters can be patched by most any decent body shop for about $1,000. The car can be painted to a modest standard for an additional $1,000, as long as you are willing to take it apart and put the pieces back together. The seats, door panels and carpets aren't hard to do yourself, and the materials will cost about $1,200.

Will you have a concours winner on your hands? No way. But for about $7,500, you'd have a decent car with freshly rebuilt mechanicals, new tires, a solid chassis and many miles left. You can even pick your own color.

Is that my plan? Naw. I'm just going to beat around in it for the winter and then sell it to make way for the next machine. We'll fool around with the seats and carpets, and maybe patch up some of the rust to keep busy over the long winter. But I'll leave the real fun for the next owner.—*Jim Schrager*

From the December 1998 issue of *SCM*.◆

> "I have made a practice in the last few years not to look at or drive most of the cars I buy. I know it sounds crazy, but there is a certain thrill to buying these wonderful old cars without actually seeing them first."

The 911 Carrera RS—Better Than a SWB

Dear Mr. Schrager: I am looking at a 1973 Carrera RS, Grand Prix White with green graphics and a black interior in superb condition. The owner calls it a "T" model. What does that mean? It has drop-dead gorgeous paint, beautiful body lines and a mint interior. The engine serial number is 611 0657 and I don't think it's original. The seller is asking $69,500. Is this a good deal for an RS in such mint condition?—**P.L., Redmond, WA**

Surtees called the 911RS the best.

The 1973 Carrera RS is one of the most valuable street 911s due to its unique spot in Porsche history. Built only in the last year of the original 911 body style, it was the first street 911 to be called a Carrera, a term reserved for the most powerful 356s of an earlier era. It was also the first production Porsche to have aerodynamic assists front and rear and wider rear wheels and tires. Special lightened steel body panels and various fiberglass and aluminum chassis and body-work components helped keep the weight well below the production cars.

Designed in a big hurry due to racing rule changes that threw the 911 in with Ferraris of bigger engine displacement, there was little time to develop, build and sell the FIA mandated 500 copies. To make matters worse, displacement of the original 2.0 911 engine was already maxed-out, having been first bored to 2.2 liters and then stroked to 2.4.

The quick solution was thinner material for the cylinder walls to fit bigger pistons in a block originally spaced for 2.0 liters displacement. But the factory discovered serious reliability problems when standard cylinder alloys were produced within the bore sizes needed. Using Nikasil, a hard nickel plating on aluminum cylinder walls, the displacement was increased to 2.7 liters.

Unlike most other Porsche factory-high-pro engines, other than new, larger pistons, cylinders and a recalibrated mechanical fuel injection, the RS engine is identical to the production 2.4 S: same cams, crankshaft, rods, case, heads, intake ports, valves, exhaust. There was no hot-rodding, most likely, because of homologation deadline pressure.

The result is a very different high-performance Porsche. Unlike the 550 Spyder, 356 Carrera four-cam, the 904, 2.0, 2.2 and 2.4 911S and even the later 3.0 Turbo Carrera (1975-77), the RS has a wide, friendly powerband with torque everywhere.

*"With just 1,580 built, an original 1973 Carrera RS is both a **wonderful car to own** and a **delight to drive.**"*

Maximum torque of the RS was 255 Nm (Newton meters) at 5,100 rpm, while the 911S had 216 Nm at 5,200. This makes the RS a joy to drive on the street and a very popular car with knowledgeable 911 enthusiasts.

This also makes it a very unusual sports/racing car, perhaps one of the reasons John Surtees, in a test of some of the finest sports cars, rated the RS as the most desirable driver's car of all time (*Classic & Sports Car*, August 1998). Other cars in this test included the Ferrari 250 SWB, Lamborghini Miura, Mercedes 300SL Gullwing, Lotus Elise, Jaguar E-type and several others.

Calling any RS a "T" is incorrect. The cars were built in three basic series: homologation cars (RS and the RSH depending on tire size), RSL road cars and RSR race cars. The car you are looking at is an RSL, with the touring conversion, M-472. This brings the interior and exterior trim up to full 911S specs.

The engine serial number you sent is for a 1971 911T which has the weaker non-forged crankshaft. It may have been rebuilt to RS specs, but the value will never be equal to one with an original motor.

A great RSL can run as high as $75,000, but the one you are looking at will run out of steam at about $45,000. Between $50,000 and $55,000 should buy a good numbers-matching #2 driver. Be wary of cars for sale in Europe. Rust remains a serious problem and in many cases European cars aren't kept in the same condition as those in the US.

With just 1,590 built, an original 1973 Carrera RS is both a wonderful car to own and a delight to drive. While they make very big prices for a used 911, we expect RSs to appreciate at the head of the market, with good cars, fairly priced, continuing to sell briskly.—*Jim Schrager*

Carerra RS: How Much Better Than a Stock 911?

Dear Mr. Schrager: *You recently wrote what a great car the 1973 911 Carrera RS is, and how they are worth about $50k. But I understand that the RS is very similar to the 1972-73 911S. I believe the RS has just 20 more horsepower than the 2.4 S. Somehow, this doesn't seem like such a big deal to me. Given that you can find a very nice 2.4 S for about $25,000, how can 20 horsepower be worth another $25,000? As a person looking for value, isn't a very good S the far better deal? I would appreciate a straightforward response, not the hopeless puffery that most of the marque magazines and club books offer. —A.J., Tulsa, OK*

A real Carrera RS is more than just a sticker kit and a pair of spoilers.

On the surface, it does seem that the Carrera RS is overvalued and/or the stock 2.4 S quite a bargain. But having owned both and driven them head-to-head on many occasions, there is a dramatic difference in the way the cars perform. It's all related to how the numbers we see relate to the performance we feel.

First, a look at the torque and horsepower, along with the rpm at which the peak readings are produced:

	HORSEPOWER (DIN)	TORQUE (NEWTON METERS)
'72-73 911S	190 @ 6,500 rpm	216 @ 5,200 rpm
'73 Carrera RS	210 @ 6,300 rpm	255 @ 5,100 rpm

On paper, the Carrera RS provides 39 more Newton meters, or 18%, more torque than the S. In real life, it seems like much, much more.

Driving an RS is a shockingly different experience than an S. I liken a good RS to driving a V8 Corvette. It has torque right when you step off from idle, all the way up to redline. Even though it has all the top-end of an S, the tremendous low-end response really transforms the car. The RS has been called the greatest 911 ever built. It takes a drive to see why.

Here's another example of how torque affects drivability. Recall the period road tests where the T, E and S models were run against each other, and how journalists preferred the lower horsepower T or E to the S for regular road use. The lower-horsepower E is also faster than the S in the benchmark 0-60-mph test.

This is because the S trades low-end torque for power high in the rpm range. In the S, at about 3,500 rpm you can begin to feel the torque, but the real screaming begins at 5,000 and runs right to the redline at 7,300. This is handy for high-speed runs on the Autobahn, but not much good when plugging around town. The E, on the other hand, doesn't pull as strong at high rpm, but runs more in the power band in a 0-60 test. The S wins the 0-100-mph test, when you use its giant top end.

But back to the RS. The value equation between an S and an RS is about more than just power curves. The Carrera is a combination street/race car that was built in very limited numbers (1,580) for just a single year (1973). One thousand to 3,000 S cars were built *each year* for seven years (1967 to 1973).

Further, the RS has a host of unique features which no early S had, including front and rear aerodynamic aids, larger rear wheel flares, larger rear wheels and tires, special lightweight body panels, special aluminum suspension pieces and so on.

So due to both rarity and performance, the RS justifies its higher value. Which is the better deal right now? They are both in big demand and we are seeing strong prices all around the world for both early S cars and the RS. With a mint early S, you'll be the envy of most everyone at your local Porsche Club meetings. With a mint RS, you can play that same role on a national scale.

Is an RS worth $25,000 more than an S? The market, which votes with its wallet, says yes. If you can afford it, an RS will provide a near-ultimate Porsche experience. However, if the standard S is what fits your budget, buy a great one and enjoy it. You'll never lose money on it if you keep it properly maintained, and you'll have a great time as well.—*Jim Schrager*

From the March 2000 issue of *SCM*.◆

> "With a mint early S, you'll be **the envy of most everyone** at your local **Porsche Club** meeting. With a mint RS, you play that same role on a national scale."

Euro Carrera Sleepers

Dear Mr. Schrager: I am looking at a European Carrera RS, complete with a correct RS 2.7-liter motor with mechanical fuel injection and 210 DIN horsepower. The car looks to be in immaculate physical and mechanical condition, with just 67,000 miles and a recent bare-metal repaint in original Chiffon White. It has a black interior, 7 and 8 x 15 Fuchs alloys with black centers and matching black graphics. The engine was just fully gone through and updated with Carrera chain tensioners and Turbo valve covers. The seller is asking $26,500.

Before you fall off your chair, this is a 1974 Carrera, which I have been told are rarer than the 1973 RS cars you have written about (April 2001 SCM, page 65). Is this car the fantastic bargain it seems to be? Will it drive like a '73 RS? Will it appreciate like a '73 RS?—**K. W., Spokane, WA**

A 1974-75 Carrera can be a huge bargain.

These cars are sleepers in the world of early 911s. Although they were made in higher quantities than the 1973 cars, they are almost completely ignored here in the US. While there were 1,590 1973 Carrera RS coupes produced, 2,184 1974-75 Euro Carrera 2.7 coupes and Targas were built. Some experts have found a few 1976 Carrera cars as well, but my sources indicate those are actually 1975 cars sold in 1976. These European cars are not to be confused with the US Carreras of 1974-75 equipped with the standard 175-hp (1974) or 165-hp (1975) 2.7 911S engine, rather than the more powerful RS-spec powerplant.

The engine for the 1974-75 Euro Carrera cars is identical to the '73 version—a 2.7-liter mechanical fuel-injected flat-six with 210 DIN horsepower and a bountiful blend of low-end torque and high-rpm power. The follow-up to the 1974-75 Carrera was the 1976-77 Carrera 3.0, with an engine rated at 200 horsepower, quite similar to the 911SC.

However, these 1974-77 European Carreras are not nearly as valuable as an original 1973. This is because all 1974-77 911 Carreras have virtually identical bodies to the 1978-83 911SCs and the 1984-89 Carreras. There were no trick lightweight body panels or special modifications to the transmission or front suspensions on these 1974-77 cars. Weight for the 1974 and newer cars was increased by 100 kilograms, or about 10% over the 1973 RS. In 1976, the European Carreras were fitted with a completely new 3.0-liter engine with the latest Bosch CIS (Continuous Injection System) fuel injection, rather than the MFI (mechanical fuel injection) of the older RS models.

Why did Porsche build the 3.0-liter when the 2.7 had power galore? Two reasons: emission controls and cost. The 911SC has the cheaper and far less complex CIS injection system that also lowers emissions. CIS injection runs much cleaner and with better gas mileage than the thirsty MFI system. Porsche realized that the CIS system made more sense for series production cars than MFI and they also realized that the 2.7-liter block, based on the 2.0/2.2/2.4 engines, was at the limits of its development.

So is this 1974 Euro Carrera a giant bargain? Well, yes, if the thrill of driving an RS matters to you. This is an inexpensive way to get much of the feel of the original. And this particular car, if it's as nice as advertised, with body and chassis in near-perfect condition, is a very good value. But will these unusual cars suddenly be discovered and race past the value of the 1973 RS models? I doubt it.

The 1973 RS was developed around the final year of the original body design. As the 911 ages, the purity and elegance of Butzi Porsche's original creation is becoming clearer. While the 1974-77 European Carreras have plenty of go power, they share a body style produced in very large numbers from 1978-89.

Further, the 1973 RS was the basis for period race cars while, by mid-1974, Porsche was turning to turbocharging and very wide bodywork to skirt the racing rules. These European 1974-75 2.7 and 1976-77 Carrera 3.0 cars weren't used much as race cars, just sweet street machines.

Considering what your options are in $26,000 Porsches (1964-65 356C/SC sunroof coupes, 1972-73 911S coupe or Targa, 1987-88 911 Carrera cabriolet), if you want well-balanced high performance coupled with a car that simply won't go down in value, this car is a logical choice.—*Jim Schrager*

From the June 2001 issue of *SCM*.◆

$16,000 for a Modified '73 S?

I am looking at a 1973 911S sunroof coupe, Guards Red with a black vinyl interior and factory air conditioning. The car was originally medium metallic green and the red repaint is showing its age with small cracks and crazes. It has 191,000 miles with paperwork showing a full engine and transmission rebuild at 150,000 in 1992. The car runs well and even the A/C seems to work. The mechanical fuel injection was recently rebuilt by Pacific Fuel Injection at a cost of $900. I don't understand why there was a switch added on the dash to prime the fuel injection for cold starts.

The interior is good, with no cracks in the dash and a recent headliner, cloth-covered Recaro seats and new carpets. The body and chassis show no rust or previous damage. However, a few items have been "updat-

Early 911s are coming on strong.

ed": 91l SC electric mirrors on both doors, a bolt-on whale tail, bolt-on SC rocker panels covers and later, 6 x 16-inch Fuchs alloys.

I've heard these are one of the best early 911s to buy, but the seller is firm at $16,000. Should I go for it?—**J.D., Indianapolis, IN**

The early 911S models (1967-73) are attracting attention among Porsche fans and prices are starting to move, leaving the more common T and E models behind. We have seen really superb cars go in the mid-twenties, with just-decent cars making the high teens.

There are three key issues to consider with an early S: originality, which means the correct engine and the correct mechanical fuel injection system; absolute integrity of the body; and finally, the good working order of the mechanicals.

From the serial numbers and the Kardex you sent, we can see you have the correct engine in the chassis. Your description of the rust-free nature of the car sounds good, but I recommend a further inspection: First, pull the carpeting and spare tire out of the front trunk and look very carefully at both battery boxes. If the area has been repainted or treated, take a small Phillips screwdriver and probe around a bit for soft metal.

Next, inspect the bottom of the outside skin of each door. Look for small bubbles in the paint, which are warning signs of rust inside. Also look near the bottom of the front fenders, just above the S aluminum rocker trim. Next, look for bubbles directly below the headlights. The chrome headlight bezels can be removed with a single retaining screw, located at the bottom of the headlight. If you have any questions, remove the bezel and inspect. The door-lock post, which is welded to the forward edge of the rear quarter panel, is another place to watch for

bubbles or worse. Finish the inspection with a careful look and poke at the rockers and rear torsion-bar areas. The floor pans on these years are galvanized and usually do not pose a problem.

For mechanical condition, compression tests are always recommended. Don't be worried about the enrichment button added for cold starts. A favorite spot for this is the open accessory hole just to the right of the steering column. Many savvy mechanics disable the automatic enriching system as this original device can stick, causing over-rich running, contaminated oil and significant damage to the engine.

For many years, mechanical fuel-injection systems had a bad reputation due to the ridiculously high prices for replacements, the tendency of the system to wear out and the inability of most mechanics to repair problems. Today, we have a few shops that can make these units run like new, and there is tremendous interest in having an original MFl system.

The car you have in your sights sounds like it just needs a fresh, complete paint job and a removal of the SC bits to be taken to the next level. You will have to decide whether to choose the original color, which Porsche simply called "metallic green," leave it Guards Red (which is wrong for this year) or select another correct color. For value, I would recommend either the original color or one appropriate for the year.

As I add up the numbers here, there is plenty of room to return the body to its original configuration and paint the car without getting buried. Or you may just want to enjoy the car as is, without painting it. I'd say this is one of those unusual cars that is a good buy regardless of whether you drive it as is or decide to take it to the next level..—*Jim Schrager*

From the May 1999 issue of *SCM*.◆

The Flaws on My 911 Are Money in the Bank That I Didn't Spend

Dear Mr. Schrager: I've been looking for an inexpensive early 911 on and off for about three years. After much research, I decided that the best years for me were 1970-73, for many of the same reasons detailed in previous columns. I found one in our local Auto Trader a few weeks ago and bought it for $6,000.

It's a 1973 911T coupe with mechanical injection and 120,000 miles on the clock. The heads were rebuilt with new valves, guides and rocker shafts at 80k, along with Carrera pressure-fed chain tensioners. Other than that, it's pretty original, with all the normal wear and tear you would expect on a 25-year-old car.

It has been in two accidents that I can see: one crash in the driver's rear quarter that looks like it was a fairly hard hit, but repaired to a decent standard, and one around the driver's headlight that is minor, but may have been repaired by the previous owner. It looks like something I might have done myself, which is not a good thing.

Depending on someone's threshold of pain for cosmetic defects, the car might seem a bit rough. But to me it will make a good daily driver.

I could easily spend $10,000 to bring this car into strong #2 range, which would mean I'd have over $16,000 in it. Even then, I'd be hard-pressed to sell it for over $10,000. I have vowed not to get buried that deep. So I am determined to be happy with what the car is, rather than what it might be. Your thoughts?—**D.S., via e-mail**

Perfect condition for a driver.

You are doing the right thing. These older, mostly original Porsches are great fun to drive and can be reasonable financial deals as long as you don't try to make them into something they aren't. One of the hardest things to do is to resist the urge to tackle all the cosmetic issues a car like this presents.

I have seen many people over-restore a car and then never drive it. You have the luxury of enjoying your car every day without being afraid to drive it to the mall on an errand.

Your priorities should be centered around ensuring that the running gear is in good shape and well maintained. Updated chain tensioners are the most important single issue on an older

"One of the hardest things to do is resist the urge to tackle all the cosmetic issues a car like this presents."

911, which you already have. Be sure to change your oil frequently. (I see nothing wrong with every 3,000 miles on a car of your vintage.) Stay up on your valve adjustments (every 15,000 miles), and watch for unusual oil leaks. Most oil leaks are not harmful to your engine, but if it's coming from the oil cooler or one of the high-pressure lines between the tank, cooler and engine block, then you need to pay attention. We do not want to run our 911s out of oil.

You didn't mention rust, and many of these older cars have a bit. It can be stopped by applying one of the epoxy-type paints right over the rust. These stop it by keeping air out of the open wound. I've seen good results with POR-15 (paint over rust) from Rest-O-Motive Laboratories in Whippany, New Jersey. (The company can be reached at 800-457-6715. This paint is carried by Classic Restorations in West Salem, Illinois, 800-225-7422.) There are other types available.

You can tackle some of the cosmetic issues as you have the time and energy without spending a fortune on a polyurethane paint job. Enjoy the car for what it is and don't obsess over the shortcomings.

To me, the flaws on my cars are money in the bank I didn't spend.—*Jim Schrager*

From the February 1998 issue of *SCM.*◆

What is a '73½ 911, Anyway?

Dear Mr. Schrager: *I have heard a great deal about the 1973 Porsche 911T and would like to know what the big deal is all about. What makes these cars so special? What type of premium should I pay for a '73½ over an early '73 car?*—**E.Z., via e-mail**

Many enthusiasts rank the mid-year 1973 911T as one of the finest all-around street 911s. Peter Zimmermann, master Porsche mechanic and author of the definitive book on buying 911s, *The Used 911 Story,* proclaims the '73½ 911T to be Porsche's first "10." Many of the rest of us have discovered that these special 911Ts feel more sophisticated and grown up than the earlier cars.

The major change made mid-year 1973 was the introduction of a new fuel-injection system, known as CIS (Continuous Injection System). Although both CIS and the earlier mechanical fuel-injection 2.4 T engines are rated at the same 140 (DIN) horsepower, CIS cars feel much smoother, both at idle and at full song. This is partially the result of milder camshaft profiles in the CIS engine, with far less valve overlap. As an extra bonus, the utter simplicity of the CIS system makes it less subject to breakdowns and far less expensive to repair.

The mechanical fuel-injection (MFI) system used on all E and S models from 1969 to 1973, and on T models in 1972 and early 1973, earned a reputation for hard starting, poor running, difficult tuning, wildly expensive replacement parts and even the clandestine destruction of engines in the following manner: To aid in starting, a solenoid is used to richen the mixture, operating automatically based on engine temperature. Unfortunately, if not carefully maintained, the solenoid can malfunction and stick open. This makes the car run very rich, allowing gasoline beyond the piston rings, which dilutes the oil and can cook your engine. Unless you are vigilant, you'll never know it until you spin a rod bearing.

More bad news: Even without a malfunctioning enriching solenoid, I have seen MFI cars set so rich that the oil is diluted with raw gas. One of my MFI cars developed a mysterious oil leak. When we investigated, we noticed the oil tank was overflowing. How could this be? A wildly rich MFI pump. Why didn't I notice? There were no symptoms. In fact, the car ran great. It could have been very ugly if we hadn't caught it.

Why was the pump set so rich? As the MFI system wears, a richer mixture hides a multitude of sins. And when an MFI system goes bad, there is much to fail. First, the pump itself can get gummed up or simply wear out. Next, the throttle bodies and their six butterfly valves and throttle shafts wear. Then there's the starting system, the altitude adjustment and the warm-up regulator. Ah, such fun. The next time SPICA-equipped Alfa

73½ 911, the best of the first generation.

owners start their caterwauling, they should spend some time in the Porsche MFI asylum.

CIS eliminates all this nonsense. At lower cost and decreased complexity, CIS allowed the 911T to meet the ever-tightening US emission control laws. Gone is the six-piston mechanical-injection pump. Instead, an airflow-controlled system working in conjunction with carefully regulated fuel pressure delivers the correct mixture demanded by the engine.

The system is called the Bosch K-Jetronic, but the name is misleading, as it has no electronics. Rather, CIS is based on an ingenious mechanical sensor, regulated by a disc which moves up and down in a cone-shaped passage. As the air flow increases, the disc, mounted on a partially counterbalanced pivoting lever, moves to allow more air to pass as the clearance between the disc and the side of the wall increases. By carefully designing the contours of the conical passage through which the disc moves, the fuel/air mixture is precisely matched to the needs of the engine.

There is one downside to the CIS system. A starting system malfunction can cause the explosion of a plastic housing (the "airbox") used to meter airflow. Carefully maintained cars can get over 100,000 miles without worry, yet many CIS cars (1973-83) have an inexpensive aftermarket device called a pop-off valve to solve this problem. Plan on $200 parts and labor if the car you are looking at doesn't have one.

With a 1973½ 911T, you have not only the exceptionally smooth and trouble-free engine, but also the last year of the original body style. These are great first Porsches, and should be worth about $2,000 more than the MFI 2.4 T. They won't appreciate like an S, but they won't cost as much to buy or maintain, and are sweet cars to drive every day.—*Jim Schrager*

From the July 2000 issue of *SCM.*◆

What's My 1974 Carrera Targa Worth?

Dear Mr. Schrager: *I'm ready to sell my 1974 Carrera Targa and would like your ideas. It has 85,000 miles and a nice, straight body with no Bondo.*

However, the driver's door fit is off. The exterior was repainted in original Viper Green a few years ago and now has some rock chips. The interior is good but needs a new carpet set, and the dash has several cracks. The wheels are Fuchs alloys, 15 x 7 inches in the front and 8 inches wide in the rear.

The original air conditioning is not hooked up. I just finished installing a rebuilt 1985 3.2-liter Carrera motor with 1978 CIS fuel injection. The transmission was also rebuilt. A stainless steel aftermarket muffler is attached to a stock header system. The car is very quick.

My dilemma is that this 911 is not a show car and not original, either. With its color, the car certainly stands out in a crowd.

My car is in fair condition and worth between $12,000 and $15,000, according to the CPI book. I've got about $8,000 invested in the motor and transmission.

What should I ask for the car to be able to sell it within four to six months? Where should I advertise it?—K.C., via e-mail

Big bumpers are not to everyone's taste.

You have an unusual car that will be a lot of fun for the right person. Unfortunately, you also have a few factors working against you.

First, the 1974 model year isn't one of the more highly desired. Due to a series of serious mechanical issues, many buyers steer clear of the '74-'77 model years. Porsche made the engines run very hot to comply with pollution-control regulations, and this often did extensive damage to the crankcase. This was more true of the '75-'77 years, but '74 is often avoided as well.

In addition, the 911 and 911S still had the narrower body of the early 911 series, but with the large and heavy federal bumpers grafted on. Most 911 buyers either like the powerful, wide look of the '78 and later cars or prefer the lighter, more vintage lines of the '73 and earlier models.

Your Carrera has the wider rear flares that followed across the 911 line in 1978. These wide rear fenders put the giant bumpers into much better perspective and this is one reason your Carrera shows a higher value than a 911S of the same year.

Second, the non-metallic, near-neon pea green is a wonderful period color and undeniably an eye-catcher. However, it is generally not preferred by buyers.

Third, the mechanical changes you have made are all improvements, with a bigger engine, more power and much better durability. But the market probably won't reward your upgrades. Hot-rod Porsches, no matter how well done, are usually not worth as much as original cars.

Finally, the flaws that remain will hurt you. The lack of crisp, fresh carpets will be an immediate turn-off, as will the cracks in the dash and the poor fit on the driver's door. You didn't mention rust, so I will assume there is none. But your car was built before the 1976 model year, when rust-resistant metal was phased in for most of the car.

On the plus side, you have the rarity of a Carrera (only 679 Carrera Targas were built out of 11,624 911s in 1974). They remain distinctive with their flared rear wheel arches, wider rear tires and early "ducktail" spoilers.

To advertise your car for sale, your best bet is your local *Auto Trader*. I'd hope to find a first-time Porsche buyer who would appreciate the newly rebuilt mechanicals and not be too worried about the mismatch of parts or the visual flaws.

Your asking price is another matter. Were it mine, I would put a modest price on the car, remembering that there are many nice, original 911SC Targas (1978-83) available at around $15,000. Although yours has a slightly larger engine (3.2 liters versus 3.0) with low miles, it will still be tough to get too close to the 911SC price, given the non-original nature of your car and also its condition.

Your CPI quotes of $12,000 to $15,000 are accurate. However, the same-year 911S Targa books from $6,750 to $11,525, so there is a big premium on the fact that your car is a Carrera. Unfortunately, you've lost some of that rarity by not having the original drivetrain. The *SCM* Price Guide shows a 1974 911S Targa worth from $9,000 to $11,000. Add a bit for your Carrera body, and there you have it: say $9,500 to $12,000.

There is a solid, active market out there for good 911s, fairly priced. If you aren't in a hurry, price the car at $13,000. If you get anxious because the phone isn't ringing, then bring the price down and keep trying. You may have to get closer to $10,000. It all depends on how badly you want to make the car go away.—*Jim Schrager*

From the May 1998 issue of *SCM.*◆

Why Sell Your '83 SC?

Dear Mr. Schrager: *I saw your advertisement offering a 1983 Porsche 911SC cabriolet with 37,000 original miles for sale. Did you get the $22,000 you were asking? This price seems high to me. And why did you sell it? After all, you are generally high on SCs.—M.H., New Bergen, NJ*

I had mixed feelings about selling our SC cabriolet as it was in great shape with completely original silver paint, an excellent burgundy full leather interior, and it even had the original top with a clear back window. With just 37,000 original miles, it had all the necessary updates and was complete with tool kit, owner's manual, original touch-up paint, correct Blaupunkt stereo and so on.

I bought it from an estate, and the previous owner hadn't driven it

A well maintained and nearly stock SC is rare.

frequently or done much maintenance. The executor was afraid of the car, as it had a glowing brake warning light and the temperature gauge ran hot on our short test drive. He understandably wanted out. I drove it home, worried about the chain tensioners. Since the car was almost 20 years old, it was time to see what things looked like inside the cam-chain housings.

Not wanting to alter the stock appearance of the engine, we used the latest Turbo tensioners rather than the Carrera pressure-fed units. We also wanted to install tensioner guards, which are small discs bolted on the tensioner shafts to prevent a complete collapse. However, the cam chains had not stretched enough to allow room on the tensioner shaft for the guards to fit, so we were unable to add them. If anyone needed proof of the low miles, I guess that was it.

The brake warning light was solved by changing a sensor. A new oil temperature sensor fixed the apparent overheating for the most part. However, on certain hot days, the gauge would move almost three-quarters of the way toward the red zone. Although it didn't go into the red portion of the gauge, I wasn't thrilled with anything past halfway. My guess was that the remote oil cooler in the front fender wasn't getting oil flow. To test this, I touched the exposed oil lines inside the passenger fender once the engine was warm. Since these were hot, the thermostat was working.

A bad gauge? A new one didn't make a difference. Was the crankcase thermostat improperly closing off flow to the main oil cooler? The thermostat in a 911 is bathed in oil and rarely fails. Even so, we replaced it. Still no difference. Finally we looked carefully at the metal oil lines running alongside the passenger side rocker panel. One of them was slightly crushed, reducing flow. Once we replaced that, all was well.

Having an original-paint Porsche reminds you of how beautifully finished these cars were when new. With a coat of wax, the gorgeous silver metallic finish looked just like the paint on a new 996.

Ultimately, I sold it because although it was a joy to behold, I rarely drove it. It sat in my warehouse while I ignored it and selected one of our early 911s to drive and fiddle with.

There was nothing wrong with this 911SC. It's just that, given my preference, I found myself enjoying the light weight, tossability and fussiness of an older 911 rather than the no-nonsense, even-keeled, almost too-perfect nature of the SC. The SC is an all-grown-up 911 with little of the vintage feel of the early cars. It didn't need me the way our older cars do. Perhaps that is part of the attraction I feel for some of the more difficult mounts in our stable.

A dealer offered me $20,000 for the car, but I had a bit more than that in it. The 1983 SC cab is rather rare, with just 4,187 produced in about a six-month period. Of course, the 1984-89 Carrera cabs are nearly identical, so for the non-fanatic, there isn't much to distinguish the SCs. Still, for the low miles and original condition, at $22,000 I figured the car would go away in a hurry. I immediately got calls but, surprisingly, not from collectors.

Rather, I heard from people looking for good used Porsches. They mostly didn't care or weren't aware of the rarity. The first guy who saw it bought it and drove it home at full asking price, but not as a collectible. Instead, he was using it as a transition car. He had plans to move up to an even newer 993 cab within a year or two.

This car sold on condition alone, which is generally the case with SCs. While that surprised me, it also reinforced the notion that cars with high production figures (over 65,000 all told for the SCs) rarely increase in value as they age. They should be bought as driving experiences, not as future investments.
—*Jim Schrager*

From the April 2002 issue of *SCM*.◆

How Much for a 36k-Mile 1980 911SC Targa?

Dear Mr. Schrager: *I am considering buying a 1980 911SC Targa, medium gray metallic, with 36,000 original miles. It's a two-owner car, apparently completely stock with original paint and complete service records, copies of which I'm enclosing here. The price is $17,500. Your thoughts?*—**S.J., Secaucus, NJ**

I believe the 911SC to be one of the best all-around Porsches ever made. Not only are they fast, well made and exciting to drive, they are also reliable and have rust-resistant galvanized bodies.

Furthermore, the 911SC represents a pinnacle of Porsche evolution that requires you to move into the 993 car sat two to three times the price level before a significant increase in speed, handling or durability can be realized. As such, the SC represents a wonderful value.

The stack of receipts you sent along indicates that this particular SC has always been the property of caring owners. However, there are some things that appear to have been left undone that will need attention if you buy this car.

The Achilles' heel of the 911SC, and all earlier 911s, are their chain tensioners. These are two small hydraulic cylinders that keep the two overhead cam chains correctly tensioned. If not renewed or upgraded, they wear out and collapse. As the 911 engine is an interference design, if a chain tensioner collapses and the cam chain skips a sprocket or two, the valves and pistons can hit each other. In other words, a repair bill in excess of $4,000. It's happened to me and it's not pleasant.

There are two solutions. Many mechanics convert to the Carrera chain tensioners introduced in 1984, which have a much longer life. These are pressurized with two special oil lines, easily visible at the very rear of the engine. The other approach is to put in a set of 930-style chain tensioners every 15 years or so. Your car is 20 years old and, even with the low mileage, I wouldn't drive it without doing one or the other. The Carrera tensioners are about $1,000, the 930 items $800 or so. Think of it as very cheap mechanical insurance.

The next issue with a very low-mileage 911SC is the clutch disc. To lower driveline vibrations, the disc had an innovative rubber center. Although it worked, we have learned that the rubber center disintegrates (usually before 50,000 miles), causing the center of the clutch to split from the outer edge of the disc and rendering the car immobile. This can also damage the flywheel surface. By now, most SCs have had the clutch disc replaced, but I don't see any records indicating that the one on

Has this SC had the Carrera tensioners upgrade?

this car has. Plan on about $1,000 parts and labor for a thorough job that addresses the pressure plate, the throwout bearing and the disc.

The SC uses a Bosch CIS (Constant Injection System) fuel injection with a plastic air box that sits between the air filter and air-flow control valve to carefully meter air and fuel flow. If the car is set too lean or too rich, a backfire at start-up can blow a hole in the box. Since CIS cars meter the gas flow by measuring the air flow, a hole in the box prevents the air-flow meter from being drawn open, thus leaving you stranded. Replacing the box is about $500 or so, and many mechanics prefer to add an aftermarket pop-off valve at the same time, which allows air to escape in case of a backfire.

The cruise control on these cars is notorious for failing, although most people use it very little. Repairing it will cost $250. The turn-signal stalk also gets tired and is not complicated to replace. Figure about $150. The fresh air blower often packs up, usually from lack of use, and costs $125 to r & r.

All 911s are sensitive to wheel balance and tire roundness, and the SC, because of its 16-inch wheels and low-profile 55-series front and 50-series rear tires, is more sensitive than most. The Fuchs forged alloys are strong and rarely fracture, even under very heavy loads. However, in absorbing a serious shock, they will bend. If you have vibrations, investigate your wheels and tires carefully for both balance and roundness.

People often complain that Targas and cabriolets leak, but I have yet to see an open 911 with its original top that had a serious problem. The fit and finish on these cars was superb. If this car has its original top and seals, chances are very good there will be few leaks. If you need to replace the top and seals, don't scrimp. For a Targa, expect to pay $450.

The SC's interior was available in vinyl, partial leather or full leather. If this car has full leather, expect the leather covering on the dash to shrink and pull away from the leading edge of the dash pad. A common solution is to install a new, non-leather dash pad to prevent this from recurring.

If you perform all the upgrades and preventative maintenance on the above list, you will have spent around $20,000, including purchase price. This is on the high side, even for such a low-mileage, original SC, but the car should provide you with decades of relatively trouble-free motoring. And you'll always be thousands of dollars ahead of someone who bought a 150,000-mile car and tried to make it nice.—*Jim Schrager*

From the October 2001 issue of *SCM*.◆

Value of a "Turbo-Look" vs. the Real Thing

Dear Mr. Schrager: *I have found an unusual 1985 911, a rare factory US-delivery wide-body car built with the Turbo bodywork and the standard 3.2-liter Carrera engine. Black on black, it's immaculate and has covered only 28k miles. I paid $32,000 and felt good about writing the check. Because of the rarity and beauty of these cars, plus the lower maintenance costs relative to a real Turbo, I would guess these will be appreciating very quickly. What will my car be worth in five to 10 years?—J.J., Riverview, MI*

I don't have good news for you. Although the cars are somewhat rare, they are not destined to be on anyone's collector car top 10 list in the foreseeable future. Generally, everyone who wants a car that looks like a Turbo also wants the thrill of a Turbo engine to go with it.

The "Turbo-look" Carreras are heavier than the standard 3.2 Carreras, slower, and have a harsher ride. They look great with their bulging fenders, are cheaper than a Turbo to buy and less costly to maintain, but collectors want the real thing.

The factory "Turbo-look" cars were a response to the elimination of the 911 Turbo from the US market between 1980 and 1985. The Turbo was unable to meet smog rules during this period, and Porsche US made a lot of noise about the 1979 930 being the "last Turbo" ever made for the US market. Oops, it didn't turn out that way. The Turbo reappeared in 1986 and has

Turbo look-alikes can't walk the walk.

been for sale off and on since then.

Having a Turbo-look Carrera is a bit like having a 356 Speedster replica. The first question everyone asks is, "Is it the real thing?" It's no fun to admit it isn't.

My advice is to realize that your car probably won't ever be worth much more than it is today. If you are looking for appreciation, you'll need to look elsewhere.—*Jim Schrager*

From the May 2002 issue of *SCM*.◆

Mystery Photo

Achtung, Franz! The new Porsche SUV is really retro!—***Victor Troha, Hudsonville, MI***

Having read *SCM*'s escalating auction results on VW vans, Bob protected his front end with a bra and spare. But what about the valuable and vulnerable flanks? Bob's vintage Italian racer had been "n/c" in the Price Guide for years. Slicing the racer in half longitudinally and bolting it to the van's sides assured future profits on his VW collectible. —***Norman Vogel, San Francisco, CA***

Dream Racer.—***Jeany Cohoe, Lake, MI***

Jaunty cross-dressing Microbus comes out of the garage.—***Walt Mainberger, Sarasota, FL***

Jim would try anything to get his bus into a four-wheel drift!—***Chris R. Henry, Michigan City, IN***

Snodgrass, in his feverish quest for a cost-effective method to check aerodynamic efficiency, failed once more and returned to his job as a design consultant for the PT Cruiser.—***John King, Libertyville, IL***

Despite frantic warnings from his spotter, Karl allowed the Vanagon to drift right up to the wall coming out of turn four, making a lasting impression on the 356 that had the outside lane.—***Jeff Hepner, Washington, PA***

If you paint it, they will come.—***Bob Lynn, Kewaskum, WI***

Further along in the Porsche SUV evolution, the Vanagon/911 concept really wasn't much better than the preceding "356 Chuckwagon" attempt. Next, perhaps a 914 hooks up with a "Thing"?—***Michael Glauberman, Huntingdon Valley, PA***

Microbus with an alter ego, according to Robert Krantz.

Make a decision today! You can't have it both ways.—***Jim Cohoe, Lake, MI***

Sure it's not correct, but does your 356 seat seven?—***Henry Kim, Toronto, ON***

The two cars were neck-and-neck all the way around the track until they came together in turn three for their first and final encounter.—***Jeff Benson, Albuquerque, NM***

Who says you can't make a silk purse out of a sow's ear? Looks like it's going 150 standing still.—***Max Hadley, Boise, ID***

Do you think the SCCA sticker is a little over the top, what with the bra and all?—***Dr. Jeff Callahan, Palm Springs, CA***

This guy Martin at *Sports Car Market* says, "A new paint job will add a couple of grand at auction."—***Ed Pasini, Henderson, NV***

You see, John. I told you I thought you cut that guy off.—***George Marshall, via e-mail***

After stealing the race car and hiding it in his van, Bob failed to remember that he had special ordered lightweight (and transparent) side panels for better gas mileage.—***Paul Black, Miami, FL***

Clarence the VW microbus was having one of his Walter Mitty dreams of greatness and glory, revealing a fleeting glimpse, to those who could see, of his alter ego Todd the Porsche, slick and cool, the guy who gets all the chicks.—***Robert M. Krantz, Sausalito, CA***

And the winner is Mr. Krantz, for realizing that, just as androids dream of electric sheep (thank you, Philip K. Dick/Blade Runner), microbuses have fantasies as well.—Keith Martin

C2/C4: Investment or Mechanical Boondoggle?

Dear Mr. Schrager: *I've recently found a 1991 911 C4 all-wheel-drive convertible for sale. It is a black-on-black, 32,000-mile, well-tended used car with condition fully appropriate for its mileage. The owner is asking $39,000, roughly in line with the Kelley Blue Book value of $38,000. Do you have any opinions about the build quality, collectibility and upside potential for such a car? Are there any mechanical "gotchas" to be wary of with these models? When I test-drove this car, it impressed me as being very fast, very pretty and actually a bit easier to drive than some of the other 911s I have sampled, thanks to a less biting oversteer, presumably due to the AWD. Any thoughts, comments or warnings you have would be of great interest to me.—**B.M., Hillsboro, OR**

Leaks between the heads and cylinders can be costly.

The C4 offers all-wheel drive and impressive power.

The 1989 Carrera 4 was a breakthrough car for Porsche. The first series-production all-wheel-drive 911 variant, it introduced the largest flat-six engine made for street use. At 3.6 liters and 247 hp, the engine was bigger and more powerful than the first 911 Turbos, and of course, without turbo lag. In addition to big power and four-wheel drive, the C4 had the first styling tweaks since the 1978 911SC, including soft, deformable front and rear bumpers, revised taillamps and new wheels with a seven-spoke silver-painted alloy known as the Design 90 rim. Changes were significant under the skin, with coil springs rather than torsion bars to suspend all four wheels, a first for the rear-engined street cars.

Given all the new ideas, I suppose it was fair to assume there would be some problems. And for the first few years of production, there were two worrisome areas in both the C4 and the two-wheel-drive sister ships, the C2. Most expensive are leaks between the cylinders and heads. Symptoms are low compression readings or oil leaks. This is a big deal, as the fix requires the installation of new-style pistons and cylinders. These redesigned parts, together with machine work on the heads, enlarges the cylinder-to-head mating surface.

Porsche was very generous on performing this update with original owners and even second buyers on cars with low miles, so check to see if it has been done. If you have to make this fix

on your own, the cost can easily exceed $6,000.

The second area of concern is the "dual mass" flywheel, which is intended to dampen driveline vibrations from the transmission. It is, as you can imagine from the name, a flywheel with dampening elements allowed to move within chambers filled with silicone grease. A neat idea, but they don't hold up and often have to be replaced with a standard flywheel. This repair runs $3,000 or so.

Both problems were resolved on cars built after June 1991. How certain is it that these problems will surface on earlier cars? The flywheel problem is more typical than the cylinder-head problem, but in reality, no one knows the incidence of the defects.

As to collectibility, right now the C2s and C4s are just used cars. Their value will continue to fall as newer and more capable Porsches are built. At some point, they may gain in value again, but it is too early to know if or when that will happen. Because of their problems, the C2/C4 cars (internally known as the 964 model) may get stuck with a bad reputation. This happened to the 1975-77 2.7-liter 911 cars and has kept their value depressed, even though many of these cars have been updated. So far, there has been little easing of the depreciation curve for the 964 cars.

I would not buy any late-model Porsche production road car for appreciation. For a car to drive, especially as the price eases and the repairs noted above are made on someone else's watch, I would gladly own and enjoy a Carrera 4 in the inclement Midwestern weather I drive in. But we have a way to go yet before the annual depreciation gets near zero. Perhaps the C4 will fall into the $15,000-$18,000 range and find some support there, as did the 911SC cars. However, the SC has a positive reputation for durability that helps as the miles roll up; the jury is still out on the C2/C4 models.

Assuming no other large problems crop up as the C2/C4s age, when their depreciation curve flattens out, a well-kept one will be a good buy. But again, not for appreciation, rather for an enormous amount of value for the dollars spent.—*Jim Schrager*

From the March 2002 issue of *SCM*.◆

Buying a "No Test Drive" 930

Dear Mr. Schrager: *How about a silver 1976 USA 930 sunroof coupe with black leather interior? The car was recently taken apart and repainted to a very high standard. The interior is all original and in nice shape. The body lines are straight and the car seems to run well. The flaws include: 132k miles; some paperwork, but no evidence of a rebuild; the oil pressure never goes above 20 pounds; the car runs steadily hotter until it reaches 230 to 240 degrees. The owner is asking $15.5k but won't let me take it for a test drive. That really scares me. However, he'll let my mechanic look it over. What is your opinion?*—**B.J.H., Denver, CO**

Be sure a competent shop checks the car over thoroughly.

If you can get through some of the flaws, $15.5k is a fine price for the car. The first USA 930 Turbo was introduced in 1976, and if in nice shape, will likely see some appreciation over the next several years. In 1976 and 1977, Porsche 930s were given the name "Turbo Carrera." An earlier Porsche to be called a Carrera was the legendary 1973 911 RS. In 1978, the 930 simply became the "911 Turbo."

The first two years of the 930 had the lightest chassis, but with the smaller 3.0-liter engine (as opposed to 3.3 from 1978-89), the early design wastegate, a smaller rear wing without an intercooler and smaller brakes. Still, the car has performance limits which can rarely be reached at legal speeds.

Turbos were built with clunky four-speeds up until 1989 and really need the fifth cog. It was just not possible to build gears strong enough to handle the turbo's explosive power and still fit five of them in the standard gearbox without an extensive redesign.

A trick to impress first-time Turbo drivers is to have them put the throttle down about a third of the way, at about 2,500 rpm, and then keep their foot steady. The car accelerates gently at first, builds a head of steam and seemingly on its own, starts flying. This happens even though they haven't pressed further on the gas. All by itself, as the turbo spools up, it's off to the races. That, of course, is an essential part of the car's charm.

The seller may be afraid to let you behind the wheel out of fear you won't know how to handle his high-spirited toy. Here are the driving rules: Stay off the boost until the engine is warm, don't put your foot into it without plenty of open road ahead and train yourself to keep on the power through high-speed corners. The testiness of this beast is overstated as long as you treat

> "The car accelerates gently at first, builds a head of steam and seemingly on its own, starts flying…That of course, is an essential part of the car's charm."

the car with respect. Yes, if you are drunk or excessivly stupid you will get into trouble, but any Turbo has road-holding capabilities far beyond most drivers' skill sets.

The Turbo you're looking at runs too hot. The most likely cause is a stuck thermostat serving the auxiliary oil cooler located in the right front fender. Test this by driving the car until it's warm. If the front oil cooler is cold, you have either a bad thermostat or a collapsed oil line. Both are straightforward to fix and shouldn't cost more than a few hundred dollars.

The oil pressure problem might be solved with either a new pressure sender or an update needed on the oil pressure relief and safety valves. If you update the pistons and springs in the oil pressure system you may experience a miraculous increase in oil pressure to near normal levels. Pressure in the range of 10 pounds per 1,000 rpm should suffice. Very low pressure at idle is not unusual. Budget another few hundred dollars for this procedure.

If those two fixes solve your overheating and oil pressure problems, the car sounds like a good buy. Of course at 132k miles, you'll need a rebuild someday. However, contrary to popular belief, well-maintained Turbos can run a long time. This is because Turbos have forged pistons, auxillary oil coolers and strong bottom ends. Factory reliability goes away quickly when performance modifications are made or when routine maintenance schedules are ignored.

Even though I can guess the reason for it, I still don't like the fact that he won't let you take it for a drive, so be sure the shop you take it to really gives it a thorough going through. If everything checks out, even after the eventual $8,000-$10,000 rebuild, you'll probably end up with a very nice car, well bought.—*Jim Schrager*

From the December 1999 issue of *SCM*.◆

Values of '96 Twin Turbos & '98 C2s

Dear Mr. Schrager: *I've found one of the most desirable Porsches ever, a 1996 Twin Turbo, with 44,000 miles, for just $74,500. This seems like a fantastic deal to me, as most of the TTs I see are close to $100,000. Is this a good price, or am I going to get hammered if I try to sell? Should I be looking for a low-mileage car, where even though I'll pay more money up front it will save money in the end? If I buy this car should I sell it before it reaches 50,000 miles?—**A.S., via email***

The 1996-97 Twin Turbo is a 993based four-wheel-drive Porsche 911 with the final development of the turbocharged air-cooled flat-six engine. It produces 400 hp and 398 foot-pounds of torque.

This is the first 911 with twin turbos, which were used to help conquer turbo lag. A smaller turbo spools faster than a large one but cannot compress enough air to feed the engine as rpm increases, hence two are needed.

Twin air-to-air intercoolers are provided to keep the air cold and dense. This makes for a seamless delivery of power, not a characteristic of earlier Porsche turbos.

The question of value has a straightforward answer: The TT, and most 911 Turbos (known in certain years and markets as 930s), are still just used cars. This means they operate with the standard used-car mechanisms. They depreciate a bit each month, and high mileage hurts the value.

That is just now beginning to change with the earliest turbos, now 25 years old. Early 3.0-liter turbo Carreras (1975-77) were crashed, bashed, thrashed and often modified within an inch of their lives. Original and correct cars are just starting to get some respect, as they are old enough and rare enough to be discovered for the astounding period performance piece that they are.

The switch from used car to collector car begins with values hitting rock bottom, priced so low that they can't drop further. For a correct and original early turbo, that price is about $15,000. From this low point, the good cars begin to creep up in value, led by concours restorations and very clean original cars.

This value movement ultimately makes it worthwhile to restore decent cars. In the last 10 years, we have witnessed this happen to the 911S models of 1969-73. The same will follow for the early turbos.

But the TT is an awesome car, one of the greatest street cars that Porsche has ever built. Won't it go up in value the way the dealers hinted it would?—A.S.

No, not for a long time. The problem is that Porsche keeps building turbos. As soon as the newer, faster 996 Turbo comes out next year, the 993 Turbo will just be last year's model. As the final air-cooled turbo, the 993 will always be special. But it won't translate into big prices for many years. Remember, even when Porsche pulled the 911 Turbo out of the U.S. market for 6 years (1980-85), there was no wild appreciation for the 1978-79 turbos that filled the gap.

But isn't the TT a future collectible, an instant classic?—A.S.

Yes, it is an instant classic. But just like Shelby Cobras, Porsche 356 Carreras, the 911 Carrera RS and even Speedsters, these cars depreciate for years before they become *valuable* classics.

The car you are looking at is a good value, but only if you realize that all TTs will depreciate for many years to come. Yours

Basking in the sun and ready to pounce.

has higher miles so it has less value to lose, but at selling time, it will be a less desirable used car and therefore sell cheaper than a low-mileage car.

Buy it, drive the heck out of it and don't worry too much about the value or the miles. You will have bought one of the greatest road cars in history at a price about equal to a new 996. And unlike the 993 Turbos with low miles that people are afraid to drive, you will have spent quality seat time in yours. It sounds like a good deal to me, but don't plan on retiring on the profits any time soon.

Dear Mr. Schrager: I'm having difficulty selling my 1998 Carrera C2S sunroof coupe. It's one of the "wide-body" special models Porsche developed to clear out the last of the air-cooled 911s, and everyone tells me the car is an instant classic. It has modest miles (11,000) and the color is silver with a gray leather interior. The car is all original except it was hit in the left rear quarter. The repair was beautifully executed, but it is no longer original paint on that part of the car. Should I have painted the whole car?

*I have been trying to sell the car, asking $72,000. This is a bit less than I paid new, but I am having trouble. Has this car turned out not to be in such great demand?—**D.B., Muskegon, MI***

Your first problem is you are asking too much for your used car. Serial-production Porsches are never worth more than their original selling price once production catches up with demand. For instance, when first introduced, both the Boxster and the Boxster S were being sold for slightly above sticker. But once all the early adopters had one, prices suddenly collapsed to list or less and all Boxsters became just used cars.

Your second problem is the body damage. No matter how skillfully repaired, any deviation from original paint takes you out of the "mint, like-new" category that collectors want and depreciates the value of your low-mileage 911. There are so many 993 C2S cars for sale, anyone who wants a car with original paint can find one. Yours will compete based on price only. If you had repainted the whole car, your situation would be even worse. A car with partial respray can at least be referred to as "mostly original paint." Nothing raises a buyer's eyebrows faster than a fairly new, low-mileage car with a complete respray.

The market, not you, is in control here. I suggest trying again, but with a price in the $60,000 to $64,000 range. —*Jim Schrager*

911s Cross the Block

"Our Experts take their pen, paper and experience to significant auctions worldwide in order to examine cars up for bid. They gather necessary information for making a prudent buying decision just as if they were to purchase the car themselves. Some examples of 911 analyses, including photos and car descriptions are below. Subscribers attest that these evaluations are the heart of *SCM*."

—Keith Martin

Early 911s (1964-1973)

#F7-**1972 PORSCHE 911T Targa.** S/N 9112111378. Odo: 94,000 miles. White/black. LHD. Fakey-doo wheels, orange peel paint, radio, but a nice solid driver. If this car runs well (I found out later it did), this was a great buy. Cond: 2. **SOLD AT $5,775.** *Was the steal of the sale. Bought by an astute* SCM *subscriber and dealer.* **Mecum, Arlington, IL, 11/99.**

#208-**1968 PORSCHE 911 2-door Coupe.** S/N 11810285. Red/black. Odo: 64,308 miles. Sportomatic. Fuchs alloys. Crumbly front, sound metal in trunk from front panel backwards. Old rusty repair around aerial hole. Blood orange originally. Engine claimed to have done only 4,000 miles since rebuild. Worth having for parts value alone. Cond: 4+. **SOLD AT $5,400.** *Here, beater beater beater. Here, beater beater beater. And a slushbox to boot! Bet Schrager wouldn't buy it for parts.* **Barrett-Jackson, Scottsdale, AZ, 1/01.**

#289-**1966 PORSCHE 912 Sunroof Coupe.** S/N 456311. White/gray leather. Odo: 62,573 miles. Later black-on-white gauges. Mileage claimed original. Later model electric seats (1982). Two owners. Small rust bubbles by engine deck lid. Very straight and attractive. Cond: 2-. **SOLD AT $9,450.** *Owner said "odometer isn't working at this moment." Huge money*

for an altered 912—enough to have bought a slightly disheveled 911, and then you'd own something. Car looked great in this color combination. **McCormick, Palm Springs, CA, 2/00.**

#133-**1970 PORSCHE 911T Targa.** S/N 9110112384. Signal orange/black. LHD. Odo: 122,746 km. Original paint apparently free of rust. Interior original and sound, too. Fuchs alloys dull. Cond: 2. **SOLD AT $20,677.** *Big result for a 2.2 Targa. These early, small-bumper cars, when in decent condition, can really get bidders going. There's no substitute for originality.* **Bonhams, Geneva, Switzerland, 3/02.**

#317-**1972 PORSCHE 911T Coupe.** S/N 9112101109. Red/black cloth seats. Rough repaint with dust and dirt, weather seals from the factory starting to show from too many run-ins with high curbs. Cond: 3-. **SOLD AT $10,815.** *A car that clearly needs some love. If it runs out well and has no rust, this was a fair price. Buying a 911 without understanding the mechanical condition always entails some risk, and that is why cars presented at auction with service records or a knowledgeable owner nearby always bring better money.* **Kruse, Atlantic City, NJ, 2/01.**

#808-**1967 PORSCHE 911 Coupe.** S/N 306229. Burgundy/tan vinyl and velour. LHD. Odo: 75,247 miles. Later-style phone-dial wheels. Fresh paint including door jambs and underhood. Front shock tower brace. Torn left door panel, well-used interior, Alpine cassette. Broken engine latch handle. RS-style spoiler. Weber carbs, lowered. Rebuilt to S specs. Cond: 4-. **SOLD AT $5,618.** *Sold at no reserve. Spot-on price for a 911 in this condition. Ready to use, just stay away from guys named Hans or Fritz who want to rebuild it and wreak havoc with your credit rating.* **eBay/Kruse, Auburn, IN, 5/02.**

#118-**1968 PORSCHE 912 Targa.** S/N 12870525. Red/black leather. LHD.

Odo: 16,262 miles. Hood and right door fit off. Rust spots behind right front tire and on gas cap. Very poor paint is faded, with two large scratches on right door. Chrome tolerable. Worn horn button. Munched sun visors. Missing right rear reflector. Evidence of Bondo. Cond: 3-. **SOLD AT $3,990.** *This was a decent buy for a summer runabout, especially if you replace the 912 badge with a 911 one to impress all your friends. Just keep the engine cover closed.* **Silver Auctions, Portland, OR, 4/02.**

#515-**1968 PORSCHE 912 Targa.** S/N 12871043. Red/black. LHD. Odo: 66,589 miles. Rare removable rear window section. AM/FM Blaupunkt, wood wheel. Fresh repaint. All the usual wear to trim pieces, but a garaged and well-cared-for example. Cond: 3. **SOLD AT $16,960.** *What just happened here? Think "survivor" more than "restored" and your mental image of this car becomes clearer.* **eBay/Kruse, Ft. Lauderdale, FL, 1/02.**

#750-**1973 PORSCHE 911 CARRERA 2.7 RS TOURING Coupe.** S/N 911 360 0347. Primrose/black. LHD. Last restored more than 10 years ago, when lightweight doors, fenders and seats were fitted. Paint and interior slightly soiled and worn. Chassis, engine and gearbox numbers all

matching. Cond: 1-. **SOLD AT $48,990.** *Shrewd buy for a retail-ready example of the Touring version of the 2.7 RS. As the years pass, the continued strength of the RS models in the marketplace is a testimony to what brilliant machines they were when new, and how well they still perform today.* **Bonhams, Olympia, UK, 12/01.**

#85-**1973 PORSCHE 911 RS/RSR FACTORY LIGHTWEIGHT Coupe.** S/N 3600196. White/black. LHD. Odo: 16,814 miles. Conversion of RS to RSR specs by Reuttmaier. Decent panel fit for a racer-type car. Right front has apparent repaired accident damage. Very presentable paint and good chrome. Underhood and interior clean, but not detailed. Mag wheels look a bit tired. Cond: 3. **SOLD AT $93,000.** *Even with the original engine, it is hard to say if this conversion represents a good value or not.* **RM Auctions, Amelia Island, FL, 3/02.**

Mid 911s (1974-1989)

#106-**1977 PORSCHE 911 CARRERA 3.0 Coupe.** S/N 9117601053. 6-cyl. White, black tape stripes/black leather.

LHD. Odo: 89,312 miles. 5-speed manual. Recaros. Factory mag wheels. Gray-market import. All gauges (including Canadian-spec speedo) turned for "9 o'clock normal" readings. CD player, trunk lid bra. Good original paint. Long laundry list of upgrade components on recent engine rebuild. Cond: 3. **SOLD AT $21,000.** *Very big money for a gray car, but VIN confirms this is original Carrera 3.0, forerunner to 1978 911SC. High-performance car should bring miles of fun.* **Mecum, Elkhart Lake, WI, 7/00.**

#253-**1989 PORSCHE 911 CARRERA SPEEDSTER 2-seat Convertible.** S/N WPOEB0913KS1737. Aquamarine blue/gray leather. LHD Odo: 1,295 miles. As-new in every respect. Mileage real. Custom color from factory to match first owner's 1958 356 Speedster. Blaupunkt AM/FM stereo, cruise control, factory air added to attractions. Cond: 1. **SOLD AT $74,800.** *Too high considering the condition and the scarcity of this model. '89 Speedsters have seen a slight uptick in prices recently. Unfortunately, to drive one is to devalue it, so you'll rarely see them on the road.* **RM Auctions, Ameilia Island, FL, 3/00.**

141-**1976 PORSCHE 911S Targa.** S/N 9116210930. Black/black vinyl. Odo: 122,757 miles. Fuchs mags. Driver's side of car resprayed, with much orange peel showing. Interior decent except for speaker hanging out of passenger door. Plastic dash cap. At least it doesn't have a huge whale tail hanging off the back. A driver. Cond: 3-. **SOLD AT $8,505.** *If the car runs out okay, a fair buy.* **McCormicks, Palm Springs, CA, 2/00.**

#255-**1980 PORSCHE 911SC Coupe.** S/N 91A0140237. Mustard yellow/black leather. Sunroof. Sporting Pennsylvania ID, car was cleaner than most, considering the nearly 71,000 miles on the clock. Seals around glass had been replaced and panels looked straight. No apparent rust despite East Coast heritage. Cond: 3. **SOLD AT $19,570.** *All the money. These later cars were not prone to rust. 71k really isn't a lot of miles for a well-taken-care-of 911SC.* **Kruse, Atlantic City, NJ, 2/01.**

#306-**1989 PORSCHE 911 CARRERA SPEEDSTER Convertible.** S/N WPOZZZ912KS152373. Guards Red/black. LHD. Odo: 16,887 km. All mint.

An original, low-mileage car. Cond: 1. **SOLD AT $31,092.** *An excellent purchase! Although, Speedster fanatics really like their cars to have negative mileage. Of course, one wonders how they ever use them without cutting their value in half.* **Bonhams, Fontvielle, Monaco, 5/02.**

#792-**1987 PORSCHE 911 TURBO Cabriolet.** S/N WPOEB0913HS1722. Red/tan leather. LHD. Odo: 59,055 miles. Slant nose, wide body. Nitrous oxide injection, roll bar, low-profile wheels and tires. All tricked out with the total boy-racer package. Plastic front spoiler cracked, repaired with glue and painted. Balance of paintwork and brightwork good. Cond: 3-. **SOLD AT $26,100.** *Sold new in New Jersey, registered in South Dakota and Kansas. Steroid-induced Porsches are fashion trends not unlike split-level houses or halter tops. This trend has long since passed on, yet the cars remain. Not funky or retro, just old. Correct price.* **eBay/Kruse, Scottsdale, AZ, 1/02.**

#445-**1989 PORSCHE 911 Carerra Speedster.** S/N WPOEB091K517318. Guards red/black. Odo: 880 miles. Stored since 1989, all original and as-new. Hopefully, next owner will enjoy driving rather than storing it. Cond: 1. **SOLD AT $55,080.** *Once checked for mechanical condition, this car will be worth more. Someone got a deal.* ***Barrett-Jackson, Scottsdale, AZ, 1/01.***

#410-1979 PORSCHE 911SC Coupe. S/N 9119200529. Silver/black. LHD. Odo: 86,053 miles. Aftermarket Turbo whale tail is cracked. Temporary Arizona tags. Aftermarket seats look very used. Black trim around doors scratched and faded. Looks like previous body damage on left door and fender. Hood not aligned. Dash has been redone. Cond: 4+. **NOT SOLD AT $12,000.** *A situation where cheap may not mean inexpensive. If this car's mechanicals were babied while its visuals were slaughtered, the high bid was close. But how often does that happen?* ***McCormick, Palm Springs, CA, 2/02.***

#264-1985 PORSCHE 930 TURBO (RUF) Coupe. Body by Porsche and Ruf. S/N WP0ZZZ93ZFS0. Guards red/tan. LHD. Alois Ruf is a well-regarded European aftermarket tuner of Porsches.

His modifications to this car include slant-nose front fenders, wider tires and BBS alloy wheels, bigger brakes, stiffer suspension, claimed 450 hp. Previous owner, Jose Canseco. Cond: 3+. **SOLD AT $30,800.** *The modifications harm the reliability and drivability of this non-US car which, in 300-hp stock trim, is already tightly wound. Fair price to both buyer and seller, if Canseco didn't drive it with the same intensity he hits a ball.* ***RM Auctions, Phoenix, AZ, 1/00.***

#415-1976 PORSCHE 911S Targa. S/N 9116211497. Blue/blue. LHD. Odo: 100,036 miles. Six-inch alloy wheels. Rear deck-lid damage. Rear quarter panels previously damaged and poorly fixed. Front hood paint poorly prepped before repaint. A high-mileage, driver 911. Cond: 4-. **SOLD AT $8,190.** *The kind of car a savvy Porsche mechanic would buy and give to you, knowing that he had just put an annuity in effect, based on repairs, that will let him buy a new pool, Jacuzzi and deck for his house.* ***McCormick, Palm Springs, CA, 2/02.***

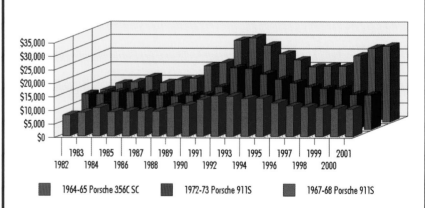

The Twenty Year Picture
COUPES FROM STUTTGART
1964-65 Porsche 356C SC, 196-68 Porsche 911S, 1972-73 Porsche 911S

Chart legend:
- 1964-65 Porsche 356C SC
- 1972-73 Porsche 911S
- 1967-68 Porsche 911S

Years: 1982 1983 1984 1985 1986 1987 1988 1989 1990 1991 1992 1993 1994 1995 1996 1997 1998 1999 2000 2001

Values: $0, $5,000, $10,000, $15,000, $20,000, $25,000, $30,000, $35,000

This value guide is provided courtesy of Cars of Particular Interest. CPI is the pocket guide most often used by credit unions and banks when dealing with loan values of collectible domestic and imported cars; www.BlackBookUSA.com.
From the June 2001 issue of *SCM* ◆

#808-1985 PORSCHE 911 Carrera Cabriolet. S/N WPOZZZ912FS1514. Golden sand metallic/dark brown. Odo: 70,912 miles. A/C. Slant-nose conversion with amateurish-looking wing-top slots. Repaired damage to front apron. Sprouting wing to scuttle trim. Very wide shiny alloy rims with Fuchs centers. Cond: 2. **SOLD AT $19,980.** *Didn't see the optional gold chain storage tray in the center console. Also missing was the requisite copy of* Bad Boys Drive Slanties. *Why do we picture the former owner on a stairstepper, watching a "How Porsches Help You Get Babes" video?* **Barrett-Jackson, Scottsdale, AZ, 1/01.**

#524-1982 PORSCHE 911 Turbo Coupe. S/N WPOZZZ93ZCS000320. Dark silver/op-art cloth and vinyl. LHD. Odo: 53,072 miles. Pep Boys "Turbo" sticker on dash. Pioneer AM/FM cassette. Turbo wide body, whale tail, Gotti wheels, sunroof. Well-done repaint, yet still a scary auction car. Cond: 4. **SOLD AT $21,200.** *Last seen at "The Auction," April 2002, where it no-saled for $19,000. Now with nine more miles. An uninspired Euro Porsche no longer in search of a new home. The seller did well; let's hope the new owner doesn't face any nasty surprises.*

Late 911s (1990-Present)

eBay/Kruse, Las Vegas, NV, 6/02.

#26-2001 PORSCHE 911 TURBO Coupe. S/N WPOAB29921S6853. Black/black. Odo: 1,319 miles. 415 horsepower, navigation device, sunroof, all power options. Murphy personnel started the car during Thursday's preview and the engine sounded strong. Chrome alloy wheels had no curb chips. Little-used and ready to roll. Cond: 2. **SOLD AT $142,800.** *Full-retail pop. Maybe local car dealers should start paying the Heinens to embezzle their inventory, so it could be recovered and auctioned off at retail. A strange marketing technique but, if it works, hey.* **James G. Murphy, Kenmore, WA, 5/01.**

#240-1995 PORSCHE 993 CARRERA Coupe. S/N WPOAA29965S3200. Blue/gray leather. Sunroof. Very well presented and preserved. Less than 30,000 miles and no visible signs of abuse. Some minor wear and tear on driver's seat. Cond: 2. **SOLD AT $38,850.** *Sold on second trip over the block. Fair-enough price for what appeared to be a decent car.* **Spectrum, Palm Springs, CA, 4/01.**

#234-1992 PORSCHE 959 S2 Coupe. S/N WPOZZZ95ZJS9002. Silver metallic/ black. Odo: 3,856 km. (Service records indicate more than 40,000 kilometers.) As-new outside and in with fresh factory-executed major service on file. Vendor is second owner. Cond: 1. **SOLD AT $203,391.** *Superb condition, but technically very complex supercar, which only factory, rather than independent shops, is able to maintain or fix here in Europe. Brought $40,000 more than last.* **Bonhams & Brooks, Monte Carlo, Monaco, 5/01.**

PART III

From 906 to 964 and Everything in Between

Welcome to the "there's a car for every pocketbook" section of *Keith Martin on Collecting Porsche.*

You'll be reading about the sleek 906s that brought Porsche so many victories on the track, and why they now cost hundreds of thousands of dollars. You'll also learn about the hapless 914s, badged as VWs in their German homeland, that can be bought for under $3,000—sometimes way under. We also point out why the ultra-cheap cars are the ones you don't want to own.

Despite being a very small car company, Porsche has built a surprising variety of interesting products over the years, many of which have generated controversy among enthusiasts. For instance, the front-engined, V8-powered 928 is regarded by some as one of the great GT cars of all time. Others dismiss it as being merely a Teutonic Corvette. In this chapter, you'll find a spirited discussion of the pros and cons of this supercar, pointing out the things to consider if you decide you need one in your garage.

How about the 944? They have a superb balance of handling and horsepower, yet their values languish. Are they just too "normal" for the typical Porsche enthusiast, who seems to want his engine cooled by air and mounted in the rear? In this chapter, you'll find a typical, no-holds-barred *SCM* analysis of this model and its stablemates.

So, if you're ready to step outside the 356 and 911 mainstream, turn the page and begin your journey.—*Keith Martin*

1973 Porsche 914-4

Chassis number: 4732919172

A completely different Porsche emerged for the 1970 model year to replace the rather short-lived 912. This one carried either the 1679-cc Volkswagen four-cylinder or the earlier 2.0-liter Porsche flat-six with its 110-horsepower rating. The big difference was that the engines were mid-mounted. The 914 was born out of a joint venture between Porsche and Volkswagen with bodies created by Karmann. The two-seat targa-topped coupe was built to a Porsche design with suspension components adopted from the 911. Four-wheel disc brakes were installed and the removable fiberglass top could be stored in the trunk. The 914 was produced in fairly large numbers until its production ended in 1976.

RM Auctions

The 914 offered here is a 1973 smog-exempt California car that has been completely restored to "as-new" showroom condition. It is finished in tangerine with black and gray interior. The options include a five-speed transmission, sunroof and alloy wheels. It has traveled 55,600 miles from new. This is a very well restored example.

This tangerine (dark orange) 1.7-liter 914 sold for $6,050 at the RM Monterey auction on the weekend of August 27 and 28, 1999. In unusually handsome condition yet offered at no reserve, this 914-4 didn't make its projected $8k to $12k pre-auction estimate.

Designed by Porsche with a body built by Karmann and a VW engine, the 914-4 attempted to be a modern interpretation of the mid-'50s 356 Speedster, a minimalist open-air two-seater with avant-garde styling, an air-cooled engine and great handling. Most shocking was the low price, as Speedsters sold for $2,995 in 1955 and the

> "In Germany, they were badged as a 'VW-Porsche' and the Wolfsburg crest was prominently placed on the steering wheel."

Year produced	1970-1976
Number produced	115,000 (approx.)
Original list price	$3,495 (1970)
SCM Price Guide	$3,500-5,000
Tune-up/major service	$120
Distributor cap	$8
Chassis #	On embossed plate in front trunk on passenger side front wheel well
Engine #	On alloy crossmember next to engine cooling fan support
Club	Porsche Club of America, P.O. Box 5900, Springfield, VA 22150
Web site	www.pca.org
Alternatives	MGB, Triumph TR-6 Fiat 124/2000 Spyder
Tier of collectibility	C

914 was introduced 15 years later at just $500 more.

The cars sold well, but due to their connection with the VW powerplant, they were often not viewed as true Porsches. In Germany, the 914 was badged as a "VW-Porsche" and the Wolfsburg crest was prominently placed on the steering wheel.

As a mid-engined car, it lives up to its promise of superb handling. The transmission is a genuine Porsche five-speed, and much of the rest of the car looks, feels and sounds right, as well. The 914-4s are frisky and fun to drive, but no one is going to call them fast, with 0-60 times in the 11- to 12-second range.

The price paid is right on the money for a 914 this nice. But I don't see much investment potential here, just a pretty car for sunny-day drives at a modest price. —Jim Schrager

(Historic description courtesy of the auction company.)

From the December 1999 issue of *SCM*.◆

1970-1976 Porsche 914-4

It was either love or hate at first sight when the 914 was introduced in 1970. Three decades later, the situation is pretty much the same.

To appreciate the 914, you have to understand its design brief: to recreate the 356 Speedster. That is, produce a simple, reliable, tossable, two-seat sports car with an immediately identifiable appearance. The biggest challenge was to produce this thoroughly modern roadster at about the same price as the final Speedsters: $3,495.

To achieve this goal, the 914 borrowed its four-cylinder boxer engine from the VW parts bin (the engine also appeared in the VW 411), and, because the Porsche factory was busy building higher-margin 911s, 914 bodies were built and assembled by Karmann (the 914/6 was completed in the Porsche factory). The standard five-speed transmission and many interior appointments were taken straight from the 911 of the era, providing at least a visual nod to the family tree. Yet, in Europe, the 914 was badged as a VW-Porsche.

Whatever you think of the styling, the 914 succeeded brilliantly in the marketplace, with over 100,000 units delivered. It was far and away the best-selling Porsche of its time and introduced a whole new generation of enthusiasts to the marque.

Although not a fast car, the 914 is fun to drive, and if you get a good one, very solid. The mid-engine location is exotic even today, and offers superb handling on the track and especially at autocross events. Porsche was clever enough to design two decent-size trunks into the car, front and back, something that the owner of a Ferrari 308 can only fantasize about. All 914s have removable targa tops.

As with any '70s collectible, watch for rust, and not just salt-induced corrosion. The location of the battery in the engine compartment can result in rust to the rear frame member directly below the battery tray. In its most destructive form, the rear wheel on the passenger side will show excessive negative camber, i.e., the top tucked in.

Try to find a car with its original Bosch fuel injection intact. Many 914s have been converted to Weber carbs, but rarely do they perform as well as the original set-up, and problems may arise when they confront emission testing. Be sure all flexible fuel lines are renewed, as they do not age gracefully and can

Love at first sight for 100,000 buyers.

"Porsche was clever enough to design two decent size trunks into the car, front and back, something that the owner of a Ferrari 308 can only fantasize about."

become a serious fire hazard. If there is slop in the shifter, replace the plastic bushings in the shift linkage and you'll be surprised by the difference.

During a pre-purchase test drive, I suggest going over a set of railroad tracks and listening for squeaks and groans from the top that may indicate critical chassis rust. The cars were quite rigid when new. If the rear window is loose, check for rust in the firewall. Many 914s have spongy brakes due to a smallish master cylinder and a trouble-prone brake-proportioning valve. Possible fixes include a bigger master cylinder from a 911.

Avoid 914s with engine problems, as even though their powerplant is VW-sourced, a complete overhaul will still run more than $4,000.

Once the king of the under-$2,000 sports car gang, the values of 914-4s have been creeping up over the past five years. Plan on spending $4,000 to $5,000 for a good 1.7L. The 2-liter cars, first introduced in 1973, are much quicker and worth the $2,000 premium they command. The most desirable 914-4 is the 1973 2.0L, due to the chrome bumpers and the lack of significant horsepower-robbing emissions equipment.

914s remain a good entry-level way to experience an air cooled Porsche. Nice cars will continue to appreciate, albeit at a modest rate. In addition, you will be quite welcome at any Porsche Club event, and probably will get to sit at the same table as the 911 group instead of being relegated to the back corner where the 924 owners are forced to huddle.—*Jim Schrager*

From the June 2002 issue of *SCM*.◆

Future Classic:
1997-1999 Porsche Boxster 2.5

The Porsche Boxster 2.5 (1997-99) was the first vehicle developed by a revamped Porsche manufacturing system capable of making low-volume yet profitable sports cars while retaining the performance and panache of a Porsche. The Boxster was no thinly veiled attempt to sell cars with a Stuttgart crest to those who couldn't afford the real thing, as the 914-4 and 924 so clearly were. As a used car, the original Boxster is quickly falling into the low to mid-thirties, and as such, represents an excellent value against similar-year 911 values that can be almost twice as much.

The Boxster is a return to the traditional Porsche virtues of crisp handling packaged in small but not tiny dimensions; a controlled ride that gives go-kart-style agility without the pounding so typical of other "high-performance" cars, and the structural soundness that has become an enduring trademark of the marque. You end up wanting to go for a drive even if you have no place to go.

On the specification sheet, the Boxster looks like a contemporary race car, with a sophisticated mid-engine layout and a sizable 2.5-liter, six-cylinder powerplant that puts out more horsepower, at 204 hp, than the 3-liter 911SC (1978-83). The Boxster shares its headlights and most of the front sheet metal with the current 911, although that will change in the next few years as the designers attempt to inject a bit of differentiation into the more costly 911.

Both the original 911 and the Boxster offer styling that is innovative and breathtaking. At the original introduction of the 911 in 1963, the body lines

"Don't go for a test drive unless you are ready to write a check, as it's a car you won't want to step out of. Twenty years from now it will definitely have a following."

Body Style . . . . .2-door roadster
Engine . . . . .6 cyl, 2.5 liter, horizontally-opposed, water-cooled alloy engine producing 204 hp
Transmission . . . . .5-speed manual or Tiptronic
Price as tested $39,980
Description . . . . .Retro/nuevo "entry-level" Porsche that harkens back in style and mid-engine layout to the world-beating 550 race cars of the '50s and early '60s.
Summary . . . . .Like the earliest Speedsters, the first-generation Boxster will have a collectible appeal for the Porsche fanatic who wants the first, purest version of a particular Porsche model. The Boxster takes the best from the past and mates it with advanced production technology to create a fully modern car still completely in touch with the original virtues of both the 356 and 911 series
Tier of Collectibility C

were immediately recognized as unique, attractive and definitive. The same can be said about the lines of the Boxster. On the road, the 911 looked ahead of its time for at least a decade, and the 996 variant still turns heads today. The lines of the Boxster are aging well, unlike so many contemporary Japanese sports cars.

The Boxster had its share of early production woes, but these were relatively quickly sorted out. With fixes made, because of the modern manufacturing techniques even the first cars are now perfectly usable, driveable machines. No collapsed chain-tensioners or elongating engine studs to worry about here.

Prices are falling, making the original Boxster $10,000-$20,000 cheaper than a new Boxster S. Don't go for a test drive unless you are ready to write a check, as it's a car you won't want to step out of. Twenty years from now, it will definitely have a following.—*Jim Schrager.*

From the August 2000 issue of *SCM.*◆

2001 Porsche Boxster S

Chassis number: WP0CB298X1U662397

As described by the seller on eBay Motors:

This 2001 Porsche Boxster S is in great condition. It is metallic silver with black leather interior. It has AM/FM stereo, CD, cruise control, power windows, all available airbags, dual power seats, power mirrors and wind screen. The engine is a six-cylinder S with a six-speed manual transmission. There is a remaining factory warranty. Chrome "turbo look" wheels are fitted and the tires are in excellent condition. The interior and exterior are in great shape, with less-than-normal wear. The car has 2,871 miles.

Porsche has not had an easy time of it when it comes to entry-level models. Both the 914 and the 924 have become classic examples of how not to take your brand downmarket, substituting some immediate sales success for longer-term brand damage.

But the Boxster, first sold here in 1997, has been different. With styling designed to be reminiscent of the fabled 550 model, and with a base six-cylinder engine that is essentially sourced from the upmarket 996, the Boxster is a real Porsche, no questions asked.

Further, the S model, introduced in 2000, was chock full of upgrades to both the interior and the performance that indicated that Porsche was treating the car as a full-fledged model of its lineup, not a sales-oriented de-contented stepchild.

When first introduced in 2000, Boxster S models were in high demand and commanded a premium of several thousand dollars over their base MSRP of $49,930. But as with all serial-production cars, once the "first-on-the-block gang" had theirs, prices slid down to MSRP, and lower.

We chose this car at random from the 20 or so that always seem to be listed on eBay Motors. With its ultra-low mileage, we expected it would sell somewhere above the $48,500 average of the cars we scanned on the national market.

But we were in for an educational experience.

This car, item #1864044565, sold on eBay at no reserve for $38,900, after 25 bids, on October 1, 2002. This price is so far below

what we thought the wholesale market to be that we did a little more investigation.

SCM ran a CARFAX, which came up clean. We contacted the selling dealer, who said the car had no surprises, and that he simply lists cars and sell them for what they will bring. As it was a private sale, we were unable to contact the buyer.

On November 14, the date this issue is sent to the printer, we made a quick scan of the eBay Motors listings. In just six short weeks, Boxster prices have taken a significant dive, with several 2001 models, one with under 6,000 miles, listed with "Buy It Now" prices of less than $41,000.

Our conclusion is that Boxsters are very soft right now, due to a confluence of factors including the economy, the onset of winter and an excessive supply of both new and used Boxsters. Porsche North America recently sent out discount coupons for new Boxsters to every PCA member: it didn't do this because sales were strong. This new-car weakness translates into poor used-car prices, as well.

When Boxsters were new in 1997 and demand far exceeded supply, you could buy a new Boxster at list, drive it for a while and sell it for about what you paid. The same was true for the Boxster S when introduced in 2000, but not for long. In today's market, Boxsters are just used cars that are depreciating, rapidly it appears.

More than 120,000 Boxsters have been produced, and they are still cranking them out. From a corporate standpoint, it has been the most successful Porsche ever, selling in large volume at big margins. However, as a collectible car, it is nowhere, due to that same large production number.

At first glance it appeared that someone got a great deal on a Boxster S, and got it for well below the current market value. But six weeks after the sale, the price appears to be just a decent deal. And by the first of the year, it will probably be full retail. Such is the way of new-car values—Jim Schrager and Keith Martin

From the December 2002 issue of *SCM*.◆

Years produced	1997-present
Number produced	120,000 and counting
Original sale price	$51,600
SCM Price Guide	$40,000-50,000
Tune-up/major service	$600
Distributor cap	$42
Chassis #	On horizontal bulkhead under front hood
Engine #	Stamped into alloy engine block
Club	Porsche Club of America, P.O. Box 5900, Springfield, VA 22150
Web site	www.pca.org
Alternatives	Mercedes SLK, BMW Z3, Nissan 350Z, Honda S2000
Tier of Collectibility	C

1986 Porsche 928S Coupe

Chassis number: WP0JB092465862641

When introduced in 1978, marque enthusiasts didn't know what to think of the 928. Like the four-cylinder 924 offered the prior year, the new car was front-engined with a water-cooled power-plant. This, then, was the future for Porsche, as the company appeared to have plans to phase out the 911, which even then had been in production for over a dozen years.

The press was much more positive about the 928 than long-time Porsche enthusiasts. It was sleek, exotic looking and very fast. The long nose behind the exposed pop-up head-lamps held an all-alloy 4.5-liter (273-c.i.) single overhead camshaft V8, producing 219 bhp in American trim.

Despite the use of aluminum panels for the doors, hood and rear hatch, the 928 weighed a less-than-svelte 3,144 pounds. The new Porsche was very refined and quieter than the 911, yet capable of reaching 60 mph in 7.0 seconds and topping out at 138 mph.

Although the base price in 1978 was a heady $28,500, that was just the starting point for what was as much a luxury vehicle as it was a closed sports car. Although power-assisted brakes and steering were standard, air conditioning, sunroof and a long list of options added to the tariff.

The 928S received a 4.6-liter engine and 234 bhp in 1983. The five-speed manual was a no-cost option, with the automatic standard. This was in the days when an automatic wasn't even available in the 911, the Sportomatic having died a quiet death in the late '70s.

By the time the example shown here was built in 1986, it cost $50,000 and sported double overhead cams for each bank of cylinders. Displacement, at just under 5 liters (302 c.i.), allowed the power output to climb to 288 bhp.

Finished in a lovely burgundy metallic, this automatic 928S has all the standard luxury equipment such as tan leather, air conditioning, electric windows, power steering and power-assisted brakes. It is truly in excellent condition and has covered just 57,000 miles since new.

This original 928S sold for $12,075, including buyer's premium at the Bonhams & Brooks auction in Aurora, Illinois, June 9, 2001. The values of all 928s continue to languish, so I view this distressing price as market correct, perhaps even a bit generous to the seller.

Unfortunately for owners, 928s are the Rodney Dangerfields of the Porsche world. Even though each 928 has a full complement of statistically significant high-performance numbers, most hard-core Porsche enthusiasts won't give 928 owners the time of day. This is due to the completely backwards manner (at

Bonham & Brooks

least from a Porsche fanatic's perspective) in which the car was designed, with a quiet, torquey, water-cooled engine in the front. Then there is the rather boring way it handles, with smooth and predictable understeer rather than the excitable hi-jinks the 911 is so well loved for.

It has also been called the Stuttgart Corvette, due to the similar layout, but if you drive any 928 and any Corvette back-to-back, the difference in the feel of the two cars is astounding. The Porsche has a rigid body structure with precise handling, while the Corvette feels much looser, with a body that creaks and groans.

Repair costs are not trivial with a used 928. Parts are wildly expensive, at times no longer available, and top-flight factory-trained technicians few and far between. I have recently followed a local 928 as it has gone from shop to shop in search of a person who could trouble-shoot a host of fuel-injection and electrical gremlins. The car has been out of service for more than six months and the end is nowhere in sight. Cubic dollars could remedy the problems, but more creative methods are required due to the modest value of the car.

This is not to say that a fully sorted 928 is unreliable, but unlike the simplicity and rugged design of the 911, the 928 is rather more fussy and the maintenance schedule must be followed carefully.

Sadly, I don't see the prices of even well-kept 928s moving upward and can imagine their values behaving more like the unloved Maserati Biturbo than their close cousin, the 911. There is a lot of performance for the money here, but the lack of upside and the potential for frightful running costs conspire to make almost any 928 a suspect investment, at best.—Jim Schrager

(Historic data courtesy of the auction company.)

From the September 2001 issue of *SCM*.◆

Years produced	1978-1992
Number produced	61,200 (approx.)
Original list price	$50,000 (1986)
SMC Price Guide	$9,000-12,000 (928S)
Tune-up/major service	$750
Distributor cap	$45
Chassis #	On horizontal bulkhead under front hood
Engine #	Stamped into alloy engine block near head
Club	Porsche Club of America, P.O. Box 5900, Springfield, VA 22150
Web site	www.pca.org
Alternatives	Mercedes 450 SLC, BMW 635 CSi, Corvette C4 coupe, Jaguar XJS coupe, Ferrari Testarossa
Tier of Collectibility	D

The 928: Fast, but Going Nowhere

Looking for a sure thing? An advertisement in a recent issue of *Hemmings Motor News* predicted the unloved 928 was just about to become appreciated and its values start to appreciate. I don't agree. 928 prices aren't going anywhere but down.

The 928 was built to succeed the 911. No small task, but Dr. Ernst Fuhrmann, creator of the legendary 356 Carrera four-cam racing engine, was the logical choice to chart the path of Porsche history.

Introduced in 1977 with a front-mounted, water-cooled, SOHC, all-alloy, 90-degree 4.5-liter V8, the 928 was a radical departure for Porsche. The giant engine (almost twice as large as the 911 of the day) developed gobs of smooth, easy power and was ideal for powering the car at triple-digit European speeds.

The avant-garde styling gave the car a striking and timeless shape, similar in approach to the original 356 and 911: smooth, apparently highly aerodynamic and distinctive without being wacky.

Enthusiasts who appreciate the value of a 928 are few.

But as a replacement for the 911, the 928 was an utter failure. In 18 years of production (1978-95), the 928 averaged about 3,400 cars per year worldwide, as compared to over 12,000 per annum for all 33 years of the 911 (1965-97).

Part of the reason for the 928's failure is that it feels and drives much differently than the 911. The 928 is fast, but not light on its feet. The 911 is all about response; the 928, terminal velocity. Think of the 928 as the world's greatest Corvette coupe. A neat idea, but unfortunately nobody cared.

Sitting in a 356 or 911, most people are amazed at the room inside. But in a 928, the giant V8 up front takes up much of the space in the center of the cockpit. As in the modern Corvette, you sit very near the floor in a 928, which is not the case in a 911.

The 928 never had a Targa or cabriolet version, as low production volumes couldn't justify the tooling costs. Can you imagine a 450 SLC without an SL? An XKE 2+2 coupe, but no roadster?

The power delivery of the 928 is different from the classic Porsche approach. Going back to the 356A four-cam Carreras, the Super 90 of the 356B series, the 911S of the 1967-73 cars and the 930 Turbo from 1976 on, sporting power meant a relatively small-displacement engine yielding high-rpm shrieks en route to power at the top of the rev range. But here was the 928, with tons of torque instead. Certainly useful, but utterly confusing to the hard-core Porsche fan.

Today, a 928 is a tremendous amount of car for the money, but cars that sold slowly when new are often very hard to sell as

"You won't be a hit at the Porsche Club with your slushbox, but it is a good match for the 928, which always seemed more suited for going to the mall than driving on the racetrack."

used cars. That is certainly the case with a 928.

I'd avoid the first two years (1978-79), as these cars had teething problems. Also, the power increases from 220 horsepower to 300 with the arrival of the 928S in 1980-83. In 1984-86, an additional 10 horsepower appear, but the best cars started in 1987, with the 5.0-liter, four-valve engines and 320 horsepower. The S4 ran for five years (1987-91), alongside the limited-production 928GT (1989-91) and the 928 GTS (1992-95).

Automatics, available in all years, started with a three-speed made by Mercedes and changed to a four-speed in 1983. You won't be a hit at the Porsche Club with your slushbox, but it is a good match for the 928, which always seemed more suited for going to the mall than driving on the racetrack.

Early 928s can be had for $5,000, but the repair bills can easily double that if you run into trouble. A decent S goes for about $12,000 and an S4 can be bought under $20,000. High miles hurts plenty, as major work on a 928 is very expensive. For $30,000 you can buy almost any 928, including a raft of late-model S4 and GT models, but these cars are still depreciating. Unlike the 911, they seem to have no bottom-value floor. I've seen '83 and '84 S models, with high miles and needing work, sell in the $3,000-$4,000 range. This is a clear indication of a lack of wide interest in the car, a malady that keeps the prices of so many interesting exotics in the cellar.

What started as a noble exercise by a brilliant engineer ended up as proof of the exclusive nature of the Porsche franchise. Luckily, the new 996 model 911 keeps its engine behind the driver, where it belongs.—*Jim Schrager*

From the July 1998 issue of *SCM*.◆

1986 Porsche 928 Factory Custom 4-door Sedan

Chassis number: POJB0921H

RM Auctions

By the early 1970s, Porsche management decided that the 911 model would eventually have to be replaced by a more modern design. The new model would feature a water-cooled V8 front-mounted engine with its transmission and differential combined in a rear-mounted transaxle for excellent weight distribution. The chassis featured all independent suspension and four-wheel disc brakes. The near equal weight distribution meant that the 928 would theoretically have far better straight-line stability than the 911 with its engine overhanging the rear axle.

In 1986 Porsche and AMG built the prototype pictured here—a custom 928 four-door sedan. One cannot help but conjecture that this variant may have been a prototype for a new 928 that would have created a completely new market niche, further distancing it from the 911.

According to current Porsche designer Harm LaGaay, this rare and unusual car was delivered to Heinz Prechter, founder and CEO of ASC (American Sunroof Corporation), whose large automotive aftermarket firm headquartered just south of Detroit enjoyed a close relationship with the factory. The workmanship of this conversion is impeccable, being the equal or better of the legendary fit and finish of a new Porsche. The entire cabin, for instance, is lined in sumptuous burgundy leather to match the exterior paintwork. Having recently enjoyed a tune-up and recharge of the air-conditioning system, this intriguing 928 runs like a new car as it should, since the odometer shows only 5,520 documented original miles.

The question is: Is this a sports car, a family sedan or the world's fastest limousine? Judging by its unique appearance and specifications, it likely qualifies as all of the above. What a marvelous way to elicit a double-take from all those snooty hotel concierges who think they know the world's exotic cars.

This unusual factory custom Porsche was offered at no reserve at the RM Monterey auction, August 16, 2002, and sold for $44,000. The sale price was slightly below the $45,000 low estimate.

In the '80s, there were constant debates inside Porsche about widening its product offering someday to include bigger sporting cars, and at several points along the way full-scale mock-ups and drivable prototype four-door and four-seat cars were developed. One look at this example (or any of the others) reaffirms one's faith in Ferry's gut reaction to each and every one of them: No thanks.

Let's take a moment to think about Porsche's latest four-door machine, the Cayenne. It's easy for the casual observer to become convinced that Porsche's focus should be the creation of a new generation of alloy-bodied, world-beating 550 Spyders or plastic-bodied 904 race cars. The reality is that these cars sold in tiny quantities, and made little money directly for Porsche, although the publicity value was significant.

The tremendous fiscal success of the Boxster has provided funds for Porsche to invest in new products, and the giant margins and high volumes afforded by the SUV segment are hard for any automotive executive to resist. Mercedes-Benz and BMW have both taken the plunge into SUV-land with great success. In fact, the M-Class now vies with the E-Class as the best-selling Mercedes in the US.

Given its technological prowess, and the relationship with VW, it seems a small leap for Porsche to enter the SUV market too. And if it succeeds in making an SUV that actually handles, it will probably sell very well.

I have already spoken with several PCA owners with deposits on Cayennes. It is indeed possible that the fiber of the Porsche brand will stretch over to this new SUV.

Of course, the overall economics of the moment have much to do with the ultimate sales volumes to be achieved. Ferry was right not to build the four-door 928. But Wendelin Weideking may also be right to build the Cayenne. My concern, given that the SUV market seems to have peaked, would be more for his lousy timing than his lousy idea.

But back to the four-door pictured here. As a one-off, the price is the price, and there is no concern about what all the other factory four-door 928s will now be worth. There are none.

Of course, you have to wonder a great deal about how this contraption will drive. I am sure the handling wasn't helped by a wheelbase approximately one foot longer than stock and an addition of hundreds of pounds in weight. And remember, the original 928 was not a light car to begin with. The factory had to use wildly expensive aluminum doors to pare some of the excess pork from its creation. Plus, any original 928 is more of a freight train rather than a nimble rally car. So this extra-long, extra-heavy version is mostly for cruising, which makes it just like most modified and hot rods: mostly for show, not too much go.

As a true Porsche factory oddity, this creation will always have some value. But I don't believe it will appreciate at the head of the market. For someone who wants to get lots of attention at the next Porsche Parade, here is just the ticket. For the rest of us, I'm not quite sure what we would do with this one for the other 51 weeks of the year.—*Jim Schrager*

(Historic data courtesy of the auction company.)

From the November 2002 issue of *SCM*.◆

Year produced	1986
Number produced	1
Original list price	N/A
Tune-up/major service	$600
Distributor cap	$40
Chassis #	On horizontal bulkhead forward of engine
Engine #	On rear-most engine case near flywheel
Club	Porsche Club of America, P.O. Box 5900, Springfield, VA 22150
Web site	www.pca.org
Alternatives	Factory custom prototypes with odd body shapes based on cars that didn't sell well
Tier of Collectibility	B

1966 Porsche Carrera 906E

Chassis number: 906.134

This superbly presented Porsche Carrera 6 began life as the Racing Team Holland car campaigned in World Championship of Makes-qualifying races by Ben Pon and fellow Dutchman Gijs van Lennep. The first time out at significant level in this 2-liter six-cylinder air-cooled coupe, they finished seventh overall and first in class in the ADAC 1,000-kilometer race at Nürburgring. After winning a home event outright on the Dutch Zandvoort circuit, Ben Pon was asked to partner with works driver Vic Elford in the 1967 Le Mans *Grand Prix d'Endurance*.

That race was to provide Elford with his first experience of the French 24-Hour classic, and he and Ben Pon finished seventh overall. At the end of that season, Ben Pon shared this car with another British driver, Tony Dean, and won the 2-liter sports category again, this time in the BOAC 1,000-kilometer at Brands Hatch.

Porsche 906 '134' was subsequently sold into amateur ownerships and reportedly "suffered one indignity after another at the hands of novices trying to keep it competitive." Ultimately it came to light in South America, being located in derelict order by Marty Yacoobian. The car was brought into the United States and sold to Bruce Canepa, the well-known restorer in Santa Cruz, California.

What followed was a mammoth 4,000-hour restoration that has been described as producing the most technically correct restoration of a 906.

When introduced in 1966, the Porsche 906—marketed generally as the 'Carrera 6'—combined a multitubular spaceframe chassis with strikingly low and curvaceous lightweight fiberglass body paneling aimed at minimum drag. The engine was a racing version of the production 911 air-cooled six-cylinder unit. This 901/20 variant's crankcase was cast in lightweight magnesium instead of aluminum, and its pistons, connecting rods, cylinder barrels and valve gear were all redesigned. With single overhead camshafts atop each cylinder bank, the new engine actually weighed 54 kg (110 lb) less than the standard 911 unit. Transmission was via a five-speed all-sychromesh transaxle with ZF limited-slip differential. The Porsche 906 became yet another classic in the German marque's enduring competition history—the model's record including outright victory in the legendary Sicilian Targa Florio race.

This 906 sold for $365,500, including buyer's commission, at the Brooks USA Auction on August 15, 1998, at Quail Lodge in Carmel, California, at the height of Porsche's 50th anniversary party.

The 906 is a tremendously important Porsche, as it marks many turning points in the firm. It was developed by a young family member, Ferdinand Piech, as his first project as racing director. Before squabbling caused Ferry Porsche to banish all family members

Brooks

Years produced	1966
Number produced	13
Original list price	............$11,500
SMC Price Guide	....$275,000-375,000
Tune-up/major service	.........$600
Distributor cap	.................$22
Chassis #	....On tubular frame, right side, near mid-engine
Engine #	....On driver's side of cooling fan, stamped on a vertical fan-support member
Club	....Porsche Club of America, P.O. Box 5900, Springfield, VA 22150
Web site	..............www.pca.org
Alternatives	...Fort GT-40, Alfa Romeo TT33/2, Ferrari 246 SP
Tier of Collectibility	................A

from active management, Piech was dedicated to making a strong impression on the firm his grandfather founded.

The 906 was built on a tubular space frame chassis rather than welded sheet-metal sections, as used in 904s and production cars. At the time, this was hailed as a departure for Porsche, but the earlier 550 cars were all built on space frames. The weight decrease was a significant feature, as the 906, a wider and longer car, weighed 174 lb less than the 904.

Although the new flat-six, SOHC engine found its way into a few of the later 904s, the 906 was built around the four-cylinder, 2.0-liter hot rod that produced 220 hp at 8,100 rpm (versus 130hp for the production 2-liter). After the initial homologation run of 52,906 cars, an additional 13 chassis were fitted with an experimental mechanical fuel-injection system, the 906E. This Bosch system gave improved throttle response and, to everyone's surprise, better mileage. A similar system was used on various 911 road cars from 1969 through 1973, including the legendary Carrera RS.

Although these were rugged endurance cars, frame breakage on crossmembers under the gearbox and half-shaft failures took their toll. As a result, Porsche decided to run important races with new 906s that had not suffered the metal fatigue born of repeated track outings.

The 906 became the first Porsche production car unable to be registered in West Germany for road use. In spite of this potential handicap, the initial production run was sold out before the official introduction.

The 906E featured here, with its race history and superb restoration, has to be one of the most desirable Porsches anywhere. While the price paid may not seem a bargain, this car will appreciate at the head of the market and always will be of interest to knowledgeable collectors.—Jim Schrager

(Historic data courtesy of the auction company.)

From the August 1999 issue of *SCM*.◆

How Not to Sell Your 906

If you have only one racing Porsche in your collection, the 906 is a great choice. It is hard to imagine a more exciting car to find at auction than a Porsche 906. A true milestone race car, 906s mark the era when Stuttgart began to build pure racing machinery. In addition to being the first Porsche unable to be certified for street use, it was the first specialized chassis developed around the new six-cylinder boxer motor, an engine destined to power 35 years of popular street and winning race cars. The manager of the 906 program was an aggressive young grandson of Professor Porsche named Ferdinand Piech.

So why did this 906 (S/N 906.137), presented Saturday afternoon, January 22 at the Barrett-Jackson auction, not attract a single serious bid? It was declared a no-sale at $250,000 and you could almost see the disappointed chandeliers clinking in the wind, for the Ford GT40 that hit the stage before it during prime time garnered serious bidding and was sold for the highest price in the auction at $429,300. Why did the 906 fall flat?

1. PROVENANCE. There were no clues about the car's race history. Who drove this car? Where did the crowds cheer it on? What cars and drivers did this 906 beat? Was it a factory car or run by a privateer? Buyers today will pay a huge premium for documented provenance. In the pits at Monterey, the new owner wants to have a little billboard showing the famous owners of the car and the famous races it has been in. Putting up a sign that says, "Mystery 906, I sure hope it has a good history," doesn't do much for an ego.

2. ORIGINALITY. Race cars live a tough life, and in many cases little is left when they are put out to pasture. We need to hear about the engine (is it correct for the car or at least the correct type?), the chassis (has it been rebuilt a few times?) and other important pieces such as the transmission. Is this an old wreck rebuilt around a chassis number, or substantially a real car?

3. SPARES. Race cars break, and if you plan to drive this car, you need spares. A detailed list of extra gear helps a potential buyer see that you are offering a turn-key package to go vintage racing. How many sets of wheels, tires, titanium connecting rods, 906 cams and 901 gear sets are included? Without these vital extras, the car is hardly usable for anything but a static display.

4. VINTAGE RACE CREDENTIALS. Many collectors feel the highest and best use of a 906 is in vintage events blasting around your favorite race track, getting a

> "So much of the value of a vintage race car is dependent on its history that presenting a six-figure car with a blank slate for a past is tantamount to showing up at a gunfight armed with a knife."

firsthand picture of what it felt like to conquer the great circuits of the world. Driving the car at speed is one of the most important reasons to buy one of these thoroughbreds. We need to understand which organizations accept this car. Has it been successfully vintage raced? Where are you likely to be invited? Will you qualify for the Monterey Historics? Even more important, is the car in "ready-to-race" condition, with key suspension components X-rayed and magnafluxed, or will it have to be taken completely apart before a new owner feels comfortable hitting the banks of Daytona in a vintage race at 160 mph?

5. PHYSICAL CONDITION. There was a large scratch on the driver's side front fender, probably done in transit. This isn't a big deal as everyone expects race cars to have been pranged and no one worries about original paint. But some effort should have been made to clean it up or even get it fixed. While not an expensive item to repair, it was a distraction and made the car look like second class merchandise. If the sellers don't care enough to primp a car for the auction block, what does that say about the level that the rest of the car is prepared to?

6. MUSIC. This car was pushed onto the auction stage. One of the most thrilling moments of B-J on Saturday afternoon was when the Ford GT40 thundered onto the stage, its Ferrari-conquering exhaust note filling the tent and sending shivers of excitement through the crowd. There is nothing like the wail of a race car to remind an enthusiast of the true meaning of life. The 906 was never started. Did it run? Would it run? Did it even *have* an engine? How fast would a crowd have materialized if the boxer music started? We'll never know.

A major auction can be an ideal place to sell a car like a 906, but the seller has to make a serious effort to educate people about its machine. So much of the value of a vintage race car is dependent on its history that presenting a six-figure car with a blank slate for a past is tantamount to showing up at a gunfight armed with a knife. Even though 906s are rare, with just 65 built in 1966, there are usually a few for sale. As an esoteric piece, 906s generally attract esoteric, well-informed buyers. Properly prepared and marketed, and with an aggressive reserve, this car should fill the stage with bidders and the tent with excitement when it crosses the block. That it didn't do any of those things at Barrett-Jackson doesn't mean that this isn't a good car, it just means that its owners have to do a far better job of presenting it.
—*Jim Schrager*

From the April 2000 issue of *SCM*.◆

1973 Porsche Carrera RSR 2.8

Chassis number: 911 360 0782
Engine number: 693 0116

In the early 1970s, the FIA decided sports car racing should use cars that more closely resembled production vehicles. Using the Carrera RS 2.7 as its homologation platform, the 2.8 RSR developed 300 (DIN) hp with the use of a twin-plug ignition, hotter camshafts, higher compression pistons and many other enhancements.

RM Auctions

The car offered here was sold to Bob Hagestad of Denver who used it to take part in IMSA and Trans-Am races including: Road Atlanta Trans-Am, April 15, 1973, R. Hagestad/P. Tracey, 8th; Lime Rock Trans-Am, May 5, 1973, R. Hagestad/Bobby Allison, DNF; Watkins Glen Trans-Am, R. Hagestad, 7th.

The car was crashed in July 1973 during practice at Trois Rivieres. Although not extensive, damage repair was time consuming, so Hagestad bought another RSR from Peter Gregg. After repairs to 0782 were completed, Hagestad sold the car to Michael Callas of Houston. Callas later sold the car to George Valerio who drove the RSR home from Texas to California without problem. After this, 0782 was sold to Dan McLoughlin, who kept the RSR a while before selling it to the Matsuda collection in Japan, where the car spent many years on display.

Recently released from the collection, 911 360 0782 is one of the very few RSR 2.8 Carreras to have escaped the modifications made to keep these race cars competitive.

Fast, light and nimble even by today's standards, the 1973 RSR Carrera ranks as one of Porsche's great competition cars.

This restored race car sold for $171,600 at the RM Auction, Amelia Island, Florida, on March 11, 2000. A look at this price helps explain the striking difference in value between race and street cars.

Although appearing similar to a standard 1973 Carrera RS, don't be deceived. The RSR is a full race car, never meant to be driven on the street. Its twin-plug engine, while just slightly bigger in displacement than the stock RS, produces nearly 50% more horsepower. It does this by throwing longevity out the window. This engine was not intended to last more than a few races between rebuilds.

From the factory build records we can verify this is one of the 55 genuine RSR cars and, unusually, still with its original engine. We can also see the original colors were Grand Prix White with a black interior and royal blue graphics, and the factory options were a limited-slip differential and a large fuel cell.

As a race car, its value is calculated in an almost entirely different manner than a street car. For a street car, accident damage hurts the value; for a race car, some damage is a virtual certainty. For a street car, original paint is highly prized; for a race car, rarely expected.

Years produced	1973
Number produced	55
Original list price	$18,000
SMC Price Guide	$175,000-300,000
Tune-up/major service	$600
Distributor cap	$250
Chassis #	On horizontal bulkhead under front lid, just aft of gas tank
Engine #	On vertical fan housing support, passenger side of engine
Club	Porsche Club of America, P.O. Box 5900, Springfield, VA 22150
Web site	www.pca.org
Alternatives	Race-prepped Mercury Capri; BMW 3.0 CS "Batmobile"; Camaro, Firebird, and Corvette, Trans Am race cars
Tier of Collectibility	A

The original engine in a street car is required to obtain a top price; since race cars are often updated, even within a single season, it does not destroy the value if a race car has a non-original engine as long as it was correct for the car as last raced. Celebrity heritage helps a street car a bit; for a race car, it helps an enormous amount. Overall paint and interior detail matter plenty in a street car; for a race car, not nearly as much.

In this RSR, we have the combination of a restoration on an original race car that previously suffered both an engine explosion and collision damage. While it was raced in its day, it never brought home any real glory for its owners. So what to do with this car?

As bought, it is over-restored for regular track work, but fine for the occasional historic race. The 2.8 RSRs were near the end of the non-Turbo 911 race cars, so they are quite a bit easier to drive than the Turbo monsters that followed. But with 300 or so horsepower, don't think for a moment this car is tame. You can get an idea of the powerband and gearing by realizing that even with about 100 extra horsepower, the RSR is slower 0 to 60 than a touring RS (5.6 versus 5.5 seconds) but faster by 3 seconds in the 0 to 100 dash (12.0 versus 15.0). Those giant 9- and 11-inch wide tires are not there for looks, but rather as a requirement to translate all that horsepower into forward motion.

The price paid was appropriately at the low range of the 2.8 RSR market, as cars that have been off the road for a long period of time often require mechanical work due to their inactivity. Once made track-ready, the value of this 2.8 RSR should move with those of the top-level group of Porsche race cars, which are today enjoying strong increases in value.—Jim Schrager

(Historic description courtesy of the auction company.)
From the August 2000 issue of *SCM.*◆

911 GT1

Bonhams

After its 1994 Le Mans victory with a decade-old design, Porsche needed a new long-term strategy for its international sports car competition. Enter the 911 GT1.

Keeping to the spirit of the regulations, Porsche used an existing 911 road car, the type 993, for the body shell. It was stiffened by a substantial roll cage that also supported the engine, gearbox, and suspension. In line with 911 tradition, the motor was a horizontally opposed six cylinder, but it was mounted ahead of the rear axle line rather than behind it like the road cars. The 3.2-liter, four-valves-per-cylinder "boxer" was water-cooled and turbocharged with a pair of intercooled KKK turbos. Maximum power of 600 hp was developed at 7,200 rpm and transmitted to a six-speed gearbox equipped with its own oil cooler.

A strong visual association with the 911 road car was necessary, so several subtle styling cues reinforced the link, but otherwise the GT1 looked every inch the purpose-built racer it was. From its huge "shark's mouth" front air intake to the high full-width wing at the rear, there was no question what the car was designed for. Beneath its predominantly carbon-fiber skin, the GT1 incorporated a number of advanced technical developments, including antilock brakes, carbon brake discs, and built-in air jacks for speedy wheel changes. Power-assisted steering helped minimize driver fatigue.

In 1997, the "Evo" GT1 saw changes that improved aerodynamics, as the race car gradually morphed away from its production-based origins. The visual connection with the production car was maintained by new kidney bean-shaped headlamps like the ones on the recently introduced type 996 production car.

Still chasing that next elusive Le Mans win, the Stuttgart firm produced a new GT1 for 1998. The car was completely redesigned with a carbon-fiber body tub, the first Porsche to use this method of construction. The gearbox was redesigned, incorporating an F1-style sequential shift mechanism. Despite facing increased competition from faster entries fielded by Mercedes and Toyota, Porsche triumphed in its 50th-anniversary year.

Regulations for the GT1 category stipulated that cars must be capable of road use to be eligible. In developing the road version of the GT1, Porsche met the most stringent EU requirements—the first car completed in January 1996 was used for compliance testing. Although there would be no series production of the GT1, the factory did produce a handful of road-going models for select customers. The road car's 544 hp and dry weight of 1,100 kg produced shattering acceleration: 0-100 kph (62 mph) in just 3.7 seconds.

Delivered new to Germany in May 1998, this 911 GT1 road car has not been used for any form of motorsport. Unmodified, it has covered a mere 4,400 km from new and is presented in outstanding condition throughout. If super exclusivity appeals to you, forget the Carrera GT. This is the car for your collection.

This rare road-going GT1 sold at the Bonhams Europe Monte Carlo auction on May 26, 2003, for $755,790, including buyer's premium.

It has been said that pretty is fast, and with the GT1, I doubt many would argue. The car—from any angle and at any speed—is the perfect picture of what a modern sports prototype should look like. I suppose someone, someday will design a better-looking car, but I surely can't imagine it today.

As the first of the historic GT1 cars to sell at auction, its market value was difficult to predict. However, we can compare this to the conceptually similar Mercedes Le Mans cars. A road version of the non-race-winning Mercedes CLK sold for over $950,000 at the same auction. By comparison, and given its tremendous corporate and race heritage, the Porsche seems like a bargain.

On the other hand, there are cheaper supercars to be had. The Ferrari F40 is around $300,000, which seems downright cheap. Or if you really want to go slumming, how about a Jaguar XJ 220? They're positively giving them away at $125,000, but you'll have to put up with their wimpy six-cylinder engines. And, of course, neither has Le Mans-winning heritage, nor are they as limited-production as the GT1.

This will always be a thin market. After all, few have the resources to buy a car like this, and even fewer have the skill to drive them properly. Will the next GT1 sell at this price? Probably, as there will likely never be more than one or two for sale at a time, and scarcity keeps prices strong. We do know this for sure: The GT1 is the most expensive road-going Porsche ever sold, new or used. Yes, the seller has suffered depreciation from his original purchase price, to the tune of $150k or so, but we can only assume that anyone who buys a million-dollar car isn't worried about trifles like a 15% loss of value.

For the Porsche fanatic of means, this was a terrific buy. Wherever he shows up, he'll be the class of the field, the envy of everyone else at the event. And chances are that as the years go by, this car will become more collectible, rather than less.—Jim Schrager

(Historic and descriptive information courtesy of Bonhams.)

From the September 2003 issue of SCM.◆

Years produced	1996-1998
Number produced	20
Original list price	$912,000
Tune-up/major service	$5,000 at factory
Distributor cap	Included in above
Chassis #	On horizontal bulkhead in front compartment
Engine #	On right side of block, forward edge
Club	Porsche Club of America, P.O. Box 5900, Springfield, VA 22150
Web site	www.pca.org
Alternatives	Ferrari F40, Jaguar XJ 220, McLaren F1 R, Mercedes CLK
Tier of Collectibility	A

A 914 With Six Appeal

Dear Mr. Schrager: *Why all the fuss about 914-6s? I know they were produced in limited quantities, which should lead to increasing values over the years. Are they great cars to drive? I assume they have a special engine that really makes the car fly. Is it a car I should consider as a first Porsche.*—**P.A., San Diego, CA**

The 914-6 is not the best choice for a first Porsche.

I do not recommend the 914-6 as a first Porsche. While Porsche tried to legitimize the 914 by inserting a genuine 911 engine, most buyers wanted the real thing (a 911) and balked at the high price of the 914-6 (less than $1,000 cheaper than the 911T, which had a bigger engine). In the end, the low volume created a car that needed further development in both the engine and suspension areas but never got it.

For the last few decades, the 914-6 has been touted as the next great collectible Porsche. Since it hasn't happened yet, it's safe to say it probably won't ever. 914-6s reached into the teens 15 years ago and haven't moved much since then. The reasons for this lack of appreciation have less to do with the humble beginnings of the 914-6 than the realities of the way they drive.

The 914-6 has the lowest-horsepower 911 engine ever produced, the 1969 2.0-liter carbureted 911T with 110 hp (measured under the German DIN horsepower rating system). Even the original 1965 production engine managed 130 hp, and of course the later E and S models up to 190. Part of the problem was that the 1969 911T engine had a number of cost-reduction items such as the first non-forged crankshaft and cast-iron cylinders.

The original 914-4 posted widely varying 0 to 60 times—11.3, 12.7, 13.0, 13.9—for an average of approximately 12.7 seconds. The 914-6 was appreciably faster with a 9.3 average. However, the 914-4 2.0 of 1973 did the 0-to-60 dash in about 9.7 seconds, almost the same as the 914-6. Although a bit lighter than the similar-year 911, the 914-6 simply doesn't have the sparkling acceleration most expect.

To go faster, you can easily switch the motor to any number of 2.2, 2.4, 2.7 or even 3.0 911 motors. As you cruise the classifieds, you'll see plenty of these for sale. In fact, a small cottage industry has developed producing the requisite parts to fit a 911 motor in a 914-4. But once you lose the originality of the car, you have little chance for investment value. You can also rebuild

"Value in the Porsche world is more than just rarity. Unlike the 356 Carrera, 911 RS and 930 Turbo, the 914-6 never was anyone's idea of an ultimate car."

the stock 914-6 engine into something more powerful, but count on $6,000-$7,000 for a thorough job.

Another issue with any 914 is interior room. Most people make frequent use of the area behind the seats in the 911. In the 914, you have a spacious front cabin, but only the twin trunks for other luggage. And you'll have to leave the kids at home.

The mid-engined 914 is a car well known for its superb handling in racing situations. But on the street, even reports in the rarely critical Porsche Club publication *Panorama* complained that the 914 ride was harsh and jarring in comparison to the 911.

The small production volume, 3,351 cars, means there shouldn't be many 914-6 cars around. Yet there are always a handful for sale. Also, value in the Porsche world is more than just rarity. Unlike the 356 Carrera, 911 RS and 930 Turbo, the 914-6 never was anyone's idea of an ultimate car.

For today's 914 buyers, the 914-4 2.0 gives about the same performance at about half the cost. In addition, the 914-4 is easier to maintain and easier to sell when you are ready to move up. While $15,000 buys a nice original 914-6, half that buys an excellent 914-4 2.0.

As an alternative, if you have your heart set on the throaty wail of the legendary six-cylinder boxer, for $15,000 you can buy a very nice early 911. In addition to increased interior room, a more refined suspension and better acceleration, the 911 should be a better investment, as well.—*Jim Schrager*

From the August 2000 issue of *SCM.*◆

$100,000 for a 914?

Dear Mr. Schrager: *I have stumbled across something I am told is a 914-6 GT. In Europe, you can't get any money for the regular 914-4s. They were marketed as VW-Porsches and are cheap as dirt. This 914-6 GT has a price tag of $100,000, though, and perhaps some racing history as well. I am shocked to hear that these old Karmann Ghia imitators can be worth even one-tenth that price tag. Can you tell me how many were made? How can I tell if this is a real one? What are they worth?—**C.G., London, England**

914-6 GT: Wilder, lighter and faster than an ordinary 914.

The 914-6 GT is a real Porsche, and worth serious money, within the range of the asking price if you are sure it is a real car. Unfortunately it is hard to know how many 914-6 GTs were produced, as the factory considered the "GT package" a series of options rather than a different model. Someone would have to sit down with the original build sheets and keep a tally of option sheets to get a production total. To date, no one has. The *SCM* Price Guide lists 11, which is our best educated guess.

The GT was built as a privateer race car, using the homologated 914-6 as a base and staying within the allowable modifications, which included structural braces, wider fenders and wider wheels but not enlarged engine displacement. The most famous of these was the French-sponsored "Sunauto" car. As a single car team, it performed admirably at Le Mans in 1970, scoring a win in its 2-liter class.

There are a number of clues you can look for that will help you determine if the car you are being offered is a real GT. It won't necessarily have each of the options listed below, but it should have close to all of them.

Most visually apparent is a pair of large fender flares, made of steel and hand-welded into place, with 6-inch and 7-inch Fuchs alloy wheels fitted beneath them.

Lightweight items include a series of fiberglass and plastic parts, including a fiberglass hood, trunk and doors, and plexiglass side and rear windows. The interior was stripped of all excess weight, including door handles, door pockets and various bits of non-essential trim. The standard seats were replaced with lightweight racing versions.

A stiffer chassis was created via a series of six stiffeners, three welded into place on each side, and a special frame just inside the top that connects the rear window body section with the windshield header. Further chassis modifications included Koni or Bilstein HD shocks and struts and large anti-sway bars in the front and rear. 914-6 GTs also had a factory-installed roll bar.

Homologation rules required the displacement to not exceed 2.0 liters, so contrary to many rumors, the cars did not have S- or RS- type engines. It instead had something far more exotic: a six-cylinder 906-spec, Weber-carbureted, 210-horsepower screamer. The engine block code is 911/20. With the exception of the titanium connecting rods, this engine had most of the 906 modifications, including dual ignition. An additional oil cooler was mounted in the front bumper.

Increased fuel capacity was provided by a large competition fuel cell in the forward compartment.

Aside from the engine, the list of modifications is relatively straightforward. There are a wide variety of fiberglass and steel replica parts available so that the home builder can produce his or her very own 914-6 GT. Consequently, the 914-6 GT is widely imitated—think Pontiac Le Mans converted to GTO specs by adding a few badges and decals.

The only sure way to verify a 914-6 GT is to inspect factory build sheets. If they are not available, the next reference point will be the engine-type number on the crankcase. Be wary of any signs that the engine designation, 911/20, appears to have been tampered with or fraudulently stamped on the case.

Given the $100,000 asking price, the seller must be convinced that he has a true, factory-built 914-6 GT. These cars have a significant following, for despite their humble 914 beginnings, the GT is a genuine factory-built race car, with some significant racing achievements.

As with any race car, pricing is done on a one-off basis, with variances in history and provenance being far more important than condition. Especially in this situation, engaging experts to help you analyze the car is critical. It's not really a question of how good a 914-6 GT this one happens to be—the primary question is "Is it a *real* 914-6 GT?" Do your homework. After all, how would you feel if you spent $100k for what turned out to be a 914 with a spoiler kit and a hopped-up 911 engine?
—*Jim Schrager*

From the July 2000 issue of *SCM*.◆

Selling My 914-6

Dear Mr. Schrager: *I noticed in the PCA magazine* Panorama *that you had a 914-6 for sale for $8,500. This seems cheap to me. Was it a real one or a conversion? What kind of shape was it in, and was it hard to find a buyer? Why did you sell this car? Are prices going to tank on these?*—**K.L.G., St. Louis, MO**

With a flat-six engine, it's the ultimate 914.

I had mixed feelings about selling our 914-6, which was Irish Green (non-metallic dark green) with a tan vinyl interior. It was correct and complete, with all its original pieces and parts. We pulled it out of a barn in Wisconsin, where it had resided immobile for many years. I sold it when I realized I didn't have the commitment needed to make it right.

The seller could not get the car to run, so we bought this one as a real unknown. Since the starter barely turned the engine over, we worried about collapsed chain tensioners, with valves hitting pistons.

We started our intervention by pulling all the spark plugs. They were drenched in oil—not old, black, smelly stuff, but new, clean fluid. Figuring we were in for big trouble, I didn't put in new plugs but just cleaned the old ones with a towel. Before reinstalling them, I decided to spin the starter. This would give me a clue as to whether the engine was okay, or if we had something truly horrible.

Boy, did it spin. And out came oil, spritzing all over the inside of the engine compartment. The previous owner had seriously overfilled the engine with oil. When I stuck the plugs back in, the car started right up, and actually ran quite well.

I was thrilled, but there was so much more to do. The brakes were shot from sitting, so we had everything rebuilt. The heat exchangers had large holes, and the engine had to be pulled to install new tensioners and a bunch of new seals.

The car was very complete, right down to the goofy passenger footrest, but everything was tired. The entire interior needed replacement, not from wear but from neglect. The body had a horrible old lacquer repaint, and rust had invaded the bottom of the passenger side and a few spots on the driver's side as well. Naturally the battery box was rusty, but luckily the frame members under it were not.

A long time ago I realized a sound piece of wisdom: You are thousands of dollars ahead when you buy an unrusty car. This is usually true even if you get the rusty car for free. In surveying the costs of making this a decent car, I decided it was beyond the time and energy I had available. If it had been my only

"A long time ago I realized a sound piece of wisdom: You are thousands of dollars ahead when you buy an unrusty car. This is usually true even if you get the rusty car for free."

Porsche, it would have been great fun. But we just have too many other projects. If I wanted a 914-6, I should simply find a better one, I reasoned.

I was surprised by the response to my ad in *Pano*. I got calls immediately, and one of the first callers asked me to hold the car while he drove from Colorado to Indiana to pick it up. I told him I would, but later that same day another fellow called from close by and wanted to visit the car right away. I told him I couldn't show it until after the first guy visited. In the meantime, several other folks indicated interest in the car and wanted pictures. I disclosed to everyone what I had written in the *Pano* ad itself, that the car needed rust repairs. The guy from Colorado was the first to look at the Porsche and drove it home on his trailer, paying the full asking price.

Do I think these prices are going to tank? Not at all. In fact, what I learned from this episode was that there is a lively market for 914-6 cars. It's made up not by 356/911 enthusiasts like me, but by people who owned 914-4s long ago and who are now interested in the most upscale 914, the 914-6. Although this crowd can't bid the cars up endlessly, they do keep the market active.

Did I sell my car too cheap? I figured it would take $10,000 or so to put the car in excellent shape, so I thought my $8,500 asking price was right on. From the response to my ad, it seems the market judged my car as a decent bargain. That's okay with me because when it is time to move on, I've always said that a fair price is the best way to make it happen.—*Jim Schrager*

From the August 2001 issue of *SCM*.◆

924s Cheap for a Reason

Dear Mr. Schrager: *I like to buy out-of-favor cars and enjoy them while the market catches up to me. Which of the following three cars would be the best for this strategy: 1977 924, white/black, 32,000 miles, near mint condition, $4,500; 1981 928, silver/black, 88,000 miles, needs a new automatic transmission, otherwise decent condition, $4,200; 1985 944, metallic gray/black, 76,000 miles, runs well, $6,500. All of these cars have been sitting on our local market for a while. Given that I am on a tight budget, which is the best buy?—A.B., Tulsa, OK*

None of the above. I like your strategy, but this plan requires that the car you purchase has a good chance to be in demand someday.

These are three Porsches the collector market has forgotten. My bet is this will not change. Understanding why will help you pick a car worth holding onto.

The 924 you are considering represents the initial model year and has the important extra of having low mileage and being in mint condition. However, there is simply no collector interest in street 924s. Although designed by Porsche, these were built by Audi and intended to be entry-level Audi sport coupes. Most 924s are underpowered and uninspiring. This car is viewed as an aberration in the long tradition of highly engineered, fun cars from Porsche. If you like this car after you drive it, there is no reason why you shouldn't enjoy owning it. But appreciation on a 924 is at best, a very long shot. If you simply get your money back when you go to sell it, you should consider yourself lucky.

The 928 is a true high-performance car, conceived by the president of Porsche, Dr. Ernst Fuhrman, to be the successor to the 911. Unlike the 924, this is a fast, powerful car with a unique and pleasant body design and exotic chassis engineering. Yet, in spite of these objective endowments, the 928 has almost no collectible value. Most traditional Porsche enthusiasts simply didn't warm up to a front-engined, water-cooled car. They still don't—notice that the Boxster is mid-engined and follows the visual theme of the early 550s. The 928 didn't follow the outline of anything from Porsche history.

928s are unlikely to ever be in the collector car flavor-of-the-month club. Because of the high cost of repair, I suggest you buy the best 928 you can, not a beater. Budget about $15,000

924s and 944s should be bought for fun, not for profit.

for a very nice 928, with all books and records up to date. Then keep your fingers crossed that the collector market adds the 928 to the approved list of desirable exotics.

Porsche got the 924 concept right with the 944, especially the post-1986 models. However, this success meant high volume, which makes the 944's day as a collectible hard to imagine. Acceptable as an entry-level Porsche for those new to the marque, they won't be sought after as examples of what the Porsche experience is all about. The 944 will probably be the most fun of the three cars you list here, but you still won't get to park in the front row at the local PCA club meeting, and your car will never appreciate in value.

What do I suggest for your budget area? For an older Porsche starting to creep up in value, I'd suggest a 914 2.0. Plan to pay about $6,000-$7,000 for a good example. If that doesn't turn you on, then you'll need to spend closer to $10,000 for a running, driving, entry-level early (pre-1973) 911. Both are regarded as "real" Porsches (the 911 far more so than the 914), will make that raspy air-cooled sound so unique to the marque and will provide a real introduction to the driving experience that makes Porsches so special.

The 924/944/928s are simply orphans in the collector car world. They may have been competent performers, but they didn't offer the kind of magic that causes Porsche owners to be so committed to their marque. Buy one of these front-engined cars for fun, but never for profit.—*Jim Schrager*

From the December 2000 issue of *SCM.*◆

"So, when you go to sell it, if you simply get your money back, you should consider yourself lucky."

Cornering the 968 Market

Dear Mr. Schrager: *I was taken aback by your "Cheap For A Reason" column (December 2000 SCM, page 65) about the lack of collectibility of the 924, 944 and 928. I have owned approximately 10 Porsches, including the rear-engine cars, such as a 911 Targa. However, I have fallen in love with a 1990 944 S2 cabriolet. I feel the key is the convertible factor. I also have a 968 cabriolet. Both cars are ultra clean, with extremely low mileage.*

Do you believe these convertibles will become collectible? At what age does the depreciation curve turn around, assuming it is an exceptional automobile? Also, what is the survival rate of any given car?

I would really appreciate hearing from you, as I am hoping to buy six to 12 of the 944 S2 cabriolets—assuming I can find them with low mileage and in ultra-clean condition—and put them away as future investments.—J.E., Versailles, OH

The 968: Unloved, now and forever.

These are fast and strong cars, but they were built in relatively large volumes and are part of the unloved 924/944/968 series. They will never be a first-tier collectible, like a 911 or a 356. Generally a car has to be highly desired when new, raced successfully and/or built in very low volumes before prices really soar. Cars with the highest appreciation potential have two or three of the above factors. Yours has none.

Further, for a mass-produced car like a '65 Mustang or a Ferrari 308 to be collectible, it has to be a car people lusted after, dreamed about, read about, stared at when they drove by and talked about with friends as something they would die to own. I don't recall seeing many posters featuring a scantily clad model in a 944 convertible.

As I've said before, the 944s and 968s are decent cars. As the final iteration of the 944, the 944 S2 (1990-91) and the 968 (1992-95) were equipped with sophisticated four-cylinder 3.0-liter engines, including a 928-derived 16-valve head. The 944 S2, with 211 horsepower, went from 0 to 60 in a respectable 6.9 seconds. The heavier cab was a few ticks slower at 7.1. The 968 benefited from a host of development work, including variable cam timing, higher compression ratio, lightened and forged rods and pistons and a fully integrated Bosch Motronic engine management system.

To give the cabriolet a unique look, the windshield was raked back and its top edge was lowered by 2.4 inches. The top and cut-down side windows were gracefully styled by Porsche designer Harm Lagaay, best known for the Boxster.

With all these attributes, why are the 944 S2 and 968 still "unloved" Porsches? Simply put, no matter how good the 944 S2 and 968 may be, they are overshadowed by the 911. The 944 and 968 were always the junior models, the starter cars, the machines that were meant to be Audi sport coupes. The 911 was never anything but the finest sports car the wizards at Zuffenhausen could dream up, with cost not a concern. The 944 and 968 was a blend of cost-conscious approaches to motoring.

The looks of the 944/968, decisively bland to begin with, were diluted even further when the clearly derivatively styled Mazda RX-7 led to a flood of similar-appearing cars on the road. "Is it a Mazda or a Porsche?" isn't the kind of question that leads to collectibility.

Furthermore, these are not rare cars. There were approximately 6,000 944 S2 cabs and 4,400 968 cabs built—large numbers by collector standards. Compare these numbers to the production numbers for the most valuable street Porsche models: 1973 Carrera 911 RS Touring—1,510; 1962 356B Twin Grille roadster—250; 1989 911 Carrera Speedster—2,065.

Due to advances in rust-prevention, the scrap rate for any post-1990 Porsche should be very low, influenced mainly by accidents and theft. So, unfortunately for future value, there will always be an abundance of 944s and 968s.

Your strategy of buying only mint and low-mileage cars doesn't matter if the car won't be collectible. For example, a mint-condition Studebaker Lark convertible is only worth a few thousand dollars more than an average one. Personally, I happen to enjoy the old Lark drop-tops, but my opinion doesn't matter. The market doesn't care a whit about the '60s compact car built in my hometown of South Bend, Indiana. That means I can have my dream car for next to nothing. It also means that when I go to sell it, I should consider myself lucky if I get my money back.

So what is the collectible future of the 944 S2 and 968 cabriolets? My guess is that they will depreciate gently until they hit a value that makes them performance and style bargains, say $10,000 to $15,000. At that price they will find a following and the price will stop dropping for nice cars. Abused cars will be worth practically nothing. I don't think their prices will ascend from there, no matter how many years pass. If you choose to bet on these cars, realize that the odds will be against you. Besides, do you really want to be known as "the guy who cornered the 968 market"?—*Jim Schrager*

From the March 2001 issue of *SCM.*◆

More Porsches Cross the Block

"The auction reports below are a collection of Porsche analyses over the last few years. They appear in the market Reports column within every issue of Sports Car Market Magazine. Each contain a photo, a descrption of the car up for sale, followed by straight to-the-point comments by one of our experts. The combination of these three facets is quintessential SCM, making our coverage both entertaining and informative. Now, enjoy these snapshots of Porsches examined by SCM experts."

— *Keith Martin,*

Mid-Engines

#20-1970 PORSCHE 914-4 Two-door. S/N 4702910254. Black/black vinyl. LHD. Odo: 8,881 miles. 5-speed. Chrome steel wheels. Original owner Wally Cleaver of "Leave it to Beaver." Cheap seat covers. Cheap paint job falling apart. Small dent to hood and driver's door latch. Trunk lid hinges loose. Rust bubbling on passenger's front fender. A beater. Cond: 4+. **SOLD AT $2,935.** *We would guess that "celebrity ownership" added exactly $935 to the value of this poor old thing. Best bet—take the "HI HUNEY" license plates and hang them on the wall, and give the car to a local charity.* **Christie's, Los Angeles, CA, 6/00.**

#405-1972 PORSCHE 914 "CHALON." Body by Mitcom. S/N 4722918590. Red/black and red cloth. LHD. Odo: 11,878 miles. Conversion job to Mitcom kit car specs has professional quality. Good paint on the exterior, but trim, trunk and door jambs show signs of major reworking. Someone spent a lot of time and money putting this one together. I just don't understand why. Cond: 3-. **SOLD AT $5,565.** *By my math, this Porsche comes out to a 919.25 (take the sum of the model numbers of the cars that the parts come from, divide by number of cars— your math may differ). Anyhow, now you have a car that looks like a Miata hit by an MR2.* **eBay/Kruse, Auburn, IN, 5/02.**

#35-1972 PORSCHE 914. S/N 4722912758. Lime green/tan vinyl. Odo: 35,855 miles. Original paint, slight crazing around wheel wells. Nice interior. Top in good shape. Minor ding in nose. Dent on driver's door and over the right rear wheel well. Cond: 2. **SOLD AT $6,136.** *914s continue to creep up in value—the result here is a surprise, given that this wasn't a perfect car by any means. Soon we'll see 912s and 914s selling for more than '74-'77 911s. Go figure.* **Silver, Portland, OR, 3/01.**

#255-1975 PORSCHE 914 Two-door. S/N 47529100678. Red/black vinyl. Odo: 49,520 miles. Recent paint over hail damage, or the worst case of fisheye yet seen. AM/FM cassette. Gaps as wide as the Missouri in places. Surprisingly clean interior. A beater with a fresh trowel full of makeup. Cond: 4. **SOLD AT $4,240.** *Someone spent some money fixing up this one, with less-than-sterling results. If your automotive desires run to cheap, red, with a clean interior and no chance for any real appreciation, this is your Porsche.* **The Auction, Las Vegas, NV, 4/01.**

#418-1970 PORSCHE 914. S/N 4702901140. Yellow/black vinyl. LHD. Odo: 114,042 miles. Michelin XZX tires on very ugly mags. Decent repaint. Interior well kept. Shows signs of some care of ownership—rare indeed on a 914 at auction. Clean in both trunks and under hood. The car card for this Porsche read "911 Targa." Cond: 3. **SOLD AT $7,560.** *It's time to stop dogging on these dogs. For the cheap money represented, I'll bet the new owner has more fun, spends less on repairs and has a better return on investment than with an MGB. We're waiting for your letters and e-mails now, MGB owners.* **The Auction, Las Vegas, NV, 4/02.**

#165-1970 PORSCHE 914-6 Roadster. S/N 9140431857. Black/black. Odo: 79,996 miles Claimed to be one-family owned from new. One of 3,360 six-cylinder roadsters built. Fuchs alloys. Shiny enough in sunshine, but really very poor paint. Top particularly scruffy. Old, dull interior. In need of total makeover. Cond: 3-. **SOLD AT $9,936.** *A tad low for a straight, original 914-6. Will be hard to restore without getting buried. Economics dictate another Porsche unless you simply must have one of these because they are unusual.* **Barrett-Jackson, Scottsdale, AZ, 1/01.**

Front Engine

#184-1984 PORSCHE 928S Coupe. S/N WPOJB0920ES8621. Bronze/tan leather. LHD. Odo: 111,709 miles.

Automatic. Sheepskins hide split and cracking leather. Fresh repaint hides wavy body. Battery, brakes, radiator, timing belt, turn signal assembly, steering U-joint, alternator, catalytic converter and A/C compressor all replaced within the past 6,000 miles. Cond: 4+. **SOLD AT $6,678.** *And in the next 6,000 miles? I think we are all ready to graduate to the 200-level course in non-ownership of cheap 928s. The former owner bailed when he saw how much damage these cars can inflict on a checkbook. We're way too smart for that now, aren't we?* **eBay/Kruse, Scottsdale, AZ, 1/02.**

#184-1987 PORSCHE 928 S4 Coupe. S/N WPOJBO928HS5861. Guards Red/tan leather. LHD. Odo: 96,438 miles. Sunroof. Hokey boy-racer rear wing. Vinyl nose and mirror bras (just like Madonna). Stick-on dash pad cover (also just like Madonna). Tired and well-used interior (let's not go there). At least the respray was well done. Cond: 3-. **SOLD AT $8,580.** *Initially a no-sale on Friday at $13,000, the dealer offering it bought too many other cars and decided to cut it loose. New owner bought it on Sunday, then tried to turn it again on Monday, but didn't let it go despite a bid of $9,100.* **Silver, Scottsdale, AZ, 1/02.**

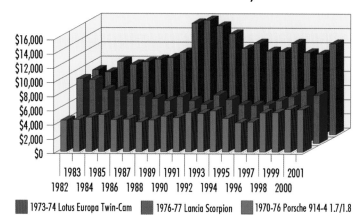

The Twenty Year Picture
MID-ENGINED MOVERS
1973-74 Lotus Europa Twin-Cam, 1976-77 Lancia Scorpion, 1970-76 Porsche 914-4 1.7/1.8

Legend:
- 1973-74 Lotus Europa Twin-Cam
- 1976-77 Lancia Scorpion
- 1970-76 Porsche 914-4 1.7/1.8

(Prices for additional cars in excellent condition. Additional data compiled from SCM archives.) This value guide is provided courtesy of Cars of Particular Interest. CPI is the pocket guide most often used by credit unions and banks when dealing with loan values of collectible domestic and imported cars; www.BlackBookUSA.com. From the February 2002 issue of *SCM* ◆

#215-1987 PORSCHE 928 S4 Coupe. S/N WPOJB0926HS8616. Red/tan leather. LHD. Odo: 37,065 miles. Very complete and original. Some wear to driver's seat bolster, but interior is otherwise clean. Built-in phone, sunroof. No paint flaws visible. Very weak tires are no help. All books, papers and Carfax. Cond: 3+. **SOLD AT $23,625.** *This may have been well above market, but if someone was simply buying a brilliant high-performance car, then it really wasn't very much, was it? And $23k won't get you this kind of scoot in any other Porsche in decent condition.* **CC Int., Branson, MO, 4/02.**

#382-1977 PORSCHE 924 MARTINI EDITION Coupe. S/N 9247104764. White with Martini sidewinders/black. RHD. Many touched-in rust bubbles along roof gutters. Very dry and crumbly windshield rubber. Torn and worn driver's seat fabric. Cond: 3-. **SOLD AT $2,221.** *Worth no more, that's for sure. If SCM ever publishes an "Unloved Cars of the Decade" album, the 924 might make a nice frontispiece.* **Bonhams & Brooks, London, UK, 2/01.**

#1-1987 PORSCHE 924S Two-door Coupe. S/N WP0AA0924HN4553. White/brown vinyl and cloth. Odo: 72,247 miles. Two-owner car. A/C, power steering, brakes and windows. Fog lights. Minor paint flaws, interior wear indicative of miles. A worn but not worn-out car. Cond: 4+. **SOLD AT $3,190.** *Cheap, even by 924S standards. The perfect starter Porsche for Hamptons kids. They can practice saying lines like, "Damn, I left my cell phone in the Porsche" at age 16.* **Kensington, Hamptons, NY, 5/01.**

#133-1985 PORSCHE 928 Coupe. S/N WP0JB092OFS8601. Red/black leather. Odo: 84,218 miles. Automatic. Wheels badly tarnished. Decent older respray. Front edge of passenger door all chewed up. Good interior. A driver. Cond: 3-. **SOLD AT $7,035.** *A 15-year-old 928 without any maintenance paperwork is a very scary car. While these are grand vehicles for high-speed touring, the costs of restoring them (or even maintaining them) make the purchase price almost irrelevant.* **McCormick, Palm Springs, CA, 2/00.**

#33-1986 PORSCHE 944 TURBO Coupe. S/N WPOAA0953GN1562. Black/cream, black vinyl. Odo: 134,615 miles. 5-speed. Polished alloys. Sunroof,

air conditioning. Momo steering wheel. Brakes upgraded to larger rotors and calipers. Recent minimalist repaint job. Lots of small interior bits were not original. Not much turbo hum. Overall, rode hard and put away wet. Cond: 4. **SOLD AT $3,952.** *Will be a good autocross car until the turbo lets go. Then will make a good kid's play structure.* **Silver, Scottsdale, AZ, 1/01.**

#284-1986 PORSCHE 928S Coupe. S/N WP0JB09296S8626. Black/black leather. LHD. Odo: 50,275 miles. Sunroof, Blaupunkt AM/FM cassette. Leather shows early signs of drying out, but still mostly supple. Total repaint is of good quality, but has some orange peel. Shows signs of continuous maintenance. Discolored mags. Michelin Pilot Sport radials. Cond: 3. **SOLD AT $12,985.** *"Well maintained" is the key here. If the owner gets away with no maintenance costs for the next year, this 928S might be the only one in the world that's a good buy. Better put a rabbit's-foot key chain and some four-leaf covers in the console just in case.* **eBay/Kruse, Ft. Lauderdale, FL, 1/02.**

#708-1979 PORSCHE 928 Coupe. S/N 9289200268. White/brown leather. LHD. Odo: 109,235 miles. Chevy 350 V8, 10-disc CD changer. Power steering and brakes. Air conditioning. A respray with plenty of overspray. Paint and leather good, with a few cracks. Dash cracking. Parts of bumper welting held in place with Scotch tape. Rear tires bald in center. Cond: 4-. **SOLD AT $9,010.** *Just about any market comment here will honk someone off, so let's give you a choice: 1. Best thing to ever happen to a 928. 2. Blasphemy! 3. 928? Porsche never made a 928. 4. A custom Chevy? Cool. 5. Great car! Great price! 6. Who cares, anyway?* **eBay/Kruse, Auburn, IN, 5/02.**

#3-1986 PORSCHE 928 FACTORY CUSTOM 4-DOOR Sedan. S/N WPOJB0921HS860136. Burgundy/burgundy leather. LHD. Odo: 6,175 miles. Automatic. Good paint, but with lots of respray work evident. Blackout trim has previous paintwork showing through. Good fit and finish to custom work. No door problems evident. Good interior has more of an American-car feel than a German one. Cond: 4+. **SOLD AT $44,000.** *The answer to a question no one dared to ask: What would a four-door 928 look like and who would want one? Unfortunately, the answer is it looks like a Porsche swallowed a Pacer. Your chance to own a four-door Porsche before the Cayenne becomes available.* **RM Auctions, Monterey, CA, 8/02.**

Race Cars

#233-1957 PORSCHE 550A Race Roadster. Body by Wendler. S/N 550-0118. Silver metallic, red flashes/black. Odo: 14,052 miles. First campaigned in SCCA events by George Barber Jr. of Alabama, and later owned in Georgia, Texas, Louisiana, Florida and Ohio before acquisition by European vendor. Removable fairing, huge woodrim wheel, headlamp stone grilles. Older repaint, some chips. Cond: 2. **SOLD AT $433,595.** *On-button and eligible for all top retro events, this customer race car was very keenly contested by four bidders, three of them by telephone. Winner had to pay mid-estimate money, establishing a new price for 550A.* **Bonhams & Brooks, Monte Carlo, Monaco, 5/01.**

#434-1964 PORSCHE 904 CARRERA GTS Coupe. S/N 904-092. Black/black. LHD. Four-cylinder, 5-speed. Complete mechanical checkup and refurbishment after many years in the Porsche Museum of Japan. One of 110 produced. Street car, no known racing history. Has carpet, mufflers, defroster. Said to be road ready, but who knows after all those years of sitting? Cond: 2. **SOLD AT $264,000.** *904s are intensely popular in high-speed European touring events like the Tour Auto. They are comfortable enough on the road, have looks to die for and are reasonably reliable so long as you don't bury the tach frequently. This was a bargain.* **RM Auctions, Monterey, CA, 8/00.**

#138-1966 PORSCHE 906 Race Car. S/N 906-122. Red/black. LHD. 5-speed manual. Ex-Scuderia Centro-Sud. Parma-Poggio winner. Complete restoration in '97 in Germany. All matching numbers. Monterey Historics winner in '98. In superb condition, surely better than it ever was when raced. Cond: 2-. **SOLD AT $253,000.** *906s are among the few sports racers that can actually be driven by someone besides Brian Redman and Hurley Haywood. The value of 906s has been climbing—another $50k wouldn't have surprised.* **RM Auctions, Monterey, CA, 8/00.**

#439-1966 PORSCHE 906 Race Car. S/N 906-145. White, red/black. LHD. 5-speed manual. From the Matsuda Porsche Museum collection in the '90s. Sold as a privateer car when new. Early race history in Japan unsubstantiated. Returned to US in '99. Showed signs of sitting. Will likely need complete mechanical refurbishment. Cond: 2-. **SOLD AT $297,000.** *Certainly faster than the 904, but more difficult to maintain, as well. Given the needs this car may have, its price, at $50,000 below low estimate, was understandable.* **RM Auctions, Monterey, CA, 8/00.**

#109-1966 PORSCHE CARRERA 6/906 Race Car. S/N 906-145. White/black. LHD. Fresh engine rebuild. Left door a bit hard to close, but overall panel fit is acceptable for a race car. Two large paint chips on right front fender. Nose is chipped and has minor cracks. Decent interior. Eight-inch crack in front windshield. Cond: 3. **NOT SOLD AT $280,000.** *A 20-year-old museum piece with no major racing history. Bid just under the low side of the SCM Price Guide. Very desirable cars, and usable in many European touring events, but estimate of $330k to $370k was just too high.* **RM Auctions, Amelia Island, FL, 3/02.**

#231-1973 PORSCHE RSR 2.8 CARRERA Coupe. S/N 911 360 0782. Eng. #693 0116. White/black cloth. LHD. Odo: 127 miles. Race-ready car that's excellent in all areas. Had been part of Matsuda Collection in Japan. Unmodified from new and now fit for more competition work. Excellent door and panel fit. Close to zero miles since new. Cond: 2. **SOLD AT $171,600.** *Very strong money, but where else can you buy a virtually new RSR 2.8 Carrera?* **RM Auctions, Amelia Island, FL, 3/00.**

#227-1961 PORSCHE 550A BECK Spyder. S/N 116582. Silver/blue. LHD. Odo: 17,543 miles. Porsche 356 pushrod engine, correct gauges. Good panel fit, paint. Supertrapp muffler. Old-style black-and-yellow California plate (expired September 1998). Nardi wood wheel taped. Minor chip on front of hood. A good-looking driver. No reserve. Cond: 2-. **SOLD AT $25,920.** *A well-built Beck, and a cheap way to have a lot of fun—but still a fake.* **Barrett-Jackson, Los Angeles, CA, 6/02.**

#103-1971 PORSCHE 917/10 CAN-AM Race Car. S/N 917 10 002. Eng. #181. Orange/black. Ex-Jo Siffert and Willi Kauhsen. Flat-12-cylinder, air-cooled 5-liter, 660-bhp engine, 5-speed Porsche transaxle, 4-wheel discs, single seater. Cond: 2-. **SOLD AT $666,000.** *The numbers 917 are magic to Porsche race fans. Great history with appearances at Mid-Ohio, Road America, Donnybrook, Laguna Seca and more with Siffert and Hockenheim, Nürburgring and Silverstone with Kauhsen in '71 and '72. Well bought.* **Christie's, Pebble Beach, CA, 8/00.**

#450-1970 PORSCHE 917K Race Car. S/N 917-022. Light blue, orange stripe/orange. Ex-Steve McQueen. Porsche had starring role in "Le Mans." Footage of "Le Mans" was played before the car was driven on the stage and the owner introduced the car personally before bidding began. A great car, with superb history. Cond: 1+. **SOLD AT $1,320,000.** *With so many bizarre, cobbled-up 917s around (they're beginning to multiply like D-types), the lack of stories surrounding this car was refreshing. The right price.* **RM Auctions, Monterey, CA, 8/00.**

PART IV
Random Thoughts

Thank you for coming this far with us. We hope you've enjoyed your *SCM*-guided trip through the world of collecting Porsches. These last few pages are just a dessert, filled with some facts, thoughts and predictions that should offer some enlightenment and entertainment to your collecting.

You'll find legal advice and buying advice. For instance, will your insurance cover you when you take your Porsche onto the track and smack into the guardrail? On the value side, just how much will 930 Turbos be worth in the future, and are they good investments?

We take a quick look at some real goofball Porsches as well. My favorite, "what were they thinking when they built this", is a 911 fitted out with badly done 959-style bodywork and a Chevy V8 engine. And how about the chopped-top 914, complete with a custom convertible top and frame?

But even these strange Porsches teach us something when they come up for auction, and we see how the market reacts to them. The same can be said for the Boxsters, 944s and 911SCs that we take a look at in this chapter.

There are several articles that make value predictions for the future. As some of them were made a few years ago, you can hold *SCM's* feet to the Price Guide fire by comparing them to the values we have in the up-to-date Price Guide included in this book.

Porsches are wonderful cars, with a tremendous and hard-earned heritage. We have appreciated this opportunity to share our thoughts about them with you.—*Keith Martin*

On Track, No Coverage

If you think your collector car is covered when you drive it on the race track, you'd better think again. When we last visited this issue (June 1999), we had no clear courtroom decision to use as a precedent.

This is no longer the case. Judge J. Borenstein has recently handed down a decision on this very issue from his bench at the Middlesex Superior Court in Massachusetts in deciding the case of Metropolitan Property and Casualty Insurance Company versus Stevens. This case is not binding authority for other courts and it will surely be appealed. Nevertheless, it is important to cover here because Borenstein's decision is the only clear statement by a court on the law that applies to determining insurance coverage for club "track events." Therefore, it will certainly be viewed as persuasive authority by other courts and, more importantly, by insurance companies facing this issue and deciding whether to pay claims arising out of these events.

Parking lot scrape or a track-day incident?

The facts of this case were much like the facts of the case I covered last year. Defendant Stevens was involved in two separate accidents on two separate occasions while driving his Porsche 911 at Bridgehampton Speedway in New York. His 911 was street legal but featured a racing seat, five-point harnesses and other performance and safety modifications. Both events were PCA (Porsche Club of America) "track events" which the club characterizes as "driving schools." No starting or finishing positions are tracked, instructors are provided (although they are not in all of the cars on the track at all times) and no lap times are recorded.

Defendant Stevens was paid for his first claim, which he reported as having occurred on a "private way." When Plaintiff Metropolitan was investigating his second claim, they discovered that both accidents had occurred at Bridgehampton Speedway. They sued Stevens, seeking to recover the money that was paid to him on the first claim and seeking a declaratory judgement stating that they did not have to pay the second claim under the "racing exclusion." The defendant counterclaimed, seeking a judgement stating that the insurance company should be forced to pay his claim because he was involved in a "driving school," not a "race speed contest." Metropolitan argued that the car was driven at racing speeds on a race track, and that the vehicle was modified for racing. Stevens claimed the modifications were for "safety and aesthetics" and that he was participating in a non-race oriented driving school where lap times and positions were not recorded.

Judge Borenstein took a very hard-line view of the case. He did not buy the argument that insurance coverage should apply because it was a driving school and not a race, nor that the vehicle's modifications were not for racing. He stated in his decision,

"The purpose of the racing exclusion in the policy was to protect insurance companies from situations where an automobile is not usually found and which present additional hazards and increased risk of loss for which the insurance

company did not contract...

In the instant case there is not a genuine issue of material fact with respect to the issue of whether the defendant was racing on the dates in question. It is clear to the court that the Defendant Stevens was engaged in 'racing' regardless of the terms he uses to describe the events.

The court finds as a matter of fact and concludes as a matter of law the following: Stevens spent a substantial amount of money to improve his vehicle for the purpose of racing, he was driving his vehicle on a known raceway, he was participating in driving 'events' sponsored by the Porsche Club of America, he was travelling at more than 70 mph during both accidents..."

Therefore, his accidents occurred while racing and indemnification is specifically excluded under the race speed exclusion. Thusly, Borenstein ruled against Stevens. He was so confident in his opinion, in fact, that he made this ruling on a Motion for Summary Judgement, not even allowing the case to be heard at trial.

Personally, I feel that the judge, clearly not a "car guy," did not fully understand the issues presented, and that he therefore could not properly distinguish between racing (not covered) and simply driving on a race track (arguably covered). Nevertheless, at least until an appeal is heard on this case, this is the only articulated case law on this issue, and it will be viewed as persuasive authority by courts and insurance companies alike. Therefore, the only safe course for the enthusiast right now, until an appeal is heard or conflicting case law is created, is to understand that the use of a vehicle on a race track in any "track event," including club "driving schools," will simply not be covered by a standard insurance policy.—*Alex Leventhal*

Mr. Leventhal is a car collector and attorney in New York. His comments here are general in nature, and are not a substitute for a consultation with an attorney.

From the February 2000 issue of *SCM.*◆

What If We Give You a New Boxster S?

Opinion surveys show car dealers, lawyers, politicians and stockbrokers lumped together in the "don't let your daughter marry one of those" category. Admittedly, some of our colleagues in these professions haven't always performed in the most stellar manner. For instance, I once represented a car dealer who sold a Ford Tempo for three times book value, financed at 18% interest, to a retarded dwarf who could not drive. Literally. This is not a joke.

And there was the dealer whose mechanics let a customer's car fall off a service lift and then told the customer, It must have come in like that. You get the idea.

In fact, however, most dealers are fair. In today's world, where customer satisfaction is so important, they really don't have much of a choice. This month's story is one with a happy ending, a situation where a dealer went above and beyond what might reasonably be expected in order to do right by a customer.

A friend called me to ask my opinion about a "make right" deal he was being offered by a Porsche dealer. He had purchased a new Porsche Boxster S from his local Porsche authorized dealer. After about 7,000 miles, the top was no longer functioning correctly, so he brought the vehicle in to the selling dealer to have it serviced under the factory warranty. The dealer did in fact fix the top during that visit, but not without scratching the roll hoops in the process. This did not thrill my friend, but when made aware of the problem, the dealer promised to buff out the scratches.

During the next visit, an unsuccessful attempt was made to buff the scratches out of the roll hoops. The scratches were lessened but not removed. Worse, this time some deep scratches were put into the front bumper. The dealer certainly appeared to have some personnel problems he needed to address, and my friend was becoming furious.

The dealer asked for one more chance to make the problem right. The car's owner was skeptical, but agreed. The dealer promised to respray the nose of the car to repair the scratched areas and to hit the roll hoops as well. The owner was concerned that the paintwork would detract from the resale value of the car, but the dealer guaranteed it would be undetectable.

Though hard to believe, this is what happened next. While the car was at the body shop to be repaired, a truck backed into it, taking out a large portion of the rear of the Porsche. At this point, the Boxster was damaged front, rear and center, and the owner was fed up. He called the dealer looking for a solution.

The owner of the dealership was mortified when he heard of the new damage. He wanted to make his customer happy, and he offered him a brand-new Boxster S for $12,000 plus the old, damaged Boxster in trade. No insurance claims, no waiting for repairs, a new car that day. My friend thought this sounded like a good deal but wanted to know what his rights were under the

Gradually demolished by the services department.

law, and whether the dealer was treating him fairly.

I told him I thought it sounded like a square deal. Legally, he was entitled to have the vehicle repaired to an as-new standard and to be compensated for the diminution in value the vehicle would suffer as a result of having been hit at all, courtesy of the dealer's insurance company (or his own company in the unlikely event that the dealer was uninsured or insolvent). That being said, convincing an insurance company or claims adjuster (or elderly judge who drives a Chrysler Cordoba) that Porschephiles are so picky that a car repaired to like-new condition still takes a hit in value is generally very difficult, and securing payment for the same is well nigh impossible without costly litigation.

In reality, without a lot of luck or legal expense, the best my friend could hope for was simply to have the repairs done well. Given his recent track record with the dealer, that didn't seem like a sure thing. In that light, the offer of a brand-new car, comparably equipped, for his car and $12,000 sounded great. The disgruntled Porsche owner would have a no-stories car that would fare much better at resale time than his repaired Boxster. And his old Boxster was sure to have depreciated $12,000 in the 7,000 miles he drove it, even had it never been hit. So, the deal was a winner as long as he had the money (which he did). To get anything more would be unlikely, even if the legal fees exceeded the $12,000 the owner had to sink into the deal. After all, he was not legally entitled to a brand-new car, only to his car being repaired properly, and to some payment for its loss in value. I told him to take the deal, which he did.

The dealership had made a very fair offer without first making feints or lowball offers. It didn't try to deny its responsibility for the damage. It should be commended for acting honorably to correct its admittedly grave errors. Now, if it can just get their service department to take care of the cars that come in instead of attacking its cosmetics with a proverbial sledgehammer, we'll have a situation where everyone is a winner.—*Alex Leventhal*

Mr. Leventhal is a car collector and attorney in New York. His comments here are general in nature, and are not a substitute for a consultation with an attorney.

From the August 2002 issue of *SCM.*◆

Spinning Into a DWI

A friend of mine purchased a Silver Rose Porsche 944 Turbo S in February. Quite happy with the car, he felt that for a purchase price of $10,000, it represented a lot of performance for the money.

Just one week after buying it, he went to the shop where it was being worked on, and after a couple of celebratory cocktails with his mechanic, chose a path home full of curvy roads. At the apex of a righthand turn (as near as can be deduced from the wreckage), he got on the gas hard at 4,000 rpm in third gear. The boost came on suddenly, and the back end broke free unexpectedly, causing the car to rotate perpendicular to the road (i.e., he lost it and spun). The car bounced off a tree and a telephone pole, rolled down an embankment and came to rest on its roof. Thankfully, no other cars, people or woodland animals were involved in the accident.

My friend found himself hanging upside down, disoriented and with a few scrapes. There were no witnesses to the accident. He walked up the road until he reached a house, asked the woman inside to call the police to come and take an accident report and tow his car away. He then went back to his car to wait. When I asked him why he did this, he said that he was a little shaken up, and running on instinct, and that instinct told him "when there is an accident, call the police." The fact that he had had two drinks before driving did not cross his mind, as he felt no effects of the alcohol and was thinking only about the horrific mass of twisted metal that had been his new car.

The police and an ambulance arrived simultaneously at the accident scene. The emergency medical crew followed protocol and put my friend in the ambulance. They began giving him oxygen, even though he reported that he was a little banged up but otherwise fine. While this was happening, the police were questioning him. After they ascertained he had consumed alcohol, they ordered the EMT workers to take blood and placed him under arrest for misdemeanor DWI. They did this without any proof that he was over the legal limit for alcohol. They simply arrested and later booked and arraigned him because his blood test *might* come back (in a few weeks) showing that he was over the limit. My friend weighs 160 pounds and had had only two drinks, so he should be under the limit, which means he should be able to get the case dismissed. This will not make up for the humiliation of being arrested, fingerprinted, questioned, arraigned and featured in the police blotter of the local newspaper under DWI.

The *prima-facie* case for DWI in New York (and generally, in all other states) requires the People to prove beyond a reasonable doubt that the defendant not only had an amount of alcohol over the statutory limit in his bloodstream, but also that he operated a motor vehicle while there was that amount of alcohol in his or her blood. This is extremely significant in the instant case, and for any reader who may occasionally have a drink and then drive.

Had my friend been so disoriented due to the accident that he stumbled off into the woods and fell asleep, awakening to deal with the problem the next day, he would not have been arrested. Had he called a friend to pick him up and take him to the hospital or home rather than calling the police, he would not have been arrested, since there would be no way to prove he had alcohol

This 944 has yet to experience a rotation perpendicular to the road.

in his system while operating the vehicle, even if the police ever questioned him (assuming he did not admit to the same).

In fact, had he sat on the wreck drinking a six-pack of beer after the accident, waiting for the police to arrive, he would still be better off, because there would be no way to prove that any drinking occurred before the accident (unless, of course, the driver admitted to the same).

Drinking and driving is a dangerous and terrible thing. People should never drink and drive, as to do so is to put themselves and others, as well as their cars, at risk. That being said, the sobriety tests and alcohol-detection apparatus are not as accurate as I would like, and people (like my friend) are often arrested and humiliated, and forced to pay attorneys, when they ultimately will be shown to have been *under the legal limit* for alcohol while driving.

Therefore, I advise readers that if you have had *anything to drink at all*, even if you are sure that you are under the legal limit, and your car becomes disabled on the side of the road due to being stuck, broken down or involved in a single-vehicle accident that involves no injury or property damage*, do not call the police or wait for the police to come and arrest you.* Go home and send a tow truck to get your car. Worry about it tomorrow. For if you are found with any alcohol in your system at all in a road-side screening, or if you admit to having had anything to drink when the police arrive, there is a good chance that you will be arrested and taken to the police station to blow into a Breathalyzer or to the hospital for a blood test.

This routine makes sense to the police, who have a duty to protect the public and who often figure they ought to take you in if you admit to drinking at all to "see what you blow" on the official Breathalyzer, since the road-side sensor is inadmissible and not very accurate. Your admission of at least some alcohol consumption gives them (arguably) probable cause to do so. Why wait and give them the opportunity to arrest you? Why suffer the humiliation of arrest when you will ultimately be let go when the Breathalyzer or blood test shows you were not over the limit? If no one was injured and your disabled car is not dangerously placed, go home and deal with it in the morning.

WARNING: Drinking and driving is wrong, dangerous and illegal. Leaving the scene of an accident (but not a disabled car) is generally illegal in most states.—*Alex Leventhal*

Mr. Leventhal is a car collector and attorney in New York. His comments here are general in nature, and are not a substitute for a consultation with an attorney.

From the April 2000 issue of *SCM.*◆

Pass the Blood Test, Go Directly to Jail

Recall my friend who wrecked his Silver Rose Porsche 944 Turbo S and was promptly arrested for DWI, even without any evidence of alcohol in his blood. ("Two for the Road," April 2000 *SCM*, page 60). The driver was involved in a single-car accident where he spun off the road and totaled his car. He then called the police, as he was taught to do years ago in high school Driver's Education. The police came and asked him if he had had anything to drink. He said yes, that he had, but had had only two drinks, several hours before. He was placed under arrest and a blood test was ordered. In short, he was arrested with no proof whatsoever of having had alcohol in his blood, simply because he admitted to having had a drink.

Temporarily out of service.

The advice offered in that column was that,if you have had *anything to drink at all*, even if you are sure that you are under the legal limit, and your car becomes disabled on the side of the road due to being stuck, broken or in a minor single-vehicle accident that involves no injury or property damage, do not call the police or wait for the police to come and arrest you. Go home and send a tow truck to get your car because if you are found with any alcohol in your system at all in a road-side screening, or if you admit to have had anything to drink, when the police arrive, there is a good chance that you will be arrested.

This was good advice, but obviously it was too late for my friend. The latest events in his case as they relate to this accident will show just how important following this advice is, and how important it is to *never* have the police believe that you have *any* alcohol in your blood, whether that belief stems from a Breathalyzer or an admission.

Recently, the eagerly awaited results of the Porsche-driver's blood test came back. In New York, blood-test results showing evidence that there was more than .1% of alcohol by weight in a person's blood shall be *prima-facie* evidence that such person was driving while intoxicated (DWI), while .07-.1% shall be *prima-facie* evidence that such a person is driving while his ability is impaired by alcohol (DWAI, a lesser offense). The fact that a *prima-facie* case is presented means that the prosecution, based on that evidence alone, has satisfied its burden for proving the elements of the crime, and creates a presumption that the defendant is guilty of the charge, allowing the prosecution to obtain a conviction unless the defense can produce evidence to disprove the presumption. A layperson could assume therefore that if my friend's blood test results were less than .07%, the alcohol-related charges would be dropped, because the law states that lesser amounts do not create a *prima-facie* case for DWI or DWAI. Unfortunately for my friend, that would be wrong.

Although it is true that alcohol levels less than .07% do not create a *prima-facie* case for the prosecution, levels between .05-.07% do not provide *prima-facie* evidence for the defense, either. Further, alcohol levels from .01-.05% do create *prima-facie* evidence for the defense, but as stated earlier, they do not prevent prosecution for DWAI, as the prosecutor is allowed to attempt to provide evidence refuting the presumption for the defense created by the *prima-facie* evidence, and thus seek a conviction.

In my friend's case, he has recently found out that his blood alcohol content (BAC) was below the .07% limit but that the prosecution intends to seek a DWAI conviction based on common law evidence because the officer that responded to the call now remembers that my friend's speech was slurred, his eyes were glassy and his gait was unstable. What's worse, the prosecutor is only offering a plea to the DWAI charge, and no better plea-bargain deal, because New York law also provides that no plea bargains outside of the alcohol category are generally allowed for alcohol offenses.

What are my friend's chances here? He can't take the plea and have an alcohol conviction on his record, so plans are being made to go to trial. Victory is not guaranteed, however, particularly if the prosecutor can shift the jury's sentiment by presenting the driver as a young, professional male with a Porsche who consumed alcohol, by his own admission, and has now hired an expensive lawyer. In short, I think the chances at trial are pretty good, but that the outcome is certainly not guaranteed.

So the question becomes, as it always does in this column, what can we take away from these facts? If you live in a state, like New York, which allows for alcohol convictions based on common law evidence such as slurred speech and the like, even when the blood- or breath-test results are below the accepted legal limit of alcohol, it is even more important to take the advice offered in my previous column on this subject as well as to take any and all other possible steps to prevent the police or legal system from ever coming to the conclusion that you have had *any* alcohol in your blood while operating a vehicle.

Particularly, the lesson to take away from this case is to be mindful of the fact that if you drive after having consumed any alcohol whatsoever, you may be prosecuted for driving while impaired by alcohol based on your other behavior which suggests impairment (such as slurred speech), even if the level of alcohol in your blood is low enough that it does not create a *prima-facie* case for the prosecution by itself.

Driving after drinking is a bad idea, no matter how little you may have had. Compounding this, be aware that in some states, even if your blood alcohol level is below the legal minimum, you may still be prosecuted. **Simply put, the only way to guarantee that you are not convicted of an alcohol-related offense is to never drive with any alcohol in your blood, because even driving with a BAC below the limit will not prevent a prosecution based on common law evidence.** This whole episode makes taking a taxi home after a splendid European-style three-hour restaurant dinner accompanied by a couple bottles of a '95 Burgundy seem like a pretty good idea.

Alex Leventhal is a car collector and attorney in New York. His comments here are general in nature, and are not a substitute for a consultation with an attorney.

From the July 2000 issue of *SCM*.◆

Porsches from $5,000 to $50,000

Here are my five Porsche picks for '98, plus two bonus selections should you find some extra space in your garage.

Under $5,000

1973-76 914 2.0: These are the best of the 914s. I recently bought one in honor of the newest 914 (some call it the Boxster), and enjoyed driving through the winter months when I wouldn't dare take our 356s or 911s out. The 2.0 engine makes a surprising difference over the 1.7 and 1.8 models. Watch out for rust, particularly below the battery tray, which can be bad enough to cause serious frame damage. Plan on spending about $4,000 for a nice one.

Under $10,000

1983-87 944: While clearly a bargain, as a Porsche, these remain a mixed bag. There is plenty of power, and the handling is excellent. Look for original paint and full maintenance books. Remember that the timing belts must be changed every 45,000 miles, and it's a good idea to replace the balance shaft belt at the same time (parts and labor, about $400). Rust is not a problem, the bottom ends can go almost forever, but plan on spending $1,300 to replace the clutch. You can be plenty tough on price, as there are tons of these around and most people want to get into a 911 as soon as their finances permit. Don't pay more than $7,000 for a nice car, less if you can.

Under $15,000

1969-71 911T coupes and Targas: These have been overlooked by the cognoscenti, as they salivate over the theoretically quicker S. Yes, the 911S is faster in Europe, where its high-revving power can be utilized in top-speed runs on the Autobahn. But here in the US, the 911T, with its abundance of low- and mid-range torque is the one to have. Remember the period comparison tests that picked the 911T over its rivals, the E and S? Not much has changed. Our editor wants us to find one for under $9,000, but that's hard without accepting big flaws. Plan on about $12,000, fully sorted. Spend more for sunroofs or Targas.

Under $20,000

1978-83 911SC coupes and Targas: These cars possess nearly bullet-proof mechanicals once set up correctly. Although 911SCs won't be appreciating anytime soon since over 67,000 were produced, they won't be going much lower either. Buy carefully, have the car fully inspected and be anxious to pay more for original paint. Cabriolets bring a big premium and may not really be worth it; Targas don't bring a premium but should; and if you buy a coupe, be sure it has a sunroof. Walk away from Euro-spec cars unless you get 25% off. Plan on $16,000 for a clean US-spec example.

Under $35,000

1979, 1986-89 930 Turbo: Yes, I know that Turbos have been slow sellers for years, but that will change, as the 930 is the 356 Speedster of our generation, a poster car and an unmistakable symbol of extreme performance. Built in limited numbers and brutally handsome, they are also wildly fast and full of fun. But be prepared to get friendly with your mechanic, as you must treat this beast with care. $30,000 should buy a nice US-spec example.

Under $45,000

1960-61 356B roadsters: These have been a bright spot in the otherwise rather stable 356 market of the last few years. Many people confuse roadsters and cabriolets, but roadsters are distinctive with their chrome-framed removable windshield and lighter, simpler tops. Although everyone wants a Speedster, few can live with its dysfunctional top and lack of roll-up windows. The roadster solves these basic issues, and in addition, provides a host of mechanical improvements over the Speedster, such as a stronger transmission, bigger oil pump and better steering gearbox. Find one with matching numbers and a solid chassis and be prepared to pay in the mid to high $30,000s.

Under $55,000

1998 Boxsters: These are great cars if you can live with just two seats, and they are slowly becoming more available. Our local dealer (Elkhart, IN) just got two 1998 models on the floor. One was in the show-car colors of silver with a lobster red leather interior and had the rare and expensive hardtop. The other was Guards Red with black leather. Both are available to drive home at sticker price. The Boxster is blessed with a rather powerful six-cylinder engine and, in many ways, is every bit as exotic as any 911. Plan on paying sticker (but no more) unless you have friends in high German places.

We'll see you at the auctions. Happy hunting in 1998.
—*Jim Schrager*

From the January 1998 issue of *SCM*.◆

Price Check

In last January's issue, I selected a group of Porsches for your consideration in 1998. Time now to see how those picks have fared and what might be ahead for the new year.

Under $5,000

1970-76 914/4: *Holding steady.* For a Porsche in this price range, you'll be surprised at how much fun these are to drive. Stick with a 2.0 if possible and get one with solid mechanicals and very little rust (be sure to look for corrosion under the battery tray). Although you'll find plenty of room for two, the mid-engine configuration means no stowage behind the seats. Don't plan on appreciation, but well bought, you shouldn't suffer much depreciation either. Someday, when enough of the over 100,000 built have rusted off the road, these cars will start to edge up in value. That won't happen in 1999.

Restored 1961 Porsche 356B T-5 roadster

Under $10,000

1983-87 944: *Declining in value.* Those are just used cars, albeit with a Porsche pedigree. This is the cheapest way to own a fully modern Porsche, with air conditioning, cruise control, a good heating system and so on. Spend a bit of time looking and you'll discover a large selection, with many anxious sellers. Don't skip the pre-purchase inspection, as mechanical work can quickly bury you. Although you can get a good car for $6,000, regardless of what you pay, it will never drive like a 911.

Under $15,000

1969-71 911T coupes and Targas: *One-time jump in value.* When California exempted 1973 and earlier cars from smog tests in 1998, it was a needed breath of fresh air for early 911 owners. Before 1998, if your car flunked the smog test, you were forced to exile your beloved 911 outside the Golden State. Today the pressure is off, so the bottom end of the market has disappeared. However, I don't believe this marks the beginning of a long-term upward spike. The production volume of Ts is quite large compared to Es or Ss, so that keeps a lid on prices. This remains a great, non-fussy car for everyday driving. Plan on about $13,000 for a nice #2 coupe, fully sorted with all updates. Pay more for cars with original paint and original interiors. Targas and sunroofs bring a premium over straight coupes.

Under $20,000

1978-81 911SC coupes and Targas: *Holding steady.* Still the best modern 911 for someone on a budget who demands a high-performance, reliable, transportation machine. Less soul than the earlier cars, but lots of torque to make up for it. Prices are flat this year as the production numbers (approximately 67,000 built) are high and the scrap rate is very low due both to bullet-proof mechanicals and galvanized sheet-metal panels. Prices will continue to hold steady in 1999, with Targas gaining a bit over coupes. Just like last year, $16,000 buys a good US-spec coupe. The prices of Euro cars remain about 25% off.

Under $35,000

1979, 1986-89 930 Turbos: *Volatile.* We have seen some older, high-mileage Turbos bring surprisingly big money (in the mid $20,000s), and we have also seen some newer, low-mileage cars sell cheap (low $30,000s). The 930 remains a landmark, coupling awesome performance with low production volume. A tremendous amount of bang for the buck, $30,000 will snare a true icon that, under acceleration, will give new meaning to the phrase tail-happy.

Under $45,000

1960-61 356B roadsters: *Prices rising.* These continue to move up, while both the more luxurious cabriolets and more Spartan Speedsters remain steady. We have seen wonderful single-grille roadsters (T-5 body style, 2,619 built) reach into the high $40,000s while the ultra-rare twin grille models (T-6 body style, 249 built) start in the low $40,000s and reach into the high $70,000s for no-excuses cars. Plan on $45,000 for an outstanding T-5 and be prepared for many admiring stares, both on the road and at the annual Porsche Parade.

Under $55,000

1998 Boxster: *Holding steady, but not forever.* Production hasn't quite caught up with demand, so these remain a bit hard to get, with owners of used cars still asking full list price. There are some early reports of engine coolant problems, so stay off the race track to keep your warranty in full force. This latest Porsche exotic will still turn heads in most parts of the world.

Watch for the Boxster S introduction. When it arrives, you will know that production has caught up with demand and prices for used Boxsters will start to soften.

Next month: the best and worst buys we saw last year, and why.—*Jim Schrager*

From the January 1999 issue of *SCM.*◆

You Paid What For That?

Chop-top 914 overpriced at $6,825

Last month I regaled you with the best buys of the year. Now it's time to drag through the dregs. Since 1998 was a wonderful year to buy a Porsche, this list of losers will necessarily be shorter than last month's list of keepers. By keeping the good and bad in perspective, you'll have the best chance of getting a great buy as 1999 unfolds.

1975 914 Speedster, $6,825

This modified 914 had its targa bar sliced off and in its place a poorly designed soft top was dropped. To its favor were nicely polished Fuchs alloy wheels and a shiny resale red paint job. However, body modifications destroyed whatever value this four-cylinder 914 had, and just to add insult to injury, there was a bit of rust on this gem. I recently saw a similar cut 914 sell in the Midwest for $1,950. Please, folks, stay away from modified Porsches unless you are willing to give them away when you are finished or enjoy being married to a sale-proof toy. (Barrett-Jackson, January '98)

1976 912E Coupe, $12,600

This one is a bit harder to understand, as it was a lovely, original car that had been carefully lowered and was genuinely attractive. Finished in pale yellow-beige, its fully polished alloys made it stand out in a crowd. Although built in low numbers, the 912E has never been a desirable car, and I will make the bold prediction it will never be one. Low build numbers are not enough to make a Porsche collectible. I can see how someone could be taken in by this car, but you must do your homework before writing the check. 912Es are slow, noisy, wildly expensive to fix and have little appeal to the Porsche crowd. Please do not confuse this with the original 912, built from 1965 to 1969, which had a genuine Porsche motor instead of the VW-derived 2.0-liter four in the 912E. I normally won't recommend a 912E at much over $5,000, but for this car, as it was so pretty, I'd allow an extra $1,000. However, that's still only half the price it sold for. (Barrett-Jackson, January '98)

1962 356B S-90 Cabriolet, $42,441

This is big-time money for a B cab, so this car had better deliver the goods. Let's start with colors: silver with a black leather

Fake 959 body work and Chevy V-8.

interior. Excellent. Now let's make sure the numbers match: Oops. The engine appears to be from a lowly 60-hp Normal, instead of the 90 horses promised on the script just below the engine lid. This is a sizeable sin when the seller is looking for big money, and it's hard to pull anything above low $30,000s on a B cab. Part of the high price paid for this particular Porsche is due to the desirability of cabs in Europe, but this is too much for a non-original car. (Brooks, Geneva, March '98)

1957 356A Speedster, $71,800

This car was recently restored and finished in its original color of ivory with a tan leather interior, with just two owners from new. However, the driver's door panel fit was off a bit and that's an important issue for any top-of-the-world 356. There are many reasons why this car might be the subject of spirited bidding: '57 and '58 are the last two years of the Speedster and the most usable, this car was very fresh, unmarked and ready to go, and Speedsters, as the most desirable 356s, have the best chance to tug at the purse strings of any enthusiast-to-be. Still, this new owner paid about $15,000 too much. (Brooks, Quail Lodge, August '98)

1972 Porsche 959 Replica, $13,375

This car makes me sad just looking at it. The body had more waves than the Atlantic Ocean and the top was as baggy as an elephant's skin, but wait, it gets worse. Someone stuffed a Chevy 350/350-hp engine where the flat-six was supposed to go. To be honest, I love custom cars. I also love Porsches. But the best thing about custom Porsches is that they usually sell for about 25 cents on the dollar. This one sold for about the same price as a real 1972 911 Targa, yet I guarantee you it will not run as well as the real thing or be worth anywhere near as much when it is time to sell. We see cars like this at obscure auctions where country folk don't encounter many real Porsches (such as in Auburn, Indiana, for example). But who would imagine this car would sell for big money right in the heart of the biggest Porsche festival ever, at Monterey? (RM Classic, Monterey, August '98)

As the year rolls on, we'll see lots of good cars. But please, be careful out there.—*Jim Schrager*

From the March 1999 issue of *SCM*.◆

Looking Back—Great Buys of '98

Looking back, 1998 was a good year at the auctions. Not only was there a wide selection of exceptional Porsches, but we saw some very sharp prices as well. In order from newest cars to oldest, here are some of the best buys of the year reported on in *SCM*.

A spare four-cam engine came with this Carrera GS.

1985 959 Prototype, $83,826

As a factory prototype for the most technologically advanced road-going Porsche in history, this car is a solid bet to appreciate. Factory prototypes, once they have reached 20 to 30 years old, seem to become wildly valuable. Witness the 901 and 902 prototypes (for the 911 and 912) that are now nearly priceless. But this 959 has extra cachet due to the fact it was a part of the Vasek Polak collection, one of Porsche's most successful privateers. As this collection is dispersed, the value of each car will rise. (Brooks, Monaco, May)

1983 911SC, $13,375

A very pretty and decent used car that sold cheaper by a few thousand than I can buy them through the classifieds. A good 911SC will shock you with its speed, handling and durability. What could be better as a daily driver? (RM Classic, Monterey, August)

1979 930 Turbo, $19,950

Body and mechanical condition is particularly important on a Turbo, but if this car checked out, it was an excellent deal. 1979 is the first year of the Turbo that doesn't require updates to be usable. This is the cheapest way to have an instantly recognizable, and very fast, automotive icon. (Barrett-Jackson, Scottsdale, January)

1973 911S Targa, $15,855

These early Ss are starting to move. We have seen wonderful '69-'73 911Ss sell in the mid $20,000s, and I know that two *SCM* readers recently purchased similar cars in that range. This car, if it drives as well as it looks, was a sweet buy. (Barrett-Jackson, Scottsdale, January)

1973 911 Carrera RS, $43,397

These are superb cars, perhaps the finest street 911 ever produced. This car, in excellent condition, simply sold too cheap. It can be resold in Europe and make a handsome profit for its new owner or held and will appreciate at the head of the market. These most expensive of all early (1965-73) 911 road cars have a significant following and a very liquid world-wide market. (Coys, Silverstone, June)

1970 911S Coupe, $13,358

Slightly less desirable than the '72-'73 Ss, as the engine on the '70-'71 cars is 2.2 versus 2.4 liters. Still, this silver car sold at an easy few thousand below market. (Autoclassic, Vancouver, April)

1961 356B Roadster, $33,075

You could sell this car for $7,500 more without doing anything more than washing it. Roadsters remain the quickest-appreciating 356 as Speedsters are already expensive and the cabriolets are held back by the fact that most people prefer the sportiness of the roadster. ("The Auction," Las Vegas, March)

1957 356A Carrera GS, $54,576

To the uninitiated, $54,000 is a ridiculously high price for an A coupe. But any 356 Carrera is a very special car. This GS was delivered with the powerful four-cam race motor, yet meant for the street and fitted with all the period luxury items such as a sunroof and Rudge knock-off wheels. The value was hurt because the original roller-bearing 1500-cc engine was missing, but the car was powered by a fresh pushrod Super 90. A later, highly desirable, plain-bearing 1600 four-cam motor came as a consolation prize. That motor alone, depending upon condition, could be worth the entire price paid. The Rudge wheels are worth maybe $8,000-$10,000 a set; the S-90 engine $4,500; and the naked body, in the stunning color of Aquamarine Metallic (a medium blue/gray metallic) done to the wonderful condition of this car, is easily worth $25,000. This Porsche, to me, was the buy of the year and if I had been at this auction, it would be in my garage today. (Brooks, Nürburgring, August)

1955 Speedster, $42,788

Here is an immaculately restored Speedster, the classic 356, in the right colors, to boot (red/black). Buy it, drive it, enjoy sunny-day outings, be the envy of the neighborhood, then sell it for every penny you paid. A sublime early Porsche at an effective cost of zero. Isn't that why you read *SCM*? (Barrett-Jackson, Scottsdale, January). —*Jim Schrager*

From the February 1999 issue of *SCM*.◆

Five Porsches That Are Going Up In Value

The 356 and 911 Porsches are among the most recognizable of collectible sports cars. With their unique, rear-mounted, air-cooled engine configuration, Porsches offer good if sometimes tricky handling, a fantastic exhaust note, decent reliability and an enormous number of parts and accessories sources. Even better, the Porsche Club of America, with over 48,000 members, is extremely active, so you'll have the chance to meet other Porsche fanatics and enjoy your car in a variety of touring and competition events.

1957-59 356A Sunroof Coupes

As the last of the original swoopy, droopy 356 body style, the 356A still captures the hearts of many Porsche lovers. Sunroofs are rare and make an already great car even better for sunny-day drives.

What to watch out for: Rust and previous collision damage, especially on the nose and front fenders. As with any 356, good gaps on the moveable body panels are important. Get the original engine or expect a healthy discount. Original colors add value, especially if they are silver or black.

Number produced: approx. 800
Fun to drive: ☆☆☆☆
Ease of ownership: ☆☆☆
Visual appeal: ☆☆☆☆☆
Appreciation potential: ☆☆☆☆
Market value in #2 cond.: $20,000

1966 911 Coupes and Sunroof Coupes

As the first full year of 911 production, these cars have a number of features not seen on other years. Standard equipment included a wood steering wheel and dash, auxiliary heater, chrome wheels and fog lights inset into the lower front valance. Sunroofs are very rare and desirable in these early cars. With 130 (DIN) horsepower, the engines are torquey and robust.

What to watch out for: Chain tensioner problems. Rust is always a problem. As other early 911 cars get "discovered," interest in these pioneers continues to accelerate.

Number produced: approx. 3,500
Fun to drive: ☆☆☆☆
Ease of ownership: ☆☆☆
Visual appeal: ☆☆☆☆
Appreciation potential: ☆☆☆☆
Market value in #2 cond.: $7,500-$10,000

1970-71 911S Coupes, Sunroofs and Targas

These 2.2-liter mechanical fuel-injected cars are often passed by in the rush to buy the last of the original S cars, the '72-'73 2.4-liter machines. But the 2.2 S has a torque curve that carries power further into the rpm range than the 2.4. As a result, for pure high-rpm hi-jinks, the 2.2 outshines the 2.4.

What to watch out for: In addition to rust and chain tensioner issues, watch out for high miles. These early Ss work hard and turn much higher rpms than the lower-horsepower T and E cars. "Those are expensive noises back there," many an S owner has been heard to say. True, but with one of these, at least you get what you pay for—high revs and great fun.

Number produced: Approx. 5,000
Fun to drive: ☆☆☆☆☆
Ease of ownership: ☆☆☆☆
Visual appeal: ☆☆☆☆
Appreciation potential: ☆☆☆☆☆
Market value in #2 cond.: $14,000-$18,000

1973 911 Carrera RS

This non-US model has slowly become one of the most collectible 911 road cars. The reason is its delightful un-race car-like performance, with gobs of torque everywhere in the powerband. Most of the cars built were the RSL models with full 911S interiors.

What to watch out for: Make sure a Carrera RS has the correct motor and a proper chassis number (911 360 XXXX). The rear wheel flares are steel, but were welded by hand so they vary a bit. All mechanical components are quite robust, and this includes the gearbox, which has its own oil pump.

Number produced: 1,580
Fun to drive: ☆☆☆☆☆
Ease of ownership: ☆☆☆☆☆
Visual appeal: ☆☆☆☆☆
Appreciation potential: ☆☆☆☆☆
Market value in #2 cond.: $45,000-$62,500

1973-76 914 2.0 Roadsters

These are the best of the 914s. Although large production volume means they will never be worth really big money, the best examples have quietly started to move upwards in price. The 2.0L drives much better than the 1.8L/1.7L cars, and makes the 914 a delightful machine to own.

What to watch out for: Check carefully for rust, particularly under the battery tray, where it can infect the subframe and rear suspension mounts. Engines are not cheap to rebuild, so make sure they are sound. The transmission is blessed with stock 911 internals, which makes it quite robust. Interiors wear poorly but aren't too expensive to redo with swap-meet parts.

Number produced: approx. 20,000
Fun to drive: ☆☆☆☆
Ease of ownership: ☆☆☆☆
Visual appeal: ☆☆☆☆
Appreciation potential: ☆☆☆☆
Market value in #2 cond.: $5,000-$7,000 ◆

Jim Schrager—2001 *SCM Pocket Price Guide.*◆

Five Porsches to Avoid

German automakers are known for their high-quality products, from the state-of-the-art Mercedes S-Class to the brilliantly executed VW Passat. Porsches have contributed their share to this reputation, with properly maintained 911 engines covering more than 200,000 miles between rebuilds, and 40-year-old 356 coupes still capable of hustling down the highway at 80 mph in relative comfort.

Warning: 924 Turbo can blow at any time.

But don't let the Stuttgart badge on the nose stand as a symbol of infallibility. While most Porsches are good, a few are bad. And some are very, very bad. The cars below are not Porsches to covet or collect. Some have design defects. Others seem to get more than their share of owner neglect or are attacked, with evil consequences, by untrained mechanics. The cars on this list are often seen selling for low prices at auction, but there's a reason for this. Remember, just because a car doesn't cost very much to buy doesn't make it a good deal. Sometimes the most expensive cars to own are the least expensive to purchase.

1. 924 Turbos
Starting with the worst first, it is hard to imagine anyone feeling good about owning a 924 Turbo. Of course, any 924 is an under-powered slug, with lousy durability and poor reliability to boot. The 924 was Porsche's attempt at an entry-level car, and the cheapening and outsourcing required to meet a low-price requirement made the car completely different from its uncle, the 911, or its cousin, the 928. Getting a 924 to perform properly required far more than slapping a turbo on the base powerplant, which had been quietly lifted from an agricultural application.

These Turbos blow up with frightening regularity. Independent mechanics often refuse to work on them. Be especially wary of low-mileage examples, as they probably never ran well enough for their owners to trust them farther than around the block.

2. 912s with questionable motors
When new, the 912 was a bargain. For $4,800, you got nearly everything that came with a $6,500 911, for almost 40% less. But as 912s aged, they often fell into the hands of budget-minded owners who did not understand the maintenance demands of this high-performance machine. Even though it is not nearly the performer that the six-cylinder 911 is, the 912 engine, producing 90 hp DIN out of 1600 cc, is a highly stressed package. It does not have a full-flow oil filter. The crankshaft's four throws are supported by just three main bearings. It does not suffer fools gladly.

A solid engine rebuild with original parts can easily top $7,500, expensive for a car that will rarely bring $10,000 in the market. So if you come across a 912 in average condition that needs engine work beyond a tune-up, in most cases you will be wise to simply walk away.

3. Heavily modified 911 Turbos
I can't understand why some 911 Turbo owners think that aftermarket tuner shops can make a better, faster, more reliable Porsche than Porsche can. Question: How many Le Mans races has the tuner shop won? Answer: None. It would seem obvious that Porsche, more than anyone else, knows how to make fast, reliable cars. So why doesn't Porsche make them go as fast as the tuner shops do?

Simply, Porsche is interested in making cars, not hand grenades. Any 911 Turbo is an extremely fast car and, if well maintained, can be enjoyed for tens of thousands of relatively trouble-free miles. The same is not true of hot-rod Turbos equipped with non-Porsche engine parts. Tuners trade reliability and longevity for power, and pay the price when an over-stressed engine lets go. If you buy one of these bad-boy tuner cars, try to enjoy it and sell it within a very short time period (i.e., before something catastrophic happens to the motor). Don't pay too much for one; when it comes time to sell, you'll find the resale market surprisingly soft. There are few buyers who are anxious to play Russian roulette with their engine each time they twist the ignition key.

4. Older 928s without full maintenance papers
These were expensive and exotic cars when new. That's not a Chevy V8 clone under the hood, but a built-from-scratch high-output OHC engine made in very low volume and developed in the field. If the maintenance books are not up to date, and, in many cases, even if they are, these cars can be an absolute nightmare to keep on the road.

To make matters worse, there are fewer and fewer competent mechanics who know these cars well. Further complicating the matter, parts are wildly expensive, as there is no aftermarket keeping Porsche's margins in check. In some very scary cases, new parts are simply unavailable. Think of this as the V12 Jaguar XJS of Porsches, with all the unpleasant connotations that conjures up. Buy at your own risk.

5. 911s with rear torsion tube rust
When the rear torsion-bar tube goes, a 911 chassis becomes a hopeless amalgam of unconnected metal. Sooner or later, completing the disintegration process, the rear suspension will collapse. Significant visual warnings of impending torsion tube problems are rust holes in the side frame rails at each end of the torsion-bar tube, just forward of the rear wheels.

Once the rust has marched that far into your chassis, repairing the damage will usually cost more than the car is worth. But it gets worse. Only a handful of shops in the US can perform this delicate repair properly. If the torsion-bar tube is installed even slightly incorrectly, the chassis will be permanently skewed and the car will forever drive down the street crabwise, due to different right and left wheelbases. This also makes for very unusual (read: dangerous) handling.

Jim Schrager—2002 *SCM Pocket Price Guide.*◆

Complete Porsche Price Guide: Values from 1954–Present

The **Price Guide** reflects a retail buying and selling range for cars in **very good to near excellent condition** significantly above a daily driver and one step below regional concours; a strong #2 on the accepted 1-6 scale, 1 being the best. These values are set by **sales activity,** primarily in the United States, as well as conversations with owners, dealers and collectors. *As condition and history are the ultimate determinants of value,* each car must be evaluated according to its own merits. Prices below assume cars with no stories attached.

An automobile priced above our guide is not necessarily overpriced, nor is one priced below a bargain. Note that exceptional #1 cars can exceed these #2 values by well over 100%. Values are as of January 2004.

*Indicates approximate production numbers.

356

50-55	356 Coupe "pre-A"	7,627	$20,000	$25,000

(Two-piece windshield until April '52. One-piece "bent" window until Oct. '55. Standard one-piece curved from then on.)

50-55	356 Cabriolet	1,685	$25,000	$32,500
54-55	356 Speedster	1,233	$45,000	$55,000
56-59	356A Coupe	13,010	$20,000	$25,000
56-59	356A Cabriolet	3,367	$27,500	$35,000
56-58	356A Speedster	2,911	$42,500	$65,000
59	356A Convertible D	1,330	$45,000	$55,000

(356, 356A: Add $2,000 for Super engine.)

56-59	356A Carrera GS Coupe	541	$80,000	$90,000

(This is total production for all GS and GT cars. Numbers below included.)

56-59	356A Carrera GS Cab.	140	$100,000	$115,000
56-59	356A Carrera Speedster	75	$125,000	$145,000
56-59	356A Carrera GT Coupe	541	$110,000	$135,000
56-59	356A Carrera GT Speedster	72	$135,000	$180,000

(There were 7 pushrod GT Speedsters built.)

60-61	356B Coupe (T-5 body)	8,556	$12,000	$15,000
60-61	365B Cabriolet (T-5)	3,091	$25,000	$32,000
60-61	356B Roadster (T-5)	2,649	$35,000	$45,000
60-61	356B Notchback (T-5)	1,048	$9,000	$13,000

(Spotter's Note: T-5 body has gas filler cap inside trunk, T-6 has external gas filler cap.)

(Add for 356 B: Super engine, add $2,000; Super-90, add $3,000.)

62-63	356B Coupe (T-6)	6,289	$16,000	$20,000
62-63	356B Cabriolet (T-6)	3,096	$30,000	$35,000
62	356B "twin grille" Rdstr. (T-6)	248	$50,000	$65,000
62	356B Notchback (T-6)	697	$10,000	$15,000
62-65	Carrera 2 GS	360	$135,000	$175,000
62-64	Carrera 2 Cab.	88	$125,000	$150,000
63-65	356C Coupe	13,507	$20,000	$25,000
63-65	356C Cabriolet	3,174	$32,500	$37,500
63-65	356 Coupe SC	inc. cpe.	$22,500	$28,000
63-65	356 Cabriolet SC	inc. Cab.	$37,500	$42,500

(Additions for all 356 Porsches: sunroof, $3,000; Rudge wheels, $10,000; hard top on a cabriolet, $1,000; hard top on a Speedster, $4,000. Deductions: wrong engine per Kardex, subtract 15% of value; improper exterior color for year of car, subtract 25% of value.)

911: Small Bumper, Short Wheelbase

65	911 Coupe 2.0	235	$10,000	$13,000
66-68	911 Coupe 2.0	10,399	$8,500	$10,000
67-68	911 Targa 2.0	1,427	$9,000	$12,000
67-68	911S Coupe 2.0	4,689	$15,000	$20,000
67-68	911S Targa 2.0	1,160	$14,000	$19,000
68	911L Coupe 2.0	1,169	$9,000	$10,000
68	911L Targa 2.0	307	$9,000	$10,500

911: Small Bumper, Long Wheelbase

69-71	911T Coupe 2.2	13,019	$8,500	$12,000
69-71	911T Targa 2.2	7,303	$9,000	$12,500
69-71	911E Coupe 2.2	5,027	$9,500	$13,000
69-71	911E Targa 2.2	935	$10,000	$13,500
69-71	911S Coupe 2.2	1,430	$16,000	$22,000
69-71	911S Targa 2.2	2,131	$16,000	$20,000

(Deduct 15% for 2.0L 1969 cars.)

72-73	911T Coupe 2.4	9,964	$10,000	$12,500
72-73	911T Targa 2.4	7,968	$10,500	$13,000

(Add $2,000 for 1973 1/2 911T with CIS injection.)

72-73	911E Coupe 2.4	2,490	$11,000	$13,000
72-73	911E Targa 2.4	1,916	$11,500	$13,500
72-73	911S Coupe 2.4	3,180	$18,000	$25,000
72-73	911S Targa 2.4	1,914	$18,000	$23,000

(Additions: sunroof, $1,000; soft-window Targa, $3,000. Deductions: four-speed transmission, $1,000; Sportomatic transmission, $1,500.)

73	Carrera RSL "Touring"	1,360	$55,000	$75,000
73	Carrera RS "Lightweight"	200	$90,000	$120,000

911: Federalized Bumper, Narrow Body

74-75	Carrera Cpe. 2.7 Euro	16,977	$18,000	$23,000
74-77	911S Coupe 2.7	inc. abv.	$7,500	$10,000
74-77	911S Targa 2.7	inc. abv.	$7,500	$9,000
74-77	Carrera Cpe. 2.7 US	inc. abv.	$9,500	$13,000
74-77	Carrera Targa 2.7 US	inc. abv.	$9,500	$13,000
76-77	Carrera Cpe. Euro 3.0	inc. abv.	$14,500	$17,000
76-77	Carrera Targa Euro 3.0	inc. abv.	$14,500	$17,000

911SC: Federalized Bumper, Wide Body

78-83	911SC Coupe	35,607	$15,000	$19,000
78-83	911SC Targa	27,678	$15,000	$19,000
80	911 "Weissach" Ed.	408	$17,500	$22,000
82	911 Ferry Porsche Ed.	200	$18,000	$22,500
83	911SC Cabriolet	4,187	$17,000	$22,000

Turbo: 930 / 911 / 993 / 996

75	930 Turbo Coupe (3.0L)	284	$16,000	$22,000
76-77	930 Turbo Coupe (3.0L)	2,596	$18,000	$23,000
78-85	930 Turbo Coupe (3.3L)	10,004	$18,000	$25,000

(2,918 US legal production. All 1975, 1980-85 930s are gray-market. Deduct 35% for gray-market, 50% if no EPA/DOT papers.)

86-89	911 Turbo (3.3L)	4,363	$22,000	$26,000
87-89	911 Turbo Cab. (3.3L)	2,002	$28,000	$35,000
87-89	911 Turbo Slant (3.3L)	675	$25,000	$35,000
87-89	911 Turbo Targa (3.3L)	657	$25,000	$35,000
91-93	C2 Turbo Cpe. (Type 964)	5,125	$35,000	$42,500

(Add 20% for 1992 380-hp S models. 80 built.)

96-97	993 Twin Turbo	n/a	$80,000	$95,000

(Deduct 25% for gray-market.)

01 996	Turbo	n/a	$85,000	$100,000

Carrera and Speedster

84-86	911 Carrera	36,834	$17,000	$19,000
84-86	911 Carrera Targa	19,502	$18,000	$20,000
84-86	911 Carrera Cabriolet	22,283	$19,000	$22,000
87-89	911 Carrera	inc.	$21,500	$24,500
87-89	911 Carrera Targa	inc.	$22,500	$25,000
87-89	911 Carrera Cabriolet	inc.	$24,500	$28,000

(Add $4,000 for factory turbo look.)

88	911 Carrera Club Sport	340	$25,000	$29,500

(339 coupes, 1 Targa.)

89	911 25th Anniv. Coupe	875	$23,500	$27,500
89	911 25th Anniv. Cab.	inc.	$27,500	$31,000

(For US, 120 coupes, 100 cabs, 80 Targas.)

89	911 Speedster	2,065	$37,500	$45,000

C2 / C4 / Smooth Bumpers

90-91	911 Carrera 2	n/a	$24,500	$28,000
90-91	911 Carrera 2 Targa	n/a	$24,500	$28,000
90-91	911 Carr. 2 Cab.	n/a	$28,000	$31,000
89-91	911 Carrera 4	n/a	$24,500	$28,500
90-91	911 Carr. 4 Targa	n/a	$24,500	$28,500
90-91	911 Carr. 4 Cab.	n/a	$30,000	$35,000
92-93	911 America Rdstr.	n/a	$42,500	$47,500
93-94	911 Carr. 2 Speedster	n/a	$42,000	$47,000

993

95-98	Carrera	46,919	$31,000	$49,000
95-96	Carrera 4 inc.		$34,500	$46,500
95-98	Carrera Cabriolet inc.		$37,500	$55,500
95-98	Carrera 4 Cabriolet inc.		$39,000	$57,500
96-98	Carrera Targa inc.		$40,000	$55,500
96-98	Carrera 4S inc.		$48,000	$61,500
97-98	Carrera S inc.		$49,000	$60,000

996

99-01	Carrera		$44,000	$60,000
99-01	Carrera Cabriolet		$50,000	$69,000
99-01	Carrera 4		$50,000	$65,000
99-01	Carrera Cabriolet 4		$55,000	$73,000

912

66-69	912 Cpe. (1.6L)	29,212	$5,000	$7,000

(Add $500 for Targa.)

76	912E Coupe (2L)	2,099	$5,000	$7,000

914

70-73	914-4 1.7L	114,479	$3,500	$5,000
70-72	914-6	3,351	$11,000	$14,000
71	914-6 GT	11	$75,000	$150,000
72	914 R	4	$75,000	$125,000
72	916 (2.7 RS- spec eng.)	20	$75,000	$125,000
72	914S (a.k.a. 914-8)	2	$100,000	$150,000

(Custom built for Porsche family members.)

73-76	914-4 2.0L	inc. abv.	$5,000	$7,500
74-76	914-4 1.8L	inc. abv.	$4,000	$5,000

924

77-82	924	122,304	$3,500	$4,000
78-83	924 Turbo	12,356	$3,500	$5,000
87-88	924S Coupe	n/a	$4,500	$5,500

928

78-82	928	n/a	$6,000	$8,000
83-86	928S	n/a	$9,000	$12,000
87-88	928S-4	n/a	$12,000	$13,500
89-90	928S-4	n/a	$18,000	$23,000
91-92	928S-4	n/a	$20,000	$24,000

(Add $1,500 for 928 GT.)

93-95	928 GTS	n/a	$28,000	$40,000

944

83-85	944 Coupe	n/a	$4,000	$6,500
86-87	944 Coupe	n/a	$5,500	$7,000
88-89	944 Coupe	n/a	$6,000	$8,000

('S' add $750, Turbo add $2,000, 'S' Turbo add $2,500.)

89-91	944S2 Coupe	n/a	$11,500	$14,000
90-91	944S2 Cabriolet	n/a	$14,500	$20,000
92-93	968 Coupe	n/a	$14,000	$18,000
92-93	968 Cabriolet	n/a	$20,000	$25,000

Boxster

97-	Boxster Roadster	n/a	$27,000	$38,000
99-	Boxster S Roadster	n/a	$40,000	$50,000

Competition Cars

(Price ranges for Competition Porsches are determined by provenance, completeness and originality. A car with all of its original parts and no stories will bring three to four times what a "bitsa" that has only a few authentic parts will.)

54-55	550	90	$325,000	$425,000
56-57	550A	39	$350,000	$450,000

(Includes Le Mans coupes. Most 550As were sold in the US and have only SCCA history. Add at least 25% for cars with international, documented provenance.)

58-59	RSK	34	$500,000	$750,000
59-62	695GS Abarth Carrera	21	$375,000	$500,000
60-61	RS 60/RS 61	35	$500,000	$700,000
64-65	904 GTS	120	$375,000	$450,000

(Production includes 104 four-cylinder 904s, 12 six-cylinder 904s, 6 eight-cylinder 904s.)

1966	906 Carrera 6	65	$300,000	$450,000
67-68	910/907	34	$350,000	$550,000
68-69	908-01/908-02/908-03	62	$500,000	$900,000
69-71	917 LH/K/10/20/30	70	$750,000	$1,750,000

(25 FIA non-turbo endurance cars, 20 Can-Am-type open cars.)

73-74	Carrera RSR 2.7	57	$55,000	$75,000
73	Carrera RSR 3.0	109	$100,000	$200,000

(15 3.0 RSRs were built in 1974 for IROC.)

73	Carrera RSR 2.8	43	$175,000	$300,000
86-88	959 "Komfort"	200*	$150,000	$175,000

(Some 959s were built up from parts, and VIN numbers higher than 290 have been observed. "Komfort" street models were equipped with power leather seats, A/C, pw, etc.)

Cayenne SUV

03	Cayenne S		$55,000	$70,000
03	Cayenne Turbo		$85,000	$95,000

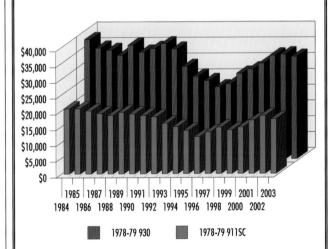

The Twenty Year Picture

1978–1979 PORSCHE 911SC AND PORSCHE 930 VALUES

This value guide is provided courtesy of Cars of Particular Interest. CPI is the pocket guide most often used by credit unions and banks when dealing with loan values of collectible domestic and imported cars; www.BlackBookUSA.com.

From the November 1997 issue of *SCM* ◆

AUCTION COMPANIES

Artcurial-Briest-Poulain-Le Fur. 33.01 42 99 20 20, fax 33.01 42 99 20 21. Maison de vente aux enchères, 7, Rond-Point des Champs Elysées, 75008 Paris, France. artcurial@auction.fr, www.poulainlefur.com.

Barrett-Jackson Auction. 480.421.6694, fax 480.421.6697. 3020 North Scottsdale Rd, Scottsdale, AZ 85251. info@barrett-jackson.com, www.barrett-jackson.com.

Bonhams. 415.391.4000, fax 415.391.4040. 220 San Bruno Avenue, San Francisco, CA 94103; **44.2072 288000,** fax 44.2075 850830. Montpelier St., Knightsbridge, London, SW7 1HH, UK. www.bonhams.com.

Christie's. 310.385.2699, fax 310.385.0246. 360 N. Camden Dr., Beverly Hills, CA 90210. www.christies.com.

Dana Mecum Auction Company. 815.568.8888, fax 815.568.6615. P.O. Box 422, Marengo, IL 60152. www.mecumauction.com.

eBay Motors, a part of eBay Inc. List your car for sale for only $40 and pay $40 more when it sells. Visit the "Services" section on www.ebaymotors.com for more details.

H&H Classic Auctions. 44.1925 730630, fax 44.1925 730830. Whitegate Farm, Hatton Lane, Hatton, Cheshire, WA4 4BZ, UK. info@classic-auctions.co.uk, www.classic-auctions.com.

Kruse International. 800.968.4444, fax 260.925.5467. P.O. Box 190, Auburn, IN 46706. www.kruseinternational.com.

Kensington Motor Group, Inc. 631.537.1868, fax 631.537.2641. P.O. Box 2277, Sag Harbor, NY 11963. KenMotor@aol.com.

Palm Springs Auctions Inc., Keith McCormick. 760.320.3290, fax 760.323.7031. 244 N. Indian Canyon Dr., Palm Springs, CA 92262. classiccarauction.com.

RM Auctions, Inc. 800.211.4371, fax 519.351.1337. One Classic Car Dr., Blenheim, ON NOP 1A0, Canada. www.rmauctions.com.

Russo and Steele. 602.252.2697. Arizona. www.russoandsteele.com.

Silver Auctions. 800.255.4485. 2020 N. Monroe, Spokane, WA 99205. silver@spokane.net, www.silverauc-tions.com.

Santiago Collector Car Auctions. 800.994.2816, fax 405.843.6251. 7321 N. Classen Blvd., Oklahoma City, OK 73116. E-mail Rocky. rockydb5@sbcglobal.net.

APPRAISALS

Dave Brownell's Vintage Auto Appraisals. 802.362.4719, fax 802.362.3007. Vermont. 25-plus years experience nationwide and internationally. Single cars or entire collections. Brass cars to contemporary supercars. Complete services from pre-purchase to insurance, donation, estate, expert witness. dbrownell@sprynet.com.

Charles W. Clarke. 860.658.2714. Hartford, Connecticut. Automotive consultant, appraiser. State of Connecticut licensed. 40-plus years automotive experience and wherewithal to address most any situation. We can travel. cwc-cars@cox.net.

Cosmopolitan Motors LLC. 206.467.6531, fax 206.467.6532. Complete appraisal services for any and all vehicles of particular note. Over 1 billion dollars in worldwide experience. We will help you in your time of need: We negotiate for you. Settlements, insurance, disputes, estates, pre-purchase, donations, etc. appraisals@cosmopolitanmotors.com.

USAppraisal. 703.759.9100. Virginia. 25 years experience with collector automobiles, available nationwide. David H. Kinney, ASA (Accredited Senior Appraiser, American Society of Appraisers). dhkinney@usappraisal.com, www.usappraisal.com.

Joseph L. Troise Appraisals. 415.332.8183. Serving SF Bay Area and northern California. Prompt, personal, professional and affordable service for insurance, legal, IRS and pre-purchase inspection. Free phone consultations. joetro@pacbell.net, www.bestyellow.com.classic.index.htm.

Auto Appraisal Group. 800.848.2886. Virginia. Serving 33 states, valuation, insurance, divorce, trusts, estates, charitable gifts, diminished value, pre-purchase inspections, expert witness. "Not just one man's opinion." aag@autoappraisal.com, www.autoappraisal.com.

Classic Car Research. 248.557.2880, fax 248.557.3511. Detroit area, will travel. 15 years in business, IAAA, for loans, estates, divorce, insurance and pre-purchase. kawifreek@msn.com, www.jmkclassiccars.com.

Dean V. Kruse. 260.927.1111, fax 260.920.2222. Indiana. Certified appraiser with 35 years in the business, appraisals completed for most of nationwide banks and insurance companies. Kruse International auctions more than 10,000 collector cars per year. One car or collections, donators, estates, disputes, pre-purchase inspections, attorneys, buyers, sellers. All inquiries kept confidential. dkruse@myvine.com.

Featherman & Co. Inc. 610.645.5595. Pennsylvania. Scott Featherman has over 20 years experience and is both a certified IAAA appraiser and ASE master technician. Complete services include appraisals, pre-purchase inspections, expert witness and advisory. Personal, prompt, confidential—available nationwide. For more information, see our listing in *SCM* Display Advertisers Index. scott@feathco.com, www.FeathermanCo.com.

AUTOMOBILIA

Spyder Enterprises. 831.659.5335, fax 831.659.5335. New York. Authentic vintage posters, postcards, memorabilia (1960s and earlier); mainly focused on Porsche, Ferrari, and racing. Leather accesories for Porsche 356; Halon fire extinguishers for your classic car; Ferrari 250.275.330 repro tool kits. Free 36 page list of all items by e-mail. singer356@aol.com.

L'art et l'automobile gallery & auction house. 631.329.8580, fax 631.329.8589. New York. 25 years of experience, 2 auctions yearly (June & December), catalog subscription $20/year or online. We carry a large collection of out-of-print books, vintage posters, prints, artwork, literature, memorabilia, etc. jvautoart@aol.com, www.arteauto.com.

COLLECTOR CAR FINANCING

J.J. Best Banc & Company. 800.USA.1965, fax 508.945.6006. Massachusetts. The largest national leader on Antique, Classic, Exotic, Rod and Sports Cars with rates starting at 7.99% and long terms from 5 to 12 years. Call, fax, or e-mail your application today for quick 10 minute approval. Efficient and professional service is what you deserve so don't hesitate, call us today to be in the driver's seat of your dream car tomorrow. www.jjbest.com.

COLLECTOR CAR INSURANCE

American Collectors Insurance. 800.360.2277. New Jersey. We've been taking the hassle—and expense—out of insuring collector vehicles since 1976. Get the collector coverage you need, at a price you won't believe! Visit us online for an instant rate quote or call toll-free. Available in all states except AK and HI. www.americancollectorsins.com.

Hagerty Collector Car Insurance. 800.922.4050. Michigan. Collector cars aren't like their late-model counterparts. These classics actually appreciate in value so standard market policies that cost significantly more won't do the job. With Hagerty, we'll agree on a fair value and cover you for the full amount. No prorated claims, no hassles, no games. See what Hagerty can do for you! www.hagerty.com.

American Hobbyist Insurance. 800.395.4835. Florida. From "brass & wood" antiques to modern day classics, our program accepts a wide range of collector vehicles. Enjoy excellent coverage & low "collector" rates. No strict mileage limitations in most states. Call toll free or visit us online. www.AmericanHobbyist.com.

COLLECTOR CAR LEASING

Premier Financial Services. 203.267.7700, fax 203.267.7773. Connecticut. With over 20 years of experience specializing in exotic, classic, and vintage autos, our Lease/Purchase plan is ideal for those who wish to own their vehicle at the end of the term as well as those who like to change cars frequently. Our Simple Interest Early Termination plan allows you the flexibility of financing with the tax advantages of leasing. We make leasing as simple as turning the key. www.WhyNotLease.com.

Putnam Leasing. 866.90.LEASE (866.905.3273). Connecticut. Never get in a car with strangers. Custom-tailored, lease-to-own financing for your dream car. Easy, fast, and dependable. Exclusive leasing agent for Barrett-Jackson, Cavallino, and Ferrari Club of America 2004 International Meet. Go with people you trust. Call toll free or visit us online. www.PutnamLeasing.com.

PHOTOGRAPHY

Bob Dunsmore Racing Photography. 503.244.4646. PO Box 80008, Multnomah, OR 97280.

RESTORATION.GENERAL

Guy's Interior Restorations. 503.224.8657, fax 503.223.6953. 431 NW 9th, Portland, OR 97209. Award-winning interior restoration. Leather dyeing and color matching.

CLASSIC CAR TRANSPORT

Cosdel International. 415.777.2000, fax 415.543.5112. California. Now in its 33rd year of international transport. Complete service, including import/export, customs clearances, DOT and EPA, air/ocean, loading and unloading of containers. Contact Martin Button. info@cosdel.com, www.cosdel.com.

Passport Transport. 800.325.4267, fax 314.878.7295. Missouri. Classic and specialty cars delivered anywhere in the USA. Special event services, including Pebble Beach, Monterey Historics, Barrett-Jackson, and Auburn. Standard-of-the-industry service since 1970. www.passporttransport.com.

TNT, INC. 518.236.4166, fax 518.236.4549. New York. Personalized auto transport service-door to door, coast to coast, open carrier or enclosed carrier. Winching and 24-hour security. First class equipment. Dependable and insured.

Intercity Lines, Inc. 800.221.3936, fax 413.436.9422. Massachusetts. Rapid, hassle-free, coast-to-coast service. Insured, enclosed transport for your valuable car at affordable prices. State-of-the-art satellite transport tracking. Complete service for vintage races, auctions, relocation moves. www.intercitylines.com.

PC BEAR Auto Transport. 717.859.1585. 135 Broad St., Akron, PA 17501. Specializing in all types: hobby, collector vehicles, toys, neat old stuff, regular cars, parts, and winching. Life long car nut. Equipment serviced and maintained by me. Clean driving record since 1959 in all states. ICCMC, US DOT insured. I sleep in my truck while transporting. Inspection and check delivery service. Door-to-door delivery. Talk to me anytime. Thank you.

Concours Transport Systems. 253.973.3987, fax 253.851.4707. Washington. Enclosed auto transport nationwide. Lift gate loading, experienced personnel. Classic & exotic cars. Special events—fully insured. Fred Koller, owner. fredkoller@ concourstransport.com, www.concours-transport.com.

356 REGISTRY

356 Registry. 810.688.9090, fax 810.688.9091. 356 Registry, 3359 Kings Mill Rd, North Branch, MI 48461. A club for those interested in 356 Porsches. The Registry Magazine is published six times a year. 356 ownership not necessary. Dues $30 annually. Membership information: Barbara Skirmants. www.356registry.org. ◆

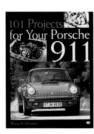

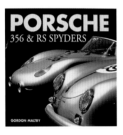

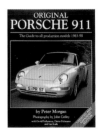